CSR, Sustainability, Ethics & Governance

In recent years the discussion concerning the relation between business and society has made immense strides. This has in turn led to a broad academic and practical discussion on innovative management concepts, such as Corporate Social Responsibility, Corporate Governance and Sustainability Management. This series offers a comprehensive overview of the latest theoretical and empirical research and provides sound concepts for sustainable business strategies. In order to do so, it combines the insights of leading researchers and thinkers in the fields of management theory and the social sciences and from all over the world, thus contributing to the interdisciplinary and intercultural discussion on the role of business in society. The underlying intention of this series is to help solve the world's most challenging problems by developing new management concepts that create value for business and society alike. In order to support those managers, researchers and students who are pursuing sustainable business approaches for our common future, the series offers them access to cutting-edge management approaches. CSR, Sustainability, Ethics and Governance is accepted by the Norwegian Register for Scientific Journals, Series and Publishers, maintained and operated by the Norwegian Social Science Data Services (NSD).

Maria-Gabriella Baldarelli · Eleonora Cardillo ·
Samuel O. Idowu
Editors

Accounting and Accountability for Social Inclusion

Interdisciplinary Dialogues for a More Sustainable World

Springer

Editors
Maria-Gabriella Baldarelli
University of Bologna
Bologna, Italy

Eleonora Cardillo
University of Catania
Catania, Italy

Samuel O. Idowu
London Metropolitan University
London, UK

ISSN 2196-7075 ISSN 2196-7083 (electronic)
CSR, Sustainability, Ethics & Governance
ISBN 978-3-032-09270-0 ISBN 978-3-032-09271-7 (eBook)
https://doi.org/10.1007/978-3-032-09271-7

This Springer imprint is published by the registered company Springer Nature Switzerland AG
The registered company address is: Gewerbestrasse 11, 6330 Cham, Switzerland

Foreword

Sustainability is not about a particular people or place. It is a global issue, both in policy terms and in ecological terms. It has been defined by the United Nations as extending beyond the ecology to include social phenomena such as inclusion of diverse populations living in different regions and parts of the world. As such, there can be no sustainability without attention to inclusion of all peoples. No single population or people has the corner on the truth—knowledge comes from the whole of the world's population. Knowledge of how exisi in life and how to survive as a species requires all people to contribute. This contribution can only occur in the context of inclusive policies and practices.

The technology for implementation of such inclusion is the same technology as is used for implementation of all types of policies—the technology of accounting and norm of accountability. The challenge of connecting broad, global social policy and implementing it through the technology of accounting is significant. There is a plethora of issues and considerations. This volume takes on these challenges through a series of research studies and essays.

These studies and essays are commendable: they are drawn from a wide variety of scholars in disparate parts of the world. Their insights are sharp and timely, illuminating the challenges in new and thoughtful ways. I commend this volume to readers of all types, and I commend the editors and scholars who have contributed to this important work.

July 2025

Professor Benedict Sheehy
University of Canberra
Canberra, Australian Capital Territory
(ACT), Australia

Preface

Sustainability and what it stands for and requires all global citizens to do is a serious business. Some fifty or so years ago the world was a little naïve and ignorant of why we should exist and operate sustainably. Thanks to the actions taken by some great global scholars and the United Nations and many of its wings. We are now less naïve and ignorant. Having said this, it should be noted that the current state of the art presents situations of profound uncertainty for the future and climatic and war conditions that generate a widespread feeling of fear and anxiety to a good number of the inhabitants of planet Earth. There is therefore an urgent need to rethink the role of public and private sector organizations and create networks that can lead to positive and hopeful circuits. Furthermore, the debate on the contents of social inclusion in sustainability development is not completely established. This is really not good enough and perhaps still unsustainable. Over time, it is hoped that despite being oriented towards considering mainly the not-for-profit sector, there would be the opportunity which would open up to welcome networks which are composed of public and private, for-profit and non-profit actors that would allow us to go beyond traditional paradigms and propose new and creative solutions to global challenges and difficulties what have come to the fore as a result of our past unsustainable practices. These would hopefully seek to restore some sanity for the emancipatory, socially responsible, accessible, inclusive and sustainable future for global citizens in general.

Global corporations that aspire to grow and prosper must be properly controlled, directed and managed. A good system of corporate governance advocates accountability, transparency and fairness. In many countries around the world a number of corporations have collapsed and failed due to inadequate governance systems being put in place by those at the helms of these corporations. Many unpalatable consequences have followed these events. The current book focuses on how accounting and accountability could facilitate social inclusion in a sustainable world. Needles to say, that would make our world a more sustainable place to exist in.

This book has the objective of preparing and equipping corporate entities to face new challenges that could emanate from the increasing use of new technologies and Artificial Intelligence. The book deals with the topic of accounting and accountability for social inclusion using interdisciplinary dialogues. Starting from how accounting and accountability could contribute in mediating between different sectors in the global economy. The book analyses the dialogue between accounting and accountability and the theoretical discourse tthat contributes to social inclusion. It also espouses how the change culture could bring about a more sustainable society.

It is hoped that the book satisfies the information needs of our global readers regardless of their sector, their callings and where they are located on planet Earth.

Bologna, Italy
Catania, Italy
London, UK

Maria-Gabriella Baldarelli
Eleonora Cardillo
Samuel O. Idowu

Acknowledgements

We would like to express our gratitude to contributors to this great piece and to our publishing team at Springer headed by the Executive Director — Books, Christian Rauscher, Barbara Bethke, Dr Prashanth Mahagaonkar, Dr Bijita Majumdar, Anette Weiss, Rocio Torresgrosa and other members of the publishing team who have supported this project and all our other projects. We are equally grateful to Professor Benedict Sheehy of the University of Canberra, Austrailia for wrting a befitting Foreword to the book. Thank you so much, Professor Sheehy.

The Editors want to express their gratitude to the anonymous referees that assisted us in ensuring that chapters in the book met acceptable standards any qualities who carefully read through the twelve chapters of the book and suggested suitable amendments to make to all the contributed chapters and the final version of the book.

Finally, we apologise for any errors or omissions that may appear anywhere in the book, please be assured that no harm was intended to anybody. Thank to everyone.

Attributions

Maria-Gabriella Baldarelli and Eleonora Cardillo Wrote Chapters: 1, 2, 3, 4, 5, 6 and 8. The attributions are of 50% of each Author of respectively chapters.

About Chapter 7: Maria-Gabriella Baldarelli wrote §7.3.1; Maria-Gabriella Baldarelli and Patrizia Petrolati wrote § 7.3.1; Federica Balluchi wrote § 7.1.1; 7.1.2; Arianna Lazzini and Paolo Di Toma wrote § 7.4; Katia Furlotti wrote § 7.2; Patrizia Petrolati wrote § 7.1.3; Stefania Vignini wrote § 7.3.2.

About Chapter 11: Maria-Gabriella Baldarelli wrote §11.2 and § 11.6, Macarena Paz Velasco Rosales wrote the other paragraphs.

Accounting and Accountability for Social Inclusion: An Introduction

Maria-Gabriella Baldarelli
University of Bologna, Bologna, Italy
maria.baldarelli@unibo.it
Eleonora Cardillo
University of Catania, Catania, Italy
cardillo@unict.it

And

Samuel O Idowu
London Metropolitan University, London, UK
s.idowu@londonmet.ac.uk

The current state of the art presents situations of profound uncertainty for the future and climatic and war conditions that generate a widespread feeling of fear amongst global citizens. There is therefore an urgent need to rethink the role of public and private sector organizations and the meaning of creating networks that can lead to positive and hopeful circuits. Furthermore, the debate on the contents of social inclusion in sustainability development is not completely established, which over time, despite being oriented towards considering mainly the not-for-profit sector, opens up the opportunity to welcome networks composed of public and private, for-profit and non-profit actors, who would consequently challenge scholars to go beyond traditional paradigms and to propose new and creative solutions. Those solutions would seek to restore hope for the emancipatory, socially responsible, accessible, inclusive and sustainable future.

Last but not least, the concept of vulnerability is considered positively in some part of the literature, as an injection of greater responsibility for those who find themselves facing situations of different abilities and circumstances.

Among other problems, inclusion is a relevant objective of the 2030 Agenda and the work contributes to outlining paths and areas in which accounting and accountability can help firms to achieve this purpose.

The book has the objective to contribute towards finding solutions new challenges also deriving from the increasing importance of new technologies and Artificial Intelligence. The chapters deal with the topic of accounting and accountability for social inclusion using also interdisciplinary dialogues. Starting from the potential of accounting and accountability in contributing to mediate in different areas, the book hopes to analyse the dialogue beween accounting and accountability and other theories to contribute to social inclusion to change culture for a more sustainable society.

In its desire to contribute to the existing theories, the book has the objective to reflect about the dialogue among accounting, accountability and Nature Based Solutions (NBS), technological Innovation and Artificial Intelligence for social inclusion. Furthermore, the book analyses some cases of sustainability drivers implementation and social inclusion best practices.

The book is divided in three parts. The first part focuses on the general overview. In this section, it proposes some theoretical frameworks and empirical experiences with the aim of evaluating and measuring social inclusion and encouraging accounting and accountability using sustainable innovative business models. In particular, espouses the "potentiality" of accounting and accountability to positively helep corporate entities regardless of their forms It also explores some definitions of accounting, accountability for social inclusion and sustainability. Finally, it uses Sustainability Reporting to evaluate how social inclusion is presented.

The second part of the book focuses on the context of specific "sectors", using cultural Institutions and the inclusion of blind and visually impaired people, analysing the importance of the experience of "touch" in tactile museums in Italy. Moreover, other very interesting cases of sustainability drivers for implementation and social inclusion in sevice sectors are analysed. After the initial analysis of conceptual Frameworks for social inclusion in cultural Institutions, social Inclusion and Nature Based-Solutions in Tactile Museum accountability and performance measurement system are presented. This part also highlights the importance of Technological Innovations in Tactile Museums and their implementation being acknowledged as best practices.

Furthermore, the state of art about the implementation of social and environmental sustainability drivers in micro and small enterprises in an Italian Region is presented and the accounting perspective of Economy of Communion research cases concludes the second part of the book.

The Third part discusses Accounting and Accountability for social inclusion in terms of interdisciplinary dialogues and the impact on higher education.

Similar topics are explored in this dialogue, such as the Accounting and Economic Inclusion of Marginalized Communities, and the Multidimensional Model for Social Tagging of Environmental Investment Costs. Furthermore, the analysis of the implementation of Sustainability Reporting in Beach Establishments in Italy is presented. Finally, Social inclusion challenges in higher education in transitioned countries is discussed.

The Introduction chapter concludes with a discussion on the problem of the fruition of vulnerable categories. It notes that issues surrounding the area are often underestimated, so this book aims to increase awareness and facilitate a better understand of the mission, governance, accounting and accountability aspects in theory and practice. The book offers suggestions on how to choose among major worthy causes and also how to measure the number of beneficial outcomes achieved both by the recipients and consequently socially responsible corporate entities themselves.

The book is aimed at Practitioners, Researchers, senior undergraduate and graduate business students, accounting and accountability, ethics, corporate social responsibility, sustainability, social inclusion and Managements courses, including students in other related disciplines such as: Economics, Accounting, Law, Social Science, Humanities several others would find the book of interest to them.

It is hoped the the book meets the requirements of our global readers who are keen to know more about the areas.

Maria-Gabriella Baldarelli, Bolognia, Italy
Eleonora Cardillo, Italy
Samuel O. Idowu, London, UK
June 2025

Contents

Editors and Contributors

About the Editors

Maria-Gabriella Baldarelli PhD, CPA, is Associate Professor of Accounting, at University of Bologna, Department of Management- Rimini Campus. Full professor availability. Envited professor at Sophia University Institute. SIDREA board member until 2018. She is a member of international scientific networks: the Centre for Social and Environmental Accounting Research (CSEAR) and the European Business Ethics Network (EBEN). Key-note Speaker 2nd International Conference on Economics, Business, Finance and Governance (ICEBFG) by Economics and Business Faculty of University of Bandar Lampung- Bali- Indonesia- Dic. 4-5, 2019. Research interests includes: accountability and gambling enterprises; corporate social responsibility; ethical, social and environmental accounting and accountability, sustainability in tourist enterprises; responsible and accessible tourism for blind people, economy of communion; gender accounting; accounting history, accounting education and Feminist Economics.

Eleonora Cardillo is Associate Professor of Business Economics—at the Department of Economics and Business of the University of Catania. She was Visiting Scholar at the CSEAR (Centre for social and environmental accounting research) School of Management of the University of St Andrews (Scotland) for the research project: "Study and analysis of the methodological and operational paths of environmental and social reporting in the evolution process of accounting information systems". Professor of Accounting and Financial Statements and Public accounting in local administrations. She was Director and Scientific Coordinator of the Master in Accounting and Control in Local Authorities, organized by the Department of Economics and Business of the University of Catania. Her research topics are public accounting systems, performance measurement, socio-environmental reporting, social inclusion in tactile museums, sustainability and accountability.

Samuel O. Idowu Samuel O Idowu is Professor of Accounting and Sustainability at the Guildhall School of Business and Law, London Metropolitan University where he is currently the course leader for the MSc Corporate Social Responsibility & Sustainability and Advanced Diploma in Professional Development (ADPD) Corporate Social Responsibility & Sustainability. Samuel is also a Professor of CSR and Sustainability at Nanjing University of Finance & Economics, China and December 1, 1918 University of Alba Iulia, Romania. He is a fellow member of the Chartered Governance Institute, a fellow of the Royal Society of Arts, a Liveryman of the Worshipful Company of Chartered Governance Institute and a named freeman of the City of London. He is the CEO and President of the Global Corporate Governance Institute an international network of CSR scholars. Samuel has published over one hundred articles in both professional and academic journals and contributed chapters in several edited books and is the Editor-in-Chief of three major global reference books by Springer – the *Encyclopedia of Corporate Social Responsibility* (ECSR), the *Dictionary of Corporate Social Responsibility* (DCSR) and the *Encyclopaedia of Sustainable Management* (ESM) and he is a Series Editor for Springer's CSR, Sustainability, Ethics and Governance books. Samuel is the Editor-in-Chief of the Journal of Sustainable Business and the American Journal of Economics and Business Administration. Samuel has been in academia for almost 4 decades winning one of the Highly Commended Awards of Emerald Literati Network Awards for Excellence in 2008 and 2014. In 2010, one of his edited books was placed in 18th position out of forty top Sustainability books by Cambridge University Programme for Sustainability Leadership and in 2016 one of his books won the outstanding Business Reference Book of the year of the American Library Association. In 2018 he won a CSR Leadership Award in Cologne, Germany and in 2019 he won the 101 Most Impactful CSR Leaders Award in Mumbai, India and in 2023, Samuel was nominated for the Gandhi CSR Award in New Delhi, India. Samuel is on the Editorial Advisory Board of the International Journal of Business Administration. He has been researching in the field of CSR since 1983 and has attended and presented papers at several national and international conferences and workshops on CSR. Samuel has made a number of keynote speeches at international conferences and workshops and written the *foreword* to a number of leading books in the field of CSR and Sustainable Development. And he has examined on a few PhD theses in the UK, Australia, South Africa, the Netherlands and New Zealand.

List of Contributors

Maria-Gabriella Baldarelli University of Bologna, Bologna, Italy

Federica Balluchi University of Parma, Parma, Italy

Eleonora Cardillo University of Catania, Catania, Italy

Katia Furlotti University of Parma, Parma, Italy

Ninel Nesheva Kiosseva University of National and World Economy (UNWE), Sofia, Bulgaria

Arianna Lazzini University of Modena and Reggio Emilia, Modena and Reggio Emilia, Italy

Lorena Mošnja-Škare Juraj Dobrila University of Pula, Pula, Croatia

Patrizia Petrolati University of Bologna, Bologna, Italy

Macarena Paz Velasco Rosales University of Bologna, Bologna, Italy

Vedrana Stermasi University of Dubrovnik, Dubrovnik, Croatia

Paolo Di Toma University of Modena and Reggio Emilia, Modena and Reggio Emilia, Italy

Stefania Vignini University of Bologna, Bologna, Italy

Ksenija Černe Juraj Dobrila University of Pula, Pula, Croatia

Part I
Accounting and Accountability for Social Inclusion: Conceptual Framework

Chapter 1
The "Potential" of Accounting and Accountability in the Current Economic System Towards an Emancipatory Change

Maria-Gabriella Baldarelli and Eleonora Cardillo

Abstract This chapter aims to reflect on some of the main aspects that characterize the state of the art of the economic-social system. This is because companies are closely connected to it and therefore are influenced and in turn influence the surrounding environment understood in a broad sense ((<author>, *La determinazione del valore creato.* CEDAM, <publisher-loc>, 2004)). The description of the main characteristics of the economic and social system is carried out by successive approximations ((Amaduzzi, A., In "Studi di Economia Aziendale. Nuova edizione delle pubblicazioni originarie in occasione della giornata di studio per ricordare Aldo Amaduzzi". 1995. Edizioni Kappa, <publisher-loc>, 1948)), starting from some interdisciplinary aspects to subsequently consider those relating to accounting and accountability.

1.1 Introduction to the State of the Economic System from Sustainable Development to Regeneration Processes in the Era of Ultra-Contemporaneity

Today it is emphasized that the problem of climate change is first and foremost an anthropological and social problem (Gianfelici 2024), and if we do not focus on these aspects, it could be much more difficult to truly pay attention to the solution of ecological problems and climate change (Gray et al. 2014). For several years, the lack of attention in accounting and accountability towards social aspects has been emphasized: "...most of the substantial attempts to engage with sustainability

M.-G. Baldarelli (✉)
University of Bologna, Bologna, Italy
e-mail: maria.baldarelli@unibo.it

E. Cardillo
University of Catania, Catania, Italy
e-mail: cardillo@unict.it

M. Baldarelli et al. (eds.), *Accounting and Accountability for Social Inclusion*, CSR, Sustainability, Ethics & Governance, https://doi.org/10.1007/978-3-032-09271-7_1

have focused on environmental sustainability, not social sustainability" (Gray et al. 2014, 230). The authors underline the difficulty of measuring the social aspects of sustainable development but that they are strongly linked to the ecological ones. Furthermore, the authors themselves launch the challenge: "Of course, this is just the sort of challenge that new researchers need to address and develop"(Gray et al. 2014, 231).

Furthermore, the chapter aims to focus attention on the characteristics of the economic and social system, which influence measurement and reporting and in particular the current meaning of accounting and accountability in the declination of social aspects and inclusion. This is in order to enter the scientific debate with the logic that, through a reflection on these aspects, we can contribute to sustainable development even in this period of "Ultra-contemporaneity" (Aceti and Moràn 2019).

For the purposes indicated above, we also add that of giving a meaning to accounting and accountability for social inclusion, which is functional to the entire discussion, which will be developed in the next chapters.

The first characteristic we consider concerns the prospect of a "regenerative" sustainable development (Gianfelici 2024). This term underlines the need for all the subjects operating in the general economic-social system to be able not only to reduce or eliminate the negative impact on the ecological and social environment, but above all to be able to regenerate the destroyed resources to activate virtuous and improving processes of the same. That is, it is no longer sufficient, for example, not to pollute, but it is necessary to have a proactive attitude to be able to improve environmental resources and the quality of life. The second characteristic is the one called ultra-contemporaneity, which derives from the constant and continuous possibility, due to the technological development of the media and communication through social media, of being in real-time contact with the entire world: "... so it is as if everything were happening on a large stage that is always populated and always available" (Aceti and Moràn 2019, 13). This aspect can generate space-time manipulation and potentially condition the lives of individuals and companies that operate in the economic and social environment. In fact, "an ultra-contemporaneous war field is continuous, flat, simultaneous, ubiquitous, systemic, productive and affects the sea, air, land, space and cyberspace" (Aceti and Moràn 2019, 14; Rodrìguez 2014, 10–11). This situation radically influences the relationships between the different subjects of the economic-social system, diverting them from their true content, in fact: "the capacities for thought and imagination that make us human, and that make our relationships something humanly rich, not relationships of simple use and manipulation... The ability to think critically, the ability to transcend localisms and to face global problems as "citizens of the world"; and finally, the ability to sympathetically represent the category of the other" (Aceti and Moràn 2019, 8; Nussbaum 2011, 21).

The third characteristic examines the technological innovation that has generated the sharing economy. The debate on the Sharing Economy (henceforth: SE) over the years has tried to analyze different areas, including the one related to the analysis of innovative business models (Qureshi et al. 2021). Especially over time, the SE, through digitalization and digital platforms, is transforming all economic activities (May et al. 2017; Zvloska et al. 2018, 2019). But this, according to some authors, does not only bring positive aspects (Oksana et al. 2020). Furthermore, other authors emphasize the role of intermediaries in poverty reduction, always from the SE perspective (Bhatt et al. 2022).

Laukkanen and Tura (2020) focus on the different types of business models that the SE considers. Among the different typologies analyzed, the area of greatest interest for our work concerns some categories that "represents the combination of the community-based and access economy, that refer to affording greater access to underutilized resources and services at the community level" (Laukkanen and Tura 2020, 6). By the authors, these two categories are considered as producers of value in themselves, because they create networks and allow the use of resources, that are not adequately used, among which also heritage is included.

In general, the SE represents a new economic and cultural model capable of rationalizing the use of resources based on the exchange or sharing of goods and services rather than their purchase (May et al. 2017; Zvloska et al. 2018, 2019, Oksana et al. 2020, Bhatt et al. 2022). Issues related to multi-channeling, the presence of skills and capabilities of users and the nature of dialectical processes in digital platforms are central in the context of a SE system extended to arts and culture. Therefore, the digital transformation process underlying the SE determines the creation of new roles and functions among the actors (Massi et al. 2021). This requires greater clarity in defining areas and opportunities for cultural users in using the potential of digital technology (Furness 2018), trying to find, in the new system of intermediation and exchange, an opportunity for socialization (Richè et al. 2016; Massi et al. 2021).

The spread of many types of "poverty" and an ever-increasing frequency of environmental, political (wars), economic (stock market crashes, etc.) "disasters" are aspects leading to the fourth characteristic of the ultra-contemporaneity time. Different forms of poverty that can emerge can be traced back to the issues of CSR and the social inclusion orientation. Literature concerning the concept of poverty is generally connected to the lack or limitation of the resources that are essential to live and manage life normally. But this concept takes on different meanings that go beyond the literal sense of the term (Sen 2000; Alkire and Foster 2011). Furthermore, some other types of poverties are arising, such as the lack of spirituality, ethics, relational goods, happiness and the arising of certain forms of addiction as compulsive gamblers (Leung and Snell 2017, Reith 2007) and "modern slavery" (Crane et al. 2021). In business literature, some research analyzed the contribution of Corporate social responsibility (CSR) to ease poverty (Muñoz and Muñoz 2020) and underlined that CSR and How the pre-existing status of CEO can influence more generosity (Xu and Ma 2021). Some scholars connect the issues of CSR to poverty and rights (Osuji and Obibuaku 2016) considering not only the human rights (Sen 2004) but also the socio-economic ones, that are part of them. Another interesting debate is about the incomplete effectiveness in solving the problem of poverty just with philanthropic interventions (Calton et al. 2013; Choi et al. 2010, Hahn 2009). However, in the context of CSR, poverty reduction has never become a central theme (Medina-Munoz and Medina-Munoz 2021), perhaps because the business case approach (if not always dominant, often privileged in CSR studies) does not fit the topic well. Therefore, for-profit organizations are of great relevance in the process of poverty reduction (Prahalad and Hammond, 2002) and the urgent need for new business models is emerging (Lartego and Mathiassen 2021, Chliova and Ringov 2017, Kristruck et al. 2011). Moreover, even in the case of for-profit organizations, profit could be considered a means and not a final goal of the enterprise (Zamagni 2016). Furthermore, previous research considered government intervention as necessary to alleviate poverty, while some scholars such as Shulist and Kistruck (2021) underlined the need to consider new approaches to "market orchestration", with the aim of re-vitalize local markets and achieve more sustainable and financial benefit for poor people and communities (Prahalad 2005). The discussion about finance and poverty and especially microfinance is very promising (Barboza and Trejos 2009) too. In this field, different views emerge but they share the idea that to solve poverty problems an integrated intervention is required, especially to increase skills of poor people, to help them to develop social and human capital and to increase the individual and social/economic system levels (Tavanti 2013; Perry and World Bank 2006). Finally, it is worth to mention the case of "chosen poverty", when a sober lifestyle is a choice (Crivelli 2020). Poverty can be linked to the concept of exclusion. Social exclusion, in fact, is embodied in the deprivation and impossibility of access to various opportunities. Some authors (Modi et al. 2021) propose a definition of social exclusion: "Social exclusion refers to the ways in which individuals or groups may become cut off from full involvement in the wider society. Social exclusion is often a corollary to poverty, and includes wide-ranging factors preventing individuals or groups from having access to opportunities open to the majority of the population" (Modi et al. 2021, p.4). This definition is associated with the concept of vulnerability. In fact, contractual relations, according to Pelligra (2008), make our lives more individualistic and less relational. The contract reigns in the mutual benefit, but when it does not respect the "rule" inherent in the contract, the "excluded" are born, because they are vulnerable and therefore cannot be included in the contract's case, since it seems that if there is no exchange, these subjects they have nothing to give. Vulnerability and dependence seem to be at the core of the social link. That goes beyond the contract and develops the logic of "cure" and that is the logic of responsibility. This definition adds to the characteristics of production, that is, a high degree of management autonomy, continuous production of services and / or products, and the high managerial. Direct effects concern the inclusion of "vulnerable" workers and users (Baldarelli and Cardillo 2022), while indirect effects represent the ability to generate relational circuits both inside and outside the firm, because they often have a strong link with the territory they act, in order to dampen and improve democracy. In summary, the presence of social links within the market and the logic of true sustainability, as understood by Nusbaum (2002), considers vulnerability, hence "different ability", not a negative aspect to sustainable development, but a constructive aspect by which who relates to vulnerable subjects feels more accountable to "do" something, that can improve the relationship. This is because vulnerable subjects appreciate social relations (Pelligra, 2008) that can regenerate culture in seeing vulnerability not as a negative aspect, but an opportunity for a new creativity.

The fifth aspect, only mentioned, concerns issues such as technological innovation and also the ever-increasing importance of Artificial Intelligence (Schmidpeter and Altenburger 2023). This topic will be considered in the following chapters, in which some specific contexts concerning cultural institutions will be discussed. In this context, the area considered is the problem of assessing the impact of technological innovation, artificial Intelligence on the accessibility and sharing of cultural products with respect to "vulnerable" people (Pelligra 2008).

After having outlined some salient aspects of the current state of the art of the economic system, the next paragraph analyses their implications on mission, governance and accountability.

1.2 The Potential of accounting and accountability for Social inclusion and the Emancipatory Change

The approach perspective to the topic, the object of analysis in this paragraph, can be traced back to two points of view, which are distant in time from each other, but which seem to be the answer to each other. The first concerns one of the classics of Accounting in Italy, which raises the question of whether this discipline has now started towards its decline: "… that young scholars discover how much is still unexplored that is offered to accounting research and work to restore to it the content and dignity that belie the feared decline" (Amodeo 1993, p. 30). In the current state of the art, obviously, we are still in the midst of the debate on various issues, which pertain to it. Therefore, rather than a decline, we can assert that we are moving towards a new Dawn of Accounting.

Gray (2013), in fact, strongly supports the importance of including sustainability within accounting, underlining that poverty, which we discussed previously, is one of the factors of un-sustainability. He states that "some of the more widely shared views are that un-sustainability is a result of: governments; bureaucracy; greed; consumption; capitalism; poverty; people; religion; men; imperfections in the market; accounting; modernity; financial markets; and so on" (Gray 2013, 313–314). Among others, Carnegie's work (2022) highlights a "new" definition of Accounting which, according to the Author, over time has had too many contributions on the technical methods of keeping Accounting (how) and few scientific contributions on the meanings (means) of accounting. "Accounting has not attained its full potential and can contribute to shaping a better world from tomorrow" (Carnegie 2022, 615). Author affirms that "the true potential of accounting as technical, social, and moral practice in helping to shape a better world currently lies close to dormant" (Carnegie 2022, 619).

The issue of the potential of accounting had already been addressed by Broadbent (1998), who underlines the absence of the feminine (female/feminist) vision of it, which does not allow accounting to fully develop its potential. Above all, the problems that have been raised after Covid 19 put these issues back at the centre of attention, which are very important, as accounting has the potential to intervene in the social and moral order and to influence all aspects of human life and companies and organizations. A new definition of accounting can be formulated: "Accounting is a technical, social and moral practice concerned with the sustainable utilisation of resources and proper accountability to stakeholders to enable the flourishing of organisations, people and nature. Importantly, this definition addresses the following questions: Technical practice: How to do accounting? Social practice: What does accounting do? Moral practice: What should accounting do? Or What should accounting not do?" (Carnegie 2022, 617).

Carnegie (2022) develops a significant criticism of the technical meaning of accounting in the traditional sense oriented to specific purposes, which he considers an extremely reductive meaning. He suggests considering accounting a social practice, because it designs social relationships and relations, extremely connected to accounting and are shaped by it. Finally, according to Carnegie (2022), accounting is the basis for decisions and therefore, in addition to a social dimension, it also has a moral dimension, which is inherent in the choices that are identified through accounting data (technical aspect) and such choices are oriented and have a great influence also on human and personal aspects. According to this approach, he states that "Inculcating a broader, more meaningful definition of accounting has 'game-changing' prospects. It would contribute to an enhanced understanding of the effects of accounting emergence and change around the globe. This project offers considerable prospects for accounting to help in shaping a better world for all humans and non-humans. This is not a risk; let us seize this opportunity" (Carnegie 2022, 625). Thus, Carnegie and Napier (2023) underline that social and moral aspects have been little analyzed in accounting and accountability and open the perspective of the importance of the social relationship consistent with the mission and purpose (Baldarelli 2023; Baldarelli and Ceraulo 2024). A definition of accountability that emphasizes the complex relationships between individuals has been formulated by Gray et al. (1997). Accountability is a concept that concerns "with the relationships between groups, individuals, organizations and the rights to information that such relationships entail. Simply stated, accountability is the duty to provide an account of the actions for which one is held responsible" (Gray et al. 1997, p. 334). Subsequently, Carnegie and Napier (2023) focus on the relationship between accounting and governance, leaving out the mission, which instead seems particularly important to us to guide the choices of the company.

This work focuses mainly on accounting and accountability, it is, however, important to reflect on three aspects, which characterize the company and that is: Mission, and therefore also purpose (Baldarelli and Ceraulo 2024), governance and accountability (from now MGA) (Matacena, 2017) inserting the variable of social inclusion within them. Matacena (Matacena 2017; Lectio Magistralis Matacena 2021) considers the for-profit company as irresponsible and strongly criticizes the scheme by asserting that there are forms of business, including social enterprises and cooperative enterprises, which also include social responsibility in the MGA. To better clarify these considerations and reasoning, we report the scheme of Matacena (2017) and then try to add some reflections on this configuration Table 1.1.

Table 1.1 Comparison between for-profit and social enterprise

SUBJECTS	PROFIT-MAKING ENTERPRISE	SUBJECTS	SOCIAL ENTERPRISE
Shareholders	Mission Capitalist benefit, that is the optimisation of yield for shareholders while pursuing an economic optimum which is sustainable in the long term. Unidimensional mission	Individual and collective users	Mission Collective benefit, that is, optimisation of individual, group and/or collective benefits while respecting maintenance of the condition of entrepreneurship as constraint on the continuity of the specific mission. Multidimensional mission
Entrepreneur actor innovator	Governance Coherent company governance with a finalistic objective, coherence gained by strong command principle made clear by a finalised hierarchical chain and realised through a coordinated directional behaviour in relation to social and economic stakeholders. Hierarchical governance	Collective entrepreneur	Governance Ultra-democratic corporate governance due to the presence, in strategic direction, of all the actors of the ethical business; ultra-democratic nature made possible by collective concerted directional behaviours in relation to economic and social stakeholders. Multistakeholder governance
Controller	Accountability Internal information system useful for management separated from external information system which has the aim of producing documents with final data and values. This system is able to produce: 1.Documents which conform to accounting obligations useful for entrepreneurship checking; 2.Financial reporting useful for investors; 3.Eventual socio-environmental reporting useful for stakeholders considered prevalent at that moment. **Unidimensional accountability**	Controller	Accountability Single information system from whence comes information able to give rise to systematic communication through which to check levels of entrepreneurship and mission pursued and achieved by way of control of the: 1.Administrative results, useful for checking obligations deriving from the presence of eventual subsidy legislation; 2.Managerial results, useful for checking constraint for entrepreneurship; 3.Institutional results, useful for checking specific social performances and activating mechanisms of fund-raising. **Multidimensional accountability**

Source Matacena 2017, 5

Matacena (2017) identifies the Social Enterprise as the model in which the aspects of social responsibility are inserted and therefore the "model" of accountability that is linked to the importance of the social and democratic purposes of the company. The theme of social inclusion represents a variable that is inserted into the theme of accountability and CSR (Idowu 2015) with respect to the MGA strand of companies, whether they are profit or non-profit. Accountability is characterized by an information system that creates both a communication system and a method of verifying the levels of entrepreneurship and the mission pursued. The company results are aimed at evaluating the specific social performances with respect to a multistakeholder governance system (Matacena 2017).

Another key concept of accountability is that of eco-justice.

Eco-justice considers the ways in which the company manages to satisfy the needs of stakeholders both internally and externally (Rusconi 2019). Eco-justice also includes the possibility of actively participating in democratic processes that develop in different nations. Finally, it also presents an intergenerational dimension, which recalls the fairness of treatment and the related methods of measuring these aspects (Gray et al. 2014, 226; Baldarelli et al., 2017, 30).

The concept of MGA can include the different areas of social inclusion, starting from the approach to accountability by Gray et al. (2014) and referring to eco-justice which is still a current principle today. This reasoning also involves a profound modification of the information system (Baldarelli et al., 2017) including the social aspects of sustainable development.

1.3 Sustainability Reporting and Risk of Manipulation

The aspects related to the mission and purpose of organizations give social and moral importance to governance, accounting and accountability processes. These areas must be paid attention to in order to reduce the problems of excessive technicality and "washing" (Gianfelici 2024). Gianfelici (2024) analyzes which are the elements that define corporate reporting and that can create the conditions for Washing. The first concerns the information asymmetry between internal and external stakeholders. Even trying to remove this asymmetry still leads to errors and distortions in the information.

A further second point concerns the problems of opportunism that generate a problem of "manipulation" (Gianfelici 2024, 64) of information. However, while in the Financial Statements theory and practice have dealt with this critical issue at length, as regards the sustainability report the risk of "manipulation" (washing) is much higher and has been addressed in a less in-depth manner. The risk of washing involves several problems. The first concerns the decrease in trust in non-financial information and above all it decreases the reputation of companies in the case in which it is highlighted that non-financial information does not correspond to the actual corporate behavior. But the most significant damage according to Gianfelici (2024) lies in the fact that even for those companies, which instead communicate information in a transparent manner and try to include in the governance what is communicated in a correct and faithful manner, a decrease in reputation and legitimacy can occur precisely due to this practice. The term washing, in literal terms, translates as "washing" and therefore has a positive meaning of cleanliness. In companies, however, it translates into negative terms as a synonym of lack of clarity and is linked to the activity of "hiding" (Gianfelici, 2024, p. 66). Furthermore, the sustainability report is more complex and less codified, so the risk of washing is greater. There are many types of washing: "green (the most famous), pink, gender, brown, etc.." (Gianfelici 2024, 66).

Washing practices create enormous distortions of information, negatively influencing the market and ultimately creating obstacles to sustainable development.

In fact, washing is currently one of the main problems to be addressed with a certain urgency, as it can have deleterious effects both on the trust that the market shows to companies, and within the company's reputation (Gianfelici 2024).

Gianfelici (2024) discussion mainly considers reporting, measurement and governance, without specifically examining the connection with the purpose (Baldarelli and Ceraulo 2024; Del Baldo 2020) and the mission. The "integrated" vision of the mission (purpose), governance and accountability represent the basis on which to act to reduce the risk of washing in the disclosure and measurement of sustainability performance. Both internally and externally, the company verifies the practices also with respect to the mission and purpose; this becomes a motivating factor to guide the entire management of the company and a path that can potentially reduce the possibility of washing. Trust, inclusiveness and openness are key factors in the collective value co-creation process that is represented in place-based and purpose-driven companies. Specifically, stakeholders contribute to the creation of value and this shows the importance of being "a purpose-driven firm, which is implementing the culture of giving and pursuing the universal fraternity" (Baldarelli and Ceraulo 2024, 193).

In the next Fig. 1.1 there is a chellange about the modification of paradigm to involve purpose and to more evalutate it inside of the Mission (Baldarelli and Ceraulo 2024).

In fact, if we do not reconnect with the purpose and the mission, we have a fragmentation which consequently generates washing.

Attention to a conscious and clear social responsibility can reduce the "irresponsibility" of companies, creating a culture more deeply oriented towards sustainable

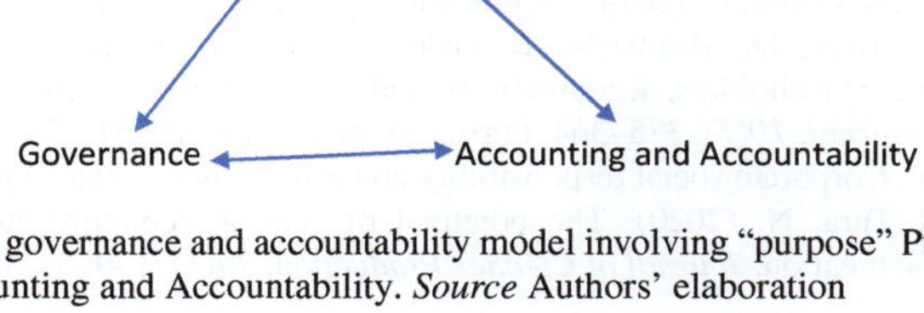

Fig. 1.1 Mission, governance and accountability model involving "purpose" Purpose and Mission Governance Accounting and Accountability. *Source* Authors' elaboration

development, where social inclusion represents a relevant element in the accounting and accountability processes.

References

Aceti, E., & Moràn, J. (2019). *Verso l'uomo. Una risposta alla povertà educativa contemporanea*, Roma: Città Nuova.

Amaduzzi, A. (1948). Il sistema produttivo dell'impresa nelle condizioni del suo equilibrio e nel suo andamento. In Studi di Economia Aziendale. Nuova edizione delle pubblicazioni originarie in occasione della giornata di studio per ricordare Aldo Amaduzzi. 1995. Roma: Edizioni Kappa.

Amodeo, D. (1993). Crepuscolo della Ragioneria, in *Scritti in onore di Carlo Masini*, Tomo I, Milano: EGEA, pp.23–30.

Baldarelli, M. G., & Cardillo, E. (2022). Managerial paths, social inclusion, and NBS in tactile cultural products: Theory and practice. *Journal of Hospitality & Tourism Research, 46*(3), 544–582.

Baldarelli, MG., & Ceraulo, S. (2024). Collective value co-creation and accountability in purpose-driven place-based companies: Theory and practice. In: Del Baldo, M., Baldarelli, MG., Righini, E. (eds*) Place based approaches to sustainability volume II*. Palgrave studies in sustainable business in association with future earth. Cham: Palgrave Macmillan. doi:https://doi.org/10.1007/978-3-031-41610-1_8; Print ISBN 978–3–031-41609-5; Online ISBN978–3–031-41610-1, pp. 177–199.

Baldarelli M. G., Del Baldo M., & Nesheva-Kiosseva N. (Eds.) (2017). *Environmental accounting and reporting. Theory and practice.* Book series: CSR, sustainability, ethics & governance (pp. 1–13). Cham: Springer. doi:https://doi.org/10.1007/978-3-319-50918-1.

Bhatt, B., Qureshi, I., & Sutter, C. (2022). (2022), how do intermediaries build inclusive markets? The role of the social context. *Journal of Management Studies, 59*, 4. https://doi.org/10.1111/joms.12796

Broadbent, J. (1998). The gendered nature of 'accounting logic': Pointers to an accounting that encompasses multiple values. *Critical Perspectives on Accounting, 9*, 267–297. https://doi.org/10.1006/cpac.1997.0158

Carnegie, G. D. (2022). Accounting 101: Redefining accounting for tomorrow. *Accounting Education, 31*(6), 615–628. https://doi.org/10.1080/09639284.2021.2014915

Carnegie, G. D., & Napier, C. J.(2023). *Introduction to the handbook of accounting, accountability and governance.* Elgar Publishing.

Catturi, G. (eds) (2004). La determinazione del valore creato, Vol II, Padova: CEDAM.

Del Baldo, M. (2020). Company case study 8: Cucinelli. Springer books, *in:* Walter Wehrmeyer & Stéphanie Looser & Mara Del Baldo *(ed.),* Intrinsic CSR and competition, chapter 0, pages 241–259, *Cham:* Springer.*DOI:* https://doi.org/10.1007/978-3-030-21037-3_15.

Gianfelici, C. (2024). *Rendicontazione di Sostenibilità e Washing. Fondamenti teorici ed evidenze empiriche*, ROMA:ARACNE.

Gray, R. (2013). Sustainability + accounting education: The elephant in the classroom. *Accounting Education, 22*(4), 308–332. https://doi.org/10.1080/09639284.2013.817795

Gray, R., Adams, C., & Owen, D. (2014). Accountability, social responsibility and sustainability:

Gray, R., Dey, C., Owen, D., Evans, R., & Zadek, S. (1997). Struggling with the praxis of social accounting: Stakeholders, accountability, audits and procedures. *Accounting, Auditing & Accountability Journal, 10*(3), 325–364. https://doi.org/10.1108/09513579710178106

Idowu, S. O. (2015). Corporate social responsibility and governance. Cham: Springer.

Laukkanen, M., & Tura, N. (2020). The potential of sharing economy business models for sustainable value creation. *Journal of Cleaner Production, 25*(3), 1–9.

Matacena, A. (2017). The subject we are dealing with: MGA model of the Enterprise. In M. G. Baldarelli, M. G., Del Baldo, M. & Nesheva-Kiosseva, N. (Eds.), *Environmental accounting and reporting. Theory and practice*, book series: CSR, sustainability, ethics & governance (pp. 1–13). Cham: Springer. doi: https://doi.org/10.1007/978-3-319-50918-1.

May, S., Königsson, M., & Holmstrom, J. (2017). Unlocking the sharing economy: Investigating the barriers for the sharing economy in a city context. *First Monday, 22*(2). https://doi.org/10.5210/fm.v22i2.7110

Modi, K., Kasana, S., Azam, A., & Madhavan, L. (2021). Education, poverty and social exclusion: Assessment of youth leaving care. *SN Social Sciences, 1*(4), 82.

Nussbaum, M.C. (2011). Non per profitto. Bologna: Il Mulino.

Oksana, M., Voytenko Palgan, Y., Bradley, K., & Zvolska, L. (2020). A decade of the sharing economy: Concepts, users, business and governance perspectives. *Journal of Cleaner Production, 269*(1), 122–215.

Pelligra, V. (2008). Vulnerabilità e dipendenza. Dal contratto alla responsabilità e ritorno [Vulnerability and addiction: From contract to liability and back]. In Pelligra, V. (Ed.), Imprese sociali: Scelte individuali e interessi comuni (pp. 1–15). Milano: Mondadori.

Qureshi, I., Bhatt, B. & Shukla, D. M. (2021). Sharing economy at the base of the pyramid: Opportunities and challenges, Cham: Springer.

Rodrìguez, S. G. (2014). Campo de Guerra. Barcellona: Anagrama.

Schmidpeter, R., & Altenburger, R. (Eds) (2023). Responsible Artificial Intelligence. *Challenges for¬ sustainable management.*, in book series: CSR, sustainability, Ethics & Governance. Cham: Springer. doi:https://doi.org/10.1007/978-3-031-09245-9.

Maria-Gabriella Baldarelli , PhD, CPA, is Associate Professor of Accounting, at University of Bologna, Department of Management—Rimini Campus. Full professor availability. Envited professor at Sophia University Institute. SIDREA board member until 2018. She is a member of international scientific networks: the Centre for Social and Environmental Accounting Research (CSEAR) and the European Business Ethics Network (EBEN). Key-note Speaker second International Conference on Economics, Business, Finance and Governance (ICEBFG) by Economics and Business Faculty of University of Bandar Lampung-Bali-Indonesia-Dic. 4–5, 2019. Research interests includes: accountability and gambling enterprises; corporate social responsibility; ethical, social and environmental accounting and accountability, sustainability in tourist enterprises; responsible and accessible tourism for blind people, economy of communion; gender accounting; accounting history, accounting education and Feminist Economics.

Eleonora Cardillo is Associate Professor of Business Economics—at the Department of Economics and Business of the University of Catania. She was Visiting Scholar at the CSEAR (Centre for social and environmental accounting research) School of Management of the University of St Andrews (Scotland) for the research project: "Study and analysis of the methodological and operational paths of environmental and social reporting in the evolution process of accounting information systems". Professor of Accounting and Financial Statements and Public accounting in local administrations. She was Director and Scientific Coordinator of the Master in Accounting and Control in Local Authorities, organized by the Department of Economics and Business of the University of Catania. Her research topics are public accounting systems, performance measurement, socio-environmental reporting, social inclusion in tactile museums, sustainability and accountability.

Chapter 2
Defining Accounting and Accountability for Sustainability and Social Inclusion

Maria-Gabriella Baldarelli and Eleonora Cardillo

Abstract The chapter examines the complex relationship between accounting and sustainability, highlighting how the role of accounting is not limited to a matter of communication and representation, but contributes to sustainable transformation and reduction of the negative impact of organizations on the environment. A section is dedicated to the definition of the key concepts of accounting, sustainability and social reporting, in order to identify their conceptual and practical areas. After highlighting the communicative role of accounting, the chapter specifically addresses the principles of sustainability and accountability. In conclusion, it highlights the importance of social inclusion as a component of social sustainability.

2.1 Accounting and Sustainability: A Complex Relationship

The development of sustainability, occurred with great speed and interest in the last ten years, has undoubtedly given greater importance to the topic of accounting. There is a relationship between accounting and socio-environmental aspects, and they exert a reciprocal influence. Understanding this mutual influence means embracing sustainability and considering accounting and reporting as elements that can support sustainable activities and actions.

Social, economic, environmental and governance issues, which are key elements of sustainability, are linked to the reporting system and can be partially measured and represented according to an accounting logic. However, the role of accounting is not limited to a question of representation, but should contribute to a sustainable transformation and to the reduction of the negative impact of organizations

M.-G. Baldarelli
University of Bologna, Bologna, Italy
e-mail: maria.baldarelli@unibo.it

E. Cardillo (✉)
University of Catania, Catania, Italy
e-mail: cardillo@unict.it

M. Baldarelli et al. (eds.), *Accounting and Accountability for Social Inclusion*, CSR, Sustainability, Ethics & Governance, https://doi.org/10.1007/978-3-032-09271-7_2

on the environment. In this sense, accounting processes represent a way to critically address the unsustainability of the world, problematize it and promote transformation (Thomson 2014).

Drawing a link between accounting system and sustainability issues from a theoretical and technical perspective implies sharing principles and criteria, which are often not easy to implement. Some authors (Walker and Wan 2012) highlight that establishing a sustainability-oriented integration between reporting, management accounting and control is difficult when internal systems for sustainable improvement are lacking.

The delicate and often contradictory relationship between accounting and socio and environmental reporting has been studied and interpreted under different profiles and fields in the literature (Broadbent and Guthrie 1992; Pallot 1992; Guthrie 1998; Steccolini 2002; Perrone 2004; Garry et al. 2005; Gray et al. 2017; Laine et al. 2021; Hamilton 2021, Ascani et al. 2021). Sometimes, contrasting reflections emerge that lead to extreme positions that establish a conflict of purposes between the two accounting systems (Gray and Bebbington 2000; Bebbington et al. 2017). International literature offers interesting conceptual and critical insights into socio and environmental accounting, linked to the in-depth analysis and substantial delimitation of different meanings relating to the historical evolution of this discipline (Moggi 2019; Barbu et al. 2022).

2.2 Defining Accounting, Sustainability Reporting and Social Accounting

The nature of accounting is linked to the collection of significant data derived from the observed and selected management phenomena, whose scope and informational content depend on the cognitive purposes to be achieved. Accounting becomes functional to the need for collecting and representing relevant information, as well as communicating the resulting outcomes. Thus, accounting system constitutes the flow of information that arrives, circulates and departs from the entity, its retrieval and use for managerial purposes. The need to control the flow of information is influenced by the complexity of organization events and this involves a process of selecting phenomena to capture those "significant for research, avoiding weighing down the investigation with the detection of phenomena that are not of interest or, even worse, that can obscure the knowledge sought" (Onida 1970). Given the multiple and diversified aspects of entities, the accounting system translates this variety into common and homogeneous values. Zappa (1927) effectively states that "business life is much more complex than it appears from our systematic surveys. Systematic surveys, necessarily synthetic, lead each phenomenon back to the homogeneous, reveal the necessary connections, in one or a few aspects, abstract a few common notes from the complex reality" (Zappa 1927). The company system is based on the technical-accounting procedures necessary to carry out the survey activity but also on the material and immaterial resources used in it and on the philosophy with which this activity is managed and organized (Airoldi et al. 2005). The economic-financial balance, theorized for a long time by business scholars (Coda 1988, 2014; D'Amico 1999; Melis 2007), is only partial or apparent if it does not also guarantee the maintenance of the general economic-social system in which the business unit is inserted (Amaduzzi 1949; Catturi 2009).

While the financial, economic and patrimonial reporting aspects are the main focus of traditional financial accounting, sustainability reporting centers mainly on social, environmental, economic and governance aspects. Sustainability reporting, as we will see in the next chapter, can adopt a dual materiality approach that considers both the impact of corporate activities on society and the environment, and the influence of society and the environment on the company.

Current development of sustainability reporting is relevant in order to understand how organizations monitor the impact of their activities on the environment, society and the economy (Adams & Whelan 2009). It represents a key tool for companies and institutions to demonstrate their commitment to sustainability and build trust with stakeholders and community.

When sustainability performance data and information are integrated with management decisions, they can create value for society, ecosystems and the territory (Porter and Kramer 2006). Sustainability reporting represents the creation of sustainability report that collects, analyzes and communicates information on sustainability (Christofi et al. 2012; Hahn and Kühnen 2013).

Another measurement area is sustainability management accounting, which uses measures and indicators to improve sustainability performance. Unlike sustainability reporting, sustainability management accounting is based on diversified methods that aim to monitor data and provide information for internal communication and reporting to support the decision-making process (Maas et al. 2016).

Sustainability is therefore measured and communicated with the aim of creating transparency and improving performance. However, to create a transparency circuit and provide support to management decisions for performance improvement, it is necessary to coordinate and organize internal processes and procedures for measuring and managing sustainability information (Table 2.1).

Table 2.1 Key sustainability measurement and management approaches from transparency and performance improvement perspectives

	Transparency	Performance improvement
Measurement	Sustainability assessment (mainly based on reporting needs)	Sustainability management accounting (mainly based on strategic objectives)
Management & communication	Sustainability reporting	(progressive) design and use of formal and informal sustainability management control

Source Maas et al. 2016, 238–242

The measurement, management, and communication processes related to an organization's sustainability path can be interpreted from a transparency and performance-management perspective (Maas et al. 2016). By enhancing clarity, accountability, and the quality of disclosed information, these processes support more informed decision-making and strengthen the organization's commitment to sustainable value creation.

In recent literature, accounting that includes the protection of the environment and ecosystems is considered an area of broader social accounting, starting from the consideration that the environment is a social issue (Gray 2002; Gray and Bebbington 2000; Bebbington et al. 2017).

Social issues are now an area that is measured by sustainability reporting, when through double materiality, the organization measures its impact on the social context and the influence of stakeholders on the company's performance. These considerations make it difficult to draw a precise demarcation between financial accounting, social accounting, and environmental accounting (Cooper et al. 2005).

In its classic definition, social reporting (accounting) refers specifically to corporate social responsibility, therefore mainly dealing with the impact of corporate activities on society and environment (Brown and Fraser 2006). From the general definition of social accounting, different meanings can be identified such as "social responsibility account" or "corporate social disclosure" or even "social accountability disclosure" that can commonly be traced back to the essential construction, presentation and communication of a social account (Gray et al. 2017), measuring social and environmental aspects of the organization. Some authors (Gray et al. 1996) defines social accounting ad "the process of communicating the social and environmental effects of organisations' economic actions to particular interest groups within society at large. As such, it involves extending the accountability of organisations, beyond the traditional role of providing a financial account to the owners of capital, in particular, shareholders. Such an extension is predicated upon the assumption that companies do have wider responsibilities than simply to make money for their shareholders". Mathews (1993) traced the term social accounting to the following areas of activity:

- *Social responsibility accounting* (SRA) which concerns the collection and dissemination of financial and non-financial, quantitative and non-quantitative information on the activities of companies. This area includes human resources accounting, employee reporting, accounting and democratic principles. Alternative terms used may be social responsibility disclosure and corporate social reporting.
- *Total impact accounting* (TIA). This term is used to report the total effects of an organization on the environment. To determine this effect, it is necessary to measure private and public costs. Due to the origins of this area of research, it is often referred to both cost-benefit analysis and social accounting and sometimes social audit, generating terminological confusion. This area currently includes the topic of accounting for sustainable development.
- *Social-economic accounting* (SEA). It represents the process of evaluating activities that derive from public funding, using financial and non-financial measures.

The entire activity should be evaluated with regard to the value of the expenditure used in relation to results achieved.

- *Social indicators accounting*. They are used to measure macro-social events, in order to establish the objectives and fix the time frame (beyond the long term) within which these objectives must be achieved. The results of this analysis should be of interest for national politics and for political decision-making processes at national and regional level.
- *Societal accounting*. This term is used to suggest a form of accounting that integrates any other form of over-interpretation or metatheory. This sphere is purely theoretical.

This division summarizes from a theoretical and systemic point of view some possible areas of social reporting, however it is really difficult to delimit from a practical point of view their measures and processes.

The concept of social responsibility (Lindblom 1983; Mathews 1993; Ramasastry 2015; Gray et al. 2017; Demirag 2018) refers to the voluntary dissemination of quantitative and qualitative information produced by an organization to inform or influence the community. The part of quantitative information can be financial and non-financial, and qualitative data and assessments of potential interest to employees, the community, owners and creditors are also included. If internal and external social communication assumes a certain value in management processes, it is appropriate that the quality of accounting systems improves with respect to the production and selection of truthful and reliable information and data.

The considerations presented above highlight that both sustainability reporting systems and social reporting systems also depend on the structure and organization of the accounting system. Therefore, socio-environmental accounting models and sustainability reports can become an integral part of reporting system, influencing its structure and information content (Ozili 2022). In this sense, accounting and accountability constitute the basis for measuring and monitoring sustainability issues and improving socio-environmental practices.

2.3 The Communicative Value of Accounting

The above reflections highlight the importance for organizations to activate accountability process to make their work more "accountable". In this sense, improving the utility that derived from the traditional accounting system requires awareness and knowledge of its limits and conventional meanings (Miller 1998).

The achievement of economic and financial balance is therefore insufficient if it is not accompanied by consideration of environmental and social impacts on the territorial context. This implies a reactive and timely behavior by companies and institutions in adapting to an ever-changing environment.

Accounting in organizations, through the processes of collecting and evaluating data and information, analyzes phenomena with economic, social, and environmental

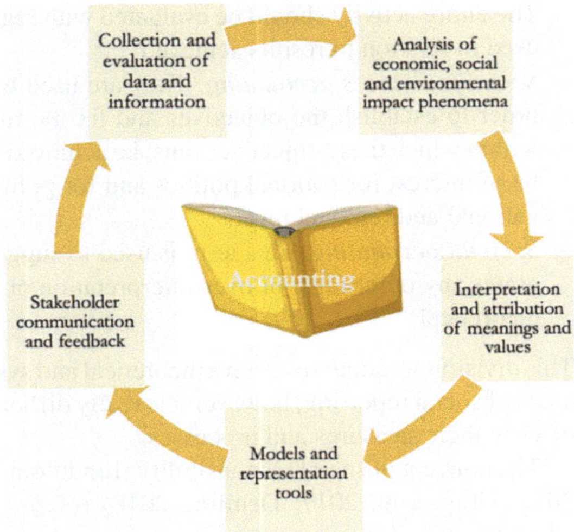

Fig. 2.1 - The communicative value of accounting. *Source* Authors' elaboration

impacts. It interprets them and attributes meanings and values that, appropriately described and represented with specific models, are communicated to stakeholders to share the semantic aspects (Fig. 2.1).

Accounting performs two essential functions within an organization: registration and collection, on the one hand, and disclosure and dissemination of information on the other. In this sense, accounting is the process of identifying, measuring, and communicating economic information to enable informed judgments and decisions by information users (Belkaoui 2000). The introduction of sustainability evaluation tools within accounting highlights the importance assumed by the methods of information disclosure; accounting is in fact conceived not only as an activity of mere measurement and selection of data but also as a relevant tool for transferring information and communicating social values and the two functions are closely connected and correlated (Salter et al. 2013; Retolaza et al. 2016). Through its dual communicative value, both internal and external, accounting conveys not only data but also the entity's system of values. Accounting, therefore, as a classification and language system, plays an essential role in shaping the perception of the social world by influencing its logic and meanings. In fact, accounting, starting from an activity of data collection and recording, provides an account of management results by activating a process that supports accountability. Accounting information used for this purpose demonstrates that resources have been allocated and distributed appropriately and employed for legitimate purposes. These considerations attribute greater significance to accounting, as accounting data, synthetic and codified expression of entity events, becomes a "symptom and symbol" of the life of the organization. In particular, it is evidence of different elements: a) the specific qualities of the entity and of the cultural elements that characterize organizational models and production methods; b) the ways of relating to the environment and managing social needs and expectations (Catturi, 2005). Accounting data enriches the symbolic and communicative dimension of organizations and entities. In an evolutionary and adaptive logic, it expresses the continuous environmental changes that entity undergoes in its development. "Thus, the corporate history described by accounting data is not only the history of a single socio-economic organism, but of the community and individuals that compose it and that express its culture; for this reason, corporate history is also the history of all the individuals that constitute the social community and of their cultural horizons; in short, by making corporate history we make social history" (Catturi 2005). In this perspective, accounting, according to the accountability approach, becomes a tool to express the social values of the organization as well as ethical and inclusive behaviors (Dillard 2014). The function assumed by accounting goes beyond the production of information and data to reach a meaning more closely linked to organizational processes and the transfer of social values. This dimension, which sees in accountability the logic of remodulation and redefinition of the accounting system, makes accounting an activity that is not purely technical but also and predominantly a means of explicating social value.

2.4 The Evolutionary Dimension of Sustainability

Sustainability can be considered as a constantly changing and fascinating concept in its changing and, sometimes, contradictory meanings (Santillo 2007). The pursuit of sustainability represents a precious goal for humanity. This concept, defined by the WCED (United Nation World Commission on Environment and Development) in 1987, known as the Bruntland Commission from the name of the Norwegian President Gro Harlem Bruntland, has been extended to different areas and therefore it is not easy to understand its real semantic boundary. Several issues emerge when one tries to define sustainability: clarifying its meaning in concrete terms, identifying the underlying ideological and political reasons and specifying the measures to put it into practice (Pezzey 2017). There is a broad consensus in considering the transition process towards sustainability as a common path to be activated, in an attempt to reduce the risk that environmental problems may compromise the survival of the human system and generate repercussions in the future of generations (Bonsu et al. 2020; Ali et al. 2023).

The definition of sustainability is therefore linked to the concept of sustainable development to which companies and organizations tend. Sustainable development is a type of development that meets the needs of the present without compromising the ability of future generations to meet their own needs. This definition comes from the WCED Brundtland Report (1987), which also highlights that "species and ecosystems must be preserved because they have an 'economic value' that is deemed crucial for development and important to human welfare" (WCED 1987, 147). Some authors (Imran et al. 2014) try to trace the complexity back to this definition, and state that "Sustainable development will then be seen as a process or approach that contributes to the well-being of ecological systems which in turn offer a better life for all living beings. It will have to address profound issues related to socio-ecological responsibility, inter-generational and intra-generational equity for all life on earth, maintaining an aggregate natural capital stock at a constant level over time, biophysical limits of the life-support system of the earth and eco-economies. This holistic and integrated approach will form the key characterization of an ecocentric dimension to sustainable development" (Imran et al. 2014).

The problem of sustainability creates the emergence of issues related to ethics, values and cultural dynamics in the relationships between individuals and society. The intergenerational problem, for example, highlights situations in which measures for the protection and safeguard of future generations could conflict with the will of present generations (for example, if a generation has to work to overcome socio-environmental problems, through the reduction of consumption and increasing investments, it assumes responsibility for damages that derive from previous generations and in this sense a situation of inequity could emerge). Sustainability includes the need to safeguard both social and environmental aspects that are expressed in the respective concepts of eco-justice and eco-efficiency (Gray and Bebbington 2001). In particular, eco-justice (which deals with social aspects) is linked to the concepts of equity and in particular to fair relationships between peoples with respect to available resources. Eco-efficiency (connected to environmental aspects) is a concept that takes on importance both because it refers to the careful use of the planet's scarce resources, and because it examines the issue of achieving a correct distribution of well-being (intragenerational equity), ensuring the growth of future generations (intergenerational equity). The development of sustainability reporting has led to a growing attention to social issues. If, in general terms, the concept of sustainability refers to the protection of present and future generations and the essential respect for their needs, it is understood that these needs are both social and environmental. Richardson (2007) states that sustainability accounting is used to refer a framework to account for financial implication of sustainability across the triple bottom line for individuals organization or company.

The approach to sustainability involves rethinking the way we organize and conduct our way of life from a social and economic point of view (Barbier and Burgess 2017). Sustainability is part of the interaction between the more complex human system and the direct implications on environmental systems. Understanding sustainability requires an understanding of the human and environmental system. The concept of sustainability is constantly evolving, and it involves continuous monitoring of the purposes and processes connected to it (Hajian and Kashani 2021). Different disciplines and schools are linked to the issue of sustainability. Natural sciences are useful for approaching geological, ecological, biological problems and for measuring changes in general, identifying trends and predicting results. It is also linked to social sciences, economics and the study of cultural values. The key to achieving sustainable development is understanding and modeling the interactions between the overall adaptive natural system and socio-economic systems. The nature of this relationship is constantly changing; just as species are born and become extinct and resources run out and others are rediscovered, in the same way socio-economic systems expand and contract. Both solutions and problems are dynamic and traced back to the different levels to which sustainability can be referred, and in particular to the individual, corporate, regional and local levels or to a country, a continent or the entire world economy. The debate around the environment leads to considering two social reasons: the social reasons for which the environment continues to be degraded and the social impact that derives from this situation. For these reasons it is impossible to maintain a distinction between the environment, sustainability and social issues.

2.5 Accountability, Sustainability and Social Inclusion

The concept of accountability, as a duty to provide an account for the actions for which one is responsible, is related to the concept of sustainability (Elkington 1998; Bovens 2007).

The basic principle that constitutes the guiding idea of social accounting models or sustainability reporting is accountability. It interprets the information responsibility of the organization, enhances the communication system, internal and external, and allows for the implementation of transparency and control. Accountability expresses the informative duty, carried out by any organization producing goods and services, with respect to the rights of stakeholders to obtain information on resources, procedural methods and results of the operational processes implemented. It arises from the general principle of social responsibility which attributes value to the informative relationships that are created between companies, institutions and social groups (Busuioc and Lodge 2017). "Organization, understood as a complex model, is a social phenomenon strongly engaged in a continuous exchange with the environment that surrounds it and which it tries to dominate, without being excessively influenced by it" (Anselmi 1993). In this sense, "in the firm, the study of the interrelationships that link parts, aspects and functions to unity, which bind operations in time and space, appears indispensable again and again to critically evaluate the information obtained from any economic analysis and to select the behaviors to be adopted in light of the repercussions that could be generated on the entire system" (Cavalieri 1999).

In the 1970s and 1980s, the concept of accountability was linked to the so-called "agency theory". In this approach, being in favor of a behavior that responds to the duty of accountability depends on the position that the subjects occupy within the company. At the basis of this model is the idea that in companies, owners are separated from managers and directors and that for the latter there is a need to report their actions to the former. In this sense, managerial accountability (Wild 1994) is developed, in which the relationships between subordinates and their superiors in hierarchical organizations are analyzed. In the 1990s, there was a growing and shared interest in social reporting processes and therefore in the logic of accountability. Perks (1993) analyses the concept under three fields of observation: accountability based on the perspective of companies, the approach with respect to the public sector and managerial accountability. For simplicity, Perks considers only two parties involved in each communication process: directors/executives report to owners, politicians to voters, secretaries to managers. The definition he attributes to this term leads back to the obligation of an organisation to provide an "account" ("Accountability means the obligation to give an account"), clarifying that to understand the purposes underlying it, it is necessary to know: who reports, to whom they report, how and what. In general, organizations and different corporate entities are led, due to the position they occupy in society, to report the results of their activity to different groups or to a reference community in a concrete and transparent way. Perks argues that if we were to assume the position of principal, we are more inclined to accept a system of accountability because the power we hold means that others are accountable to us for their actions. If we are agents, perhaps we are less inclined to accept a system that may be restrictive of our freedom of action. According to Gray and Jenkins (1993), there are three different types of accountability as result of combinations of different logics (legal, economic, technical, social and political) and in particular they are "financial accountability", "managerial accountability" and "professional accountability".

Gray et al. (1997) consider accountability as an emancipatory concept that support organizations in exposing, enhancing and developing social relationship through a re-examination and expansion of established rights to information. They also state that social accountability "arises only if organizations have a social responsibility otherwise there is no social accountability to discharge". In this sense, the concept of accountability, manifesting itself in a moral and sometimes formal duty, arises from the responsibility of individuals and organizations to account for their activities. The realization of the concept of accountability involves not only the availability of information, but also that it is reliable and qualitatively satisfactory, understandable and accessible. Kearns (1996), arguing that society should consider creating an "accountability environment", identifies different meanings of the concept. First, one meaning is that related to public needs and requirements. Furthermore, being accountable requires a negotiation activity and an appropriate response to the demand of customers, particular group interests and other potential stakeholders. Other times, accountability is defined in terms of discretionary judgments, calculated risks and business activities. Finally, accountability is expressed in relation to administrative duty, when governments and non-profit organizations interpret and communicate the needs of citizens to the higher authorities that have power and financial resources to meet such needs. When examining the profiles of accountability, three distinct dimensions can be identified (Bovens 1998):

a) an external profile that concerns the external communication of the results achieved. The communication of the results achieved is even more important when society and the community feel the need and/or the right to receive information. The need for accountability arises in some contexts from the request for popular participation and the need to activate mechanisms of collaboration among interested parties;
b) a second profile is the internal one, related to the "responsibilization" of the subjects holding decision-making power in the organizational system. These

subjects perceive social needs and verify the results achieved and the deviations from the planned objectives;

c) a third profile of accountability is the accounting one. In this sense, the most suitable accounting reporting system is identified to define and record objectives and results not only in financial terms but also in economic and sectoral terms.

Munro (1996) states that, on the one hand, we have "accounts" understood as stories, explanations and reasons and, on the other, "accounts" understood as codified representations, documents expressed in numerical form. In today's language, this term is often referred to as something that should be achieved rather than as a formally constituted element. The difference lies in considering accountability as a statically represented element, through a document for example, or looking at accountability as a process in which different subjects interact and carry out a communicative exchange. Mulgan (2000) describes several elements and actions underlying accountability: the preparation of an account requested by external subjects or entities; the activation of social interactions and exchange, through a communication and feedback process; the consideration of the authority's rights to answer for those actions for which it is called to answer and for which it is sanctionable.

The concept can be defined also as a personal or organizational virtue or as a social relationship or mechanism (Bovens 2010). The term accountability in the sense of virtue, refers to substantive norms and principles for the actors behavior and to actions and measures regarding transparency and control. The concept of accountability as a mechanism is linked to the nature of the obligation to give an account which may arise from a hierarchical or principal-agent relationship, from a contractual agreement or obligations assumed voluntarily (Table 2.2).

Source Bovens 2010, 959–960.

According to some doctrinal orientations (Odongo and Wang 2018), accountability constitutes a form of responsibility towards society and surrounding entities, which, being directly or indirectly affected by the organization, fully hold moral rights and a right to information (Tamvada, 2020). In this sense, within the scope of a firm's activity, the ethical dimension coexists with the economic dimension, with the latter unable to be truly separated from the former or analyzed in isolation (Cavalieri and Franceschi 2010).

Table 2.2 Two concept of accountability

Accountability as a	Virtue	Mechanism
Locus	Behaviour of actor	Relation actor-forum
Focus	Evaluative/prescriptive	Analytical/descriptive
	Substantive standards	Effect of arrangements
Field of study	Good governance	Political and social control
Research design	Dependent variable	Independent variable
Importance	Legitimacy	Various goals
Deficit	Inappropriate behaviour	Absent or malfunctioning mechanisms

Accountability, even in its current meaning, represents the principle that characterizes the communication models of organizations that provide information on their work and it is an expression of their duty of responsibility. The recognition of responsibility translates into a reactive or sensitive behavior of the organization by creating a connection with society or interested parties (Masiero et al. 2020; Wong et al. 2021; Samans and Nelson 2022). In the context of building a process of social interaction, different levels of implementation of accountability can be identified. It can be achieved through accounting tools and standards that are linked to responsible, ethical and moral behavior. However, today there are new accountability tools that have innovated the communication channels between organizations and citizens, for example the use of social media or the implementation of digital communication strategies (Yusuff et al. 2023).

Several elements, including the pandemic period and the growing awareness of the community on the importance of environmental protection and safeguarding, have stimulated a strong and frenetic cultural movement in the last decade that has led the EU and the governments of nations to pay attention to environmental and social issues. The UN Agenda 2030 has defined sustainability objectives (SDGs) with the aim of improving the overall conditions of the world and the degree of accountability for human actions towards the community. Social inclusion plays an important role within the action program of the Agenda 2030. In fact, this theme is transversal to various targets linked to the different SDGs. Social inclusion represents a sustainability objective (Mendoza-del Villar et al. 2020) that plays a crucial role in promoting shared participation and equal opportunities for citizens across different contexts and areas, while overcoming discriminatory and racist practices.

For example, Goal 4 highlights the importance of ensuring inclusive and equitable quality education and promoting lifelong learning opportunities for all. It also highlights the need to build adequate and child-responsive, disability- and gender-sensitive education facilities and provide safe, non-violent, inclusive and effective learning environments for all. Goal 5 aims to eliminate all forms of violence against all women and girls in the public and private spheres, including trafficking for prostitution, sexual exploitation and other forms of exploitation. Goal 8 aims to promote sustained, inclusive and sustainable economic growth, full and productive employment and decent work for all. Goal 9 promotes inclusive and sustainable industrialization through the development of quality, reliable, sustainable and resilient infrastructure. Goal 10 aims to promote social, economic and political inclusion for all, regardless of age, gender, disability, race, ethnicity, origin, religion, economic status. Goal 16 promotes peaceful and more inclusive societies for sustainable development, providing access to justice for all and creating effective, accountable and inclusive institutions. It also aims to ensure responsive, inclusive, participatory and representative decision-making at all levels.

Social inclusion and a sense of belonging are important components of social sustainability (Dempsey et al. 2011). However, creating a socially inclusive environment where people feel a sense of belonging may be a theoretical ideal, as in workplaces or urban communities there is a complex and contradictory reality (Kohon 2018). Inclusive processes aim to reduce social inequalities that lead to divisions among different population groups. In this context, the decisions of institutions and governments, the transformation of politics and the improvement of public services can foster inclusive, targeted, collaborative and responsible systems (Mir et al., 2024).

2.6 Conclusions

The chapter has tried to identify the relationship between reporting and socio-environmental aspects and their mutual influence. The nature of reporting is linked to the collection of significant data deriving from management phenomena whose information content depends on the cognitive objectives that are intended to be achieved. Accounting and reporting should constitute elements to support measurement and sustainable activities.

The development of sustainability reporting is relevant to understand how organizations monitor the impact of their activities on environment, society and economy.

Sustainability assessment and communication have the objective of creating transparency and improving performance. To favor transparency circuit and provide support to management decisions, it is necessary to coordinate and organize the internal processes of measurement and management of sustainability information.

To this end, the chapter has highlighted the role of accounting in this context. In fact, through the processes of data and information collection and evaluation, it analyzes phenomena with economic, social and environmental impacts and communicates them to stakeholders to share their semantic aspects. Two essential concepts are the basis of socio-environmental reporting systems: sustainability and accountability. The definition of sustainability is linked to the concept of sustainable development. At its base emerges the need for species and ecosystems to be preserved because they have an "economic and social value"considered crucial for development and important for human well-being. Accountability, a constantly evolving concept, implies the presence of different elements: the preparation of a report requested by subjects to account for activities; the activation of social interactions and exchanges; the right/duty to answer for the actions for which the organization is responsible. In line with the principles of accountability, social inclusion represents a sustainability objective that takes on great importance in achieving shared participation and equal opportunities. These reflections are in line with SDG Goal 4 of the Agenda 2030 which underlines the relevance of ensuring quality, inclusive and equitable education and promoting lifelong learning opportunities for all.

References

Adams, C. A., & Whelan, G. (2009). Conceptualising future change in corporate sustainability reporting. *Accounting, Auditing & Accountability Journal, 22*(1), 118–143.

Airoldi, G., Brunetti, G., & Coda, V. (2005). *Corso di economia aziendale.* Il mulino.

Ali, S. M., Appolloni, A., Cavallaro, F., D'Adamo, I., Di Vaio, A., Ferella, F.,.& Zorpas, A. A. (2023). Development goals towards sustainability. *Sustainability,* 15(12), 9443.

Amaduzzi, A. (1949). *Conflitto ed equilibrio di interessi nel bilancio dell'impresa.* Francesco Cacucci.

Anselmi L. (1993), Economicità e socialità nell'azienda pubblica, in *Scritti in onore di Carlo Masini, Strategia e organizzazione delle aziende,* Milano: Egea.

Ascani, I., Ciccola, R., & Chiucchi, M. S. (2021). A structured literature review about the role of management accountants in sustainability accounting and reporting. *Sustainability, 13*(4), 2357.

Barbier, E. B., & Burgess, J. C. (2017). The sustainable development goals and the systems approach to sustainability. *Economics, 11*(1), 20170028.

Barbu, E. M., Ionescu-Feleagă, L., & Ferrat, Y. (2022). The evolution of environmental reporting in Europe: The role of financial and non-financial regulation. *The International Journal of Accounting, 57*(02), 2250008.

Bebbington, J., Russell, S., & Thomson, I. (2017). Accounting and sustainable development: Reflections and propositions. *Critical Perspectives on Accounting, 48,* 21–34.

Belkaoui, A. R. (2000). Accounting theory *(Fourth Ed.).* Business press, Thomson Learning.

Bonsu, N. O., TyreeHageman, J., & Kele, J. (2020). Beyond agenda 2030: Future-oriented mechanisms in localising the sustainable development goals (SDGs). *Sustainability, 12*(23), 9797.

Bovens, M. (2007). Analysing and assessing accountability: A conceptual framework 1. *European Law Journal, 13*(4), 447–468.

Bovens, M. (2010). Two concepts of accountability: Accountability as a virtue and as a mechanism. *West European Politics, 33*(5), 946–967.

Bovens, M. A. P. (1998). The quest for responsibility: Accountability and citizenship in complex organisations. Cambridge: Cambridge university press.

Broadbent, J., & Guthrie, J. (1992). Changes in the Public Sector: A Review of Recent Alternative Accounting Research. Accounting, Auditing & Accountability Journal, 5(2).

Brown, J., & Fraser, M. (2006). Approaches and perspectives in social and environmental accounting: An overview of the conceptual landscape. *Business Strategy and the Environment, 15*(2), 103–117.

Busuioc, M., & Lodge, M. (2017). Reputation and accountability relationships: Managing accountability expectations through reputation. *Public Administration Review, 77*(1), 91–100.

Catturi, G. (2005). Dato contabile, sistema di scritture del valore aggiunto e dimensione "politica" dell'azienda. *Contabilità e Cultura Aziendale, V(2).*

Catturi, G. (2009). Linguaggio e comunicazione degli organismi aziendali. *Pecunia: revista de la Facultad de Ciencias Económicas y Empresariales, 9,* 85–109.

Cavalieri E. (1999), Considerazioni sull'evoluzione delle teorie economico-aziendali, in Cavalieri E., Ranalli F., *Economia aziendale, 2,* Giappichelli.

Cavalieri, E., & Franceschi, R. F. (2010). *Economia aziendale* (Vol. 1). Giappichelli.

Christofi, A., Christofi, P., & Sisaye, S. (2012). Corporate sustainability: Historical development and reporting practices. *Management Research Review, 35*(2), 157–172.

Coda, V. (1988). *L'orientamento strategico dell'im-presa.* Unione Tip.-Ed. Torinese.

Coda, V. (2014). Enrico Cavalieri, il contributo alla teoria dell'equilibrio aziendale. *Contabilità e cultura aziendale: rivista della Società Italiana di Storia della Ragioneria: XIV*(2), 2014, 21–30.

Cooper, C., Taylor, P., Smith, N., & Catchpowle, L. (2005). A discussion of the political potential of social accounting. *Critical Perspectives on Accounting, 16*(7), 951–974.

D'Amico, L. (1999). Profili del processo evolutivo negli studi di economia aziendale. In *schemi di analisi per" paradigmi" e" programmi di ricerca scientifici"*. Giappichelli.

Demirag, I. (Ed.). (2018). *Corporate social responsibility, accountability and governance: Global perspectives*. Routledge.

Dempsey, N., Bramley, G., Power, S., & Brown, C. (2011). The social dimension of sustainable development: Defining urban social sustainability. *Sustainable Development, 19*(5), 289–300.

Dillard, J. (2014). Legitimating the social accounting project: An ethic of accountability. *Sustainability accounting and accountability*, 233–247.

Elkington, J. (1998). Accounting for the triple bottom line. *Measuring Business Excellence, 2*(3), 18–22.

Gray, A., & Jenkins, B. (1993). Codes of accountability in the new public sector. *Accounting, Auditing & Accountability Journal, 6*(3).

Gray, R. (2002). The social accounting project and accounting organizations and society privileging engagement, imaginings, new accountings and pragmatism over critique? *Accounting, Organizations and Society, 27*(7), 687–708.

Gray, R., Adams, C., & Owen, D. (2017). *Social and environmental accounting. In the Routledge companion to critical accounting*. Routledge.

Gray, R., & Bebbington, J. (2000). Environmental accounting, managerialism and sustainability: Is the planet safe in the hands of business and accounting? In *Advances in environmental accounting & management* (pp. 1–44). Emerald Group Publishing Limited.

Gray, R., Dey, C., Owen, D., Evans, R., & Zadek, S. (1997). Struggling with the praxis of social accounting: Stakeholders, accountability, audits and procedures. *Accounting, Auditing & Accountability Journal, 10*(3), 325–364.

Gray, R., Owen, D., & Adams, C. (1996). *Accounting & accountability: Changes and challenges in corporate social and environmental reporting*. Prentice hall.

Gray, R. H., & Bebbington, J. (2001). *Accounting for the Environment (Second ed.)*London: SAGE.

Guthrie, J. (1998). Application of accrual accounting in the Australian public sector–rhetoric or reality. *Financial accountability & management, 14*(1), 1–19.

Hahn, R., & Kühnen, M. (2013). Determinants of sustainability reporting: A review of results, trends, theory, and opportunities in an expanding field of research. *Journal of Cleaner Production, 59*, 5–21.

Hajian, M., & Kashani, S. J. (2021). Evolution of the concept of sustainability. From Brundtland report to sustainable development goals. In *Sustainable resource management* (pp. 1–24). Elsevier.

Hamilton, K. (2021). Accounting for sustainability. In *Approaches to sustainable development* (pp. 21–30). Routledge.

Imran, S., Alam, K., & Beaumont, N. (2014). Reinterpreting the definition of sustainable development for a more ecocentric reorientation. *Sustainable Development, 22*(2), 134–144.

Kearns, K. P. (1996). *Managing for accountability: Preserving the public Trust in Public and Nonprofit Organizations*. Jossey-Bass.

Kohon, J. (2018). Social inclusion in the sustainable neighborhood? Idealism of urban social sustainability theory complicated by realities of community planning practice. *City, Culture and Society, 15*, 14–22.

Laine, M., Tregidga, H., & Unerman, J. (2021). *Sustainability accounting and accountability*. Routledge.

Lindblom, C. K. (1983). The concept of organizational legitimacy and its implications for corporate social responsibility disclosure. *American Accounting Association Public Interest Section*, 220–221.

Maas, K., Schaltegger, S., & Crutzen, N. (2016). Integrating corporate sustainability assessment, management accounting, control, and reporting. *Journal of Cleaner Production, 136*, 237–248.

Masiero, E., Arkhipova, D., Massaro, M., & Bagnoli, C. (2020). Corporate accountability and stakeholder connectivity. *A case study. Meditari Accountancy Research, 28*(5), 803–831.

Mathews, M. R. (1993). *Socially responsible accounting*. Chapman & Hall.

Melis, A. (2007). Financial statements and positive accounting theory: The early contribution of Aldo Amaduzzi. *Accounting, Business & Financial History, 17*(1), 53–62.

Mendoza-del Villar, L., Oliva-Lopez, E., Luis-Pineda, O., Benešová, A., Tupa, J., & Garza-Reyes, J. A. (2020). Fostering economic growth, social inclusion & sustainability in industry 4.0: A systemic approach. *Procedia Manufacturing, 51*, 1755–1762.

Miller, P. (1998). The margins of accounting. *European Accounting Review, 7*(4), 605–621.

Mir, G., Durrani, N., Julian, R., Kimei, Y., Mashreky, S., & Doan, T. D. (2024). Social inclusion and sustainable development: Findings from seven African and Asian contexts. *Sustainability, 16*(11), 4859.

Moggi, S. (2019). Social and environmental reports at universities: A Habermasian view on their evolution. *Accounting Forum, 43*(3), 283–326.

Mulgan, R. (2000). Accountability: An ever-expanding concept? *Public Administration, 78*(3), 555–573.

Munro, R. (1996). Alignment and identity work: The study of accounts and accountability. *In Accountability: Power, Ethos and the Technologies of Managing*, R. Munro and Mouritsen J. International Thomson Business Press.

Odongo, N. H., & Wang, D. (2018). Corporate responsibility, ethics and accountability. *Social Responsibility Journal, 14*(1), 111–122.

Onida, P. (1970). La logica ed il sistema delle rilevazioni quantitative d'azienda, Giuffrè.

Ozili, P. K. (2022). Sustainability accounting. In *Managing risk and decision making in times of economic distress, part a* (pp. 171–180). Emerald Publishing Limited.

Pallot, J. (1992). Elements of a theoretical framework for public sector accounting. *Accounting, Auditing & Accountability Journal, 5*(1).

Perks, R. W. (1993). *Accounting and society*. Chapman & Hall.

Perrone, P. (2004). La responsabilità sociale degli enti locali e la comunicazione dei risultati. *Azienda Pubblica, n. 2.*

Pezzey, J. (2017). Sustainability: An interdisciplinary guide. In *The economics of sustainability* (pp. 103–144). Routledge.

Porter, M. E., & Kramer, M. R. (2006). The link between competitive advantage and corporate social responsibility. *Harvard Business Review, 84*(12), 78–92.

Ramasastry, A. (2015). Corporate social responsibility versus business and human rights: Bridging the gap between responsibility and accountability. *Journal of Human Rights, 14*(2), 237–259.

Retolaza, J. L., San-Jose, L., & Ruíz-Roqueñi, M. (2016). *Social accounting for sustainability: Monetizing the social value, 53–55*. Springer.

Richardson, B. J. (2007). Financing environmental sustainability. *Corporate Governance and Sustainability: Challenges for Theory and Practice,* 122.

Salter, S. B., Kang, T., Gotti, G., & Doupnik, T. S. (2013). The role of social values, accounting values and institutions in determining accounting conservatism. *Management International Review, 53*, 607–632.

Samans, R., & Nelson, J. (2022). Corporate reporting and accountability. In *Sustainable Enterprise value creation: Implementing stakeholder capitalism through full ESG integration* (pp. 187–218). Springer International Publishing.

Santillo, D. (2007). Reclaiming the definition of sustainability (7 pp). *Environmental Science and Pollution Research, 14*(1).

Steccolini, I. (2002). Local government annual report: an accountability medium?. *SDA Bocconi Research Division Working Paper*, (02–81).

Tamvada, M. (2020). Corporate social responsibility and accountability: A new theoretical foundation for regulating CSR. *International Journal of Corporate Social Responsibility, 5*(1), 2.

Thomson, I. (2014). Mapping the terrain of sustainability and accounting for sustainability. In *Sustainability accounting and accountability* (pp. 15–29). Routledge.

Wild, J. J. (1994). Managerial accountability to shareholders: Audit committees and the explanatory power of earnings for returns. *The British Accounting Review, 26*(4), 353–374.

Wong, C. W., Wong, C. Y., Boon-Itt, S., & Tang, A. K. (2021). Strategies for building environmental transparency and accountability. *Sustainability, 13*(16), 9116.

Yusuff, K., Whittle, A., & Mueller, F. (2023). Accounting for the "harms" of social media firms: Dialogic accountability and discursive contestation in public hearings. *Accounting, Auditing & Accountability Journal, 38*(3), 1019–1040. https://doi.org/10.1108/AAAJ-11-2022-6165

Zappa, G. (1927). Tendenze nuove negli studi di ragioneria: discorso inaugurale dell'anno accademico 1926-27 nel R. In *Instituto Superiore di Scienze Economiche e Commerciali di Venezia.* S.A. Istituto Editoriale Scientifico.

Maria-Gabriella Baldarelli PhD, CPA, is Associate Professor of Accounting, at University of Bologna, Department of Management-Rimini Campus. Full professor availability. Envited professor at Sophia University Institute. SIDREA board member until 2018. She is a member of international scientific networks: the Centre for Social and Environmental Accounting Research (CSEAR) and the European Business Ethics Network (EBEN). Key-note Speaker second International Conference on Economics, Business, Finance and Governance (ICEBFG) by Economics and Business Faculty of University of Bandar Lampung-Bali-Indonesia-Dic. 4–5, 2019. Research interests includes: accountability and gambling enterprises; corporate social responsibility; ethical, social and environmental accounting and accountability, sustainability in tourist enterprises; responsible and accessible tourism for blind people, economy of communion; gender accounting; accounting history, accounting education and Feminist Economics.

Eleonora Cardillo is Associate Professor of Business Economics, at the Department of Economics and Business of the University of Catania. She was Visiting Scholar at the CSEAR (Centre for social and environmental accounting research) School of Management of the University of St Andrews (Scotland) for the research project: "Study and analysis of the methodological and operational paths of environmental and social reporting in the evolution process of accounting information systems". Professor of Accounting and Financial Statements and Public accounting in local administrations. She was Director and Scientific Coordinator of the Master in Accounting and Control in Local Authorities, organized by the Department of Economics and Business of the University of Catania. Her research topics are public accounting systems, performance measurement, socio-environmental reporting, social inclusion in tactile museums, sustainability and accountability.

Chapter 3
Sustainability Reporting Tools and Social Inclusion Evaluation: Conceptual Network

Maria-Gabriella Baldarelli and Eleonora Cardillo

Abstract The purpose of this chapter is to provide a systematization of different social reporting tools that have been developed over time. The different reporting documents are described in order to reach the sustainability reporting model introduced by the CSRD (Directive 2464/2022). A section is dedicated to the main topics of the sustainability report and the concept of double materiality. The chapter also offers insights for assessing stakeholder engagement and social inclusion, presenting the key themes that may serve as potential measurement areas.

3.1 Sustainability Reporting Tools: Purposes and Approaches

The innovation of accounting systems aims to meet the growing need for accountability and for information on the social and environmental impacts generated by organizations. Socio-environmental reporting systems pose important and different challenges to companies and institutions. Some of these challenges are: assessing the company's non-financial impacts on socio-environmental areas and stakeholders; making increasingly complex and detailed information available to the outside world; responding to the increased sensitivity of consumers and citizens towards social, ethical and environmental issues; placing the concept of "value" at the center of companies' evaluation systems (corporate value-public value); broadening the scope of measurement, which becomes not only economic-financial but also social and environmental; integrating traditional accounting with sustainability reporting.

Over time, various socio-environmental measurement and reporting tools have been developed, shaping public policies and supporting the adoption—often on a

M.-G. Baldarelli
University of Bologna, Bologna, Italy
e-mail: maria.baldarelli@unibo.it

E. Cardillo (✉)
University of Catania, Catania, Italy
e-mail: cardillo@unict.it

M. Baldarelli et al. (eds.), *Accounting and Accountability for Social Inclusion*, CSR, Sustainability, Ethics & Governance, https://doi.org/10.1007/978-3-032-09271-7_3

voluntary basis—of instruments governed by guiding principles or reference models. This has gradually created a problem that is considered far from secondary, which is that of "terminology" (Rusconi 2024). The proliferation of multiple models implies above all the risk of conceptual confusion and misunderstandings that are also reflected in practice. Rusconi (2024) argues that a contribution to reducing the distorted use of claims of being 'socially responsible and sustainable' can come from the way social and sustainability reporting is presented to all interested stakeholders.

Sustainability reporting is being adopted by companies around the world that require greater transparency on both environmental and social issues (Al-Shaer et al. 2022). To this end, the methodological tools adopted, such as ESRS (European Sustainability Reporting Standards), Global Reporting Initiative (GRI), AA1000 and Carbon Disclosure Project (CDP), are important in the progress of companies towards achieving sustainability goals. However, the existence of different frameworks, criteria, ratings, standards and methodologies has created considerable complications and complex implementation processes (Siew 2015).

In this regard, Rusconi (2024, 5) emphasizes that "with regard to the various forms of reporting on the set of three economic, social and environmental aspects, the importance of terminology is particularly evident when examining proposals, guidelines and standards that have been gradually proposed, including in particular: Gruppo di Studio per il Bilancio Sociale (hereinafter GBS, which recently changed its title), GRI, Integrated Reporting (hereinafter IR) and Environment Social Governance indices (hereinafter ESG indices), the latter concerning overall assessments of the environment, sociality and governance, which primarily serve to inform investors, but which in any case can provide useful information, even if not exhaustive, to all interested stakeholders".

The definition of different documents poses different interpretative problems and confuses the scopes not only of the different types of reports but also of the underlying theoretical approaches.

The content and purpose of one document compared to another is not always clear. We will simply say that the social report neglects the environmental dimension and that an environmental report neglects the social dimension. But it is also true that the environment and the protection of ecosystems are important social issues. This makes the environmental sphere not perfectly separable from the social one. Similarly, the ESG approach is not perfectly differentiable from that of the TBL.

However, many of these approaches and models were born in specific historical periods, in moments of growth of awareness, in phases in which the commitment of the institutions towards the protection of the territory emerged and in critical moments in which people understood the importance of protecting the planet.

Starting from these premises, the following section does not aim to provide univocal definitions that rigidly delimit contents or scope. The end is to try to follow an evolutionary path of the main tools and purposes of socio-environmental reporting that even if they can be considered misleading or reductive, they strive to offer a framework of the different meanings and models that express in any case the transformation of reporting models towards the logic of sustainability.

3.2 Social and Environmental Reporting Tools: Differences and Similarities

Within the framework of systems for measuring companies' sustainable activities, a variety of accounting documents have been developed over the years which, despite their differences, still share several points of contact.

The *Environmental Report* is a communication tool that companies can use to analyze environmental issues related to their production system (Baldarelli et al. 2017).

European documents developed especially in the early 2000s, when the European Union (Recommendation of 30 May 2001 of the European Commission, Collection, evaluation and representation in the balance sheet of environmental information and Recommendation of 2 March 2004 of the Council of Europe, on the need to integrate traditional accounting with forms of environmental balance sheet) made explicit the theme of environmental accounting and its advantages at government level. The environmental report has been characterized by an evolutionary process that has led it towards a broader logic of sustainability (Hohnen 2012). Today the purposes of the environmental balance sheet are included in the concept of sustainability and in the related SDGs goals. In fact, just like the sustainability report, the environmental balance sheet represents an informative document, which exposes the relationships between company and environment and is aimed at evaluating the environmental performance of production activities (Barbu et al. 2022). It indicates the main environmental problems, reporting the strategic and management initiatives adopted for environmental protection and preserving. Through analysis, data, statistics, and indicators, the extent of the environmental impact on the territory and the community is assessed.

Social reporting is an expression of the social responsibility of companies and organizations (Unerman 2000). Social reporting can represent a form of new governance to ensure stakeholder accountability (Hess 2007). The European Union establishes the importance of social reporting and defines social responsibility as a voluntary action relating to the social and environmental concerns of companies in their commercial operations and in their relationships with interested parties (Green Paper—Promoting a European framework for corporate social responsibility, European Commission 18/7/2001). This notion has been extended over time to identify "the responsibility of enterprises for their impacts on society" (Communication of 25 October 201 n. 681). The social report, through a series of qualitative and quantitative indicators, evaluates the social performance of a company with respect to the strategies and policies adopted (Haniffa & Cooke 2005). It is linked to the financial statement, making explicit the accounting items with respect to the different categories of stakeholders. Some reference standards are the Accountability 1000 Series of Standards Framework. In Italy the commonly adopted standard is that of the Social Report Study Group (GBS) which has defined the principles for drafting the Social Balance Sheet. They provide useful indications for drafting the social balance sheet in order to outline a transparent and complete process.

The *social and environmental report* is a document that considers both dimensions (social and environmental), and that reports its performance in terms of environmental impact and with respect to a context and a community (Vourvachis & Woodward 2015). It represents an essential document to ensure clear, responsible and transparent communication by companies regarding the activities carried out and their impact on the environment and society (Contrafatto 2014; Spence 2009). Given the ever-increasing attention of consumers and the community on the effects of the activities carried out by organizations, this document expresses not only the company's social and environmental commitment but can also represent a source of competitive advantage.

The *sustainability report* reports the economic, environmental and social impacts of a company or organization. It broadens the observation vision and focuses on the evaluation of the three dimensions underlying the social responsibility of firms. Specifically, the different dimensions, economic, social and environmental, constitute the three traditional fundamental pillars of sustainability attributable to the Triple bottom line logic. This approach is achieved with the integration of the three dimensions that are related as the activities of one necessarily impact the others. In its general meaning, the concept highlights the existence of a paradigm that can lead to a pluralistic dimension of social life through which different entities require obtaining specific responses from corporate entities (Elkington 1999). The sustainability report is structured on the basis of principles and standards, among which the GRI (Global Reporting Initiative, 2016—www.globalreporting.org/standards) is among the most widespread (Quilice et al. 2018). It provides guidelines and procedures for setting up an appropriate evaluation and communication of economic, social and environmental performance. Other widespread standards are those defined by the SASB (Sustainability Accounting Standards Board) and the TCFD (Task Force on Climate-related Financial Disclosures).

Starting from the characteristics of social and environmental report described above, it can be said that their contents converge within the sustainability report. It becomes the main vehicle for communicating information regarding the actions undertaken by firms in terms of sustainability (Siano 2014, 2020; Persico & Rossi 2016; Bortoli 2023).

From this description, it is evident that while each document analyzes specific areas, they also share points in common. Specifically, the socio and environmental report and the sustainability report are two similar documents. With reference to the scope of analysis, the social and environmental report focuses specifically on social and environmental impacts, while the sustainability report also includes the economic aspect. With respect to the purposes, the social and environmental report aims to disclose in detail the social and environmental performance of an organization; the sustainability report, instead, aims to demonstrate how the company integrates sustainability in all areas of its activity. The structure of the two documents is usually different. The sustainability report in general follows a more comprehensive approach, integrating financial measures with social and environmental indicators, while the social and environmental report can be more specific and sectoral. Furthermore, the sustainability report is generally aimed at a broader audience, including investors and financial institutions, who seek a comprehensive view of corporate sustainability. The social and environmental report, furthermore, can be particularly useful for local institutions and non-profit organizations that focus less on economic impacts measurement.

Another form of sustainable reporting is the *Integrated Reporting*, which is conceived according to a broader and more integrated vision than the previous types. It aims to provide a comprehensive assessment of the value creation process, through the production of complete information for interested parties. The measurements of different aspects are brought back to an organic framework that constitutes the integrated balance sheet. The document provides an overall vision of the company's ability to create value (economic balance sheet), considering the needs of stakeholders (social balance sheet) and the environment (sustainability balance sheet-environmental balance sheet). The value represented in the integrated balance sheet derives not only from tangible assets (balance sheet/assets) but also from intangible ones. The preparation of the balance sheet is based on reference standards that are provided by the International Integrated Reporting Council (IIRC), which builds the integrated report model on the basis of specific requirements including comparability and verifiability (Mongiello 2017; Magnaghi 2014).

Another type of reporting is the *intangible assets balance sheet* that manages and valorises the intellectual capital of a company (Lev 2000). The aforementioned intellectual capital includes human capital, relational capital created by relationships with stakeholders and organisational capital that derives from the set of internal skills of the company. An important part of the intangible assets balance sheet is the determination of indicators that measure internal and external phenomena. The purpose of the document is based on the awareness that the strategic orientation of companies is directed towards the creation of value strongly linked to intangible capital. Internal and external reporting of intangible assets presents several challenges in relation to the application of rules and the definition of valuation practices. For example, the major complexities are related to: the factors that drive decisions on the allocation of corporate resources between tangible and intangible assets; the links between corporate strategic investment decision models and external competitive processes; the collection of internal data that, on average, seems to be insufficient to allow a complete identification and management of intangible investments; the regulations on external financial reporting that define assets including resources that generate future benefits, but exclude many intangible assets; the processing of statistical data that follows a more macroeconomic logic without defining a conceptual framework or common data collection tools (Cañibano & Sánchez 2004). Literature has examined existing and promulgated U.S. GAAP (Generally Accepted Accounting Principles), UK, and IASC (International Accounting Standards Committee) accounting principles relating to intangible assets, finding inconsistencies in the measurement and reporting of intangible assets (Eckstein 2004). In 2021, the European Financial Reporting Advisory Group (EFRAG) published a Discussion Paper entitled «Better Information on Intangibles. Which is the Best Way to go?», in which it recognizes the need to renew the accounting principles on intangibles and proposes a series of possible solutions to improve the criteria for recognizing and measuring internally produced intangibles, the methods for determining costs and the disclosure on key intangibles.

Finally, a reporting method introduced by the European Union is the *Non-Financial Statement*, made mandatory by Directive 2014/95/EU for large companies Non-Financial Reporting Directive (NFRD 2014/95/EU). It requires a level of detail and standardization of non-financial information that has recently been further strengthened by the Corporate Sustainability Reporting Directive (CSRD 2464/2022) which we will discuss in the next paragraph. The NFRD aims to report and disclose all information and elements of the business model in terms of social, environmental and governance aspects, through the use of specific performance indicators. It has therefore become a tool for disseminating Corporate Social Responsibility (CSR) policies and actions to achieve the Sustainable Development Goals of the UN Agenda 2030. The NFRD defines the requirements for some large companies to follow in order to include a non-financial statement in the management report, which follows the logic of the *Sustainability Report*. These requirements are applicable to so-called "public interest" companies that have more than 500 employees: this includes listed companies, banks and insurance companies.

Based on the contributions of Persico and Rossi (2016) and Bortoli (2023), a summary table of the main socio-environmental reporting models developed and refined over time has been drawn up.

3.3 The Sustainability Reporting in the CSRD

The introduction of the EU directive (Directive 2464/2022—CSRD) has improved the level of environmental and social disclosure of companies and organizations, identifying specific conceptual profiles and measurement areas. The aim is to promote greater environmental and social awareness, transparency in the disclosure of environmental practices and reliable reporting, free from any trace of greenwashing. Frameworks that promote sustainability reporting have increasingly integrated the 17 United Nations Sustainable Development Goals, placing a strong focus on performance measurement (Abeysekera 2022; Beyne et al. 2021).

The CSRD (Directive 2464/2022), an acronym for Corporate Sustainability Reporting Directive, is the EU regulation that requires European companies, including qualified EU subsidiaries of non-European companies, to publicly disclose their social and environmental impact, as well as the effect of their actions relating to the environment, social sphere and governance (ESG) on their business. The CSRD significantly expands the scope, disclosure and reporting requirements for sustainability compared to the previous EU Directive 2014/95 NFRD (Non-Financial Reporting Directive). Currently, approximately 11,700 companies across Europe prepare the Non-Financial Statement (NFS) required by the NFRD, while with the new CSRD the number of companies will expand to approximately 50,000, of which 6000 in Italy. The aim of the CSRD is to make environmental sustainability information more transparent and accessible for investors and consumers,

Table 3.1 Comparison of the main social and environmental reporting models

Typologies	Performance	Purpose	Characteristics
Sustainability Report (GRI approach)	Social, environmental and economic	Analyze the social, environmental and economic dimensions and the relationship between these	The sustainability report highlights the data relating to each area and their interdependence, highlighting the results according to a triple bottom line logic
Social report	Social	Analyse the social dimension of the company from the stakeholders'perspective	The report examines the social dimension exclusively and the data express the value produced in relation to the structure of the society
Environmental report	Environmental	Analyse the environmental dimension of the company and the impact of the activity on ecosystems	The report examines the environmental dimension exclusively and the document expresses data and information on the impacts exerted by the organization on the environment.
Financial statement	Economic and financial	The civil balance sheet is a formal document that measures the economic, financial and patrimonial performance	The document highlights the economic performance and the valuation of the company's assets
Integrated report	Social, environmental, economic and competitive	Analyze through a modular, synthetic and supplementary approach, the data reported in the economic, sustainability and environmental report	The integrated report also provides information on how an organization is able to create value over time. The document is therefore also configured as a strategic and competitive tool.

(continued)

Table 3.1 (continued)

Typologies	Performance	Purpose	Characteristics
Non -financial declaration	Social, environmental and governance (ESG)	Reporting the results achieved over time from an environmental, social and governance (ESG) perspective and on the basis of single materiality	The document measures the social, environmental and governance dimensions, reporting data and information on ethical values, transparency of the corporate structure, diversity policies of the composition of the Board of Directors, control procedures, behavior of top management and corporate compliance.
Sustainability Report (CSRD)	Social, environmental and governance (ESG)	The reports are drawn up on the basis of the European sustainability reporting standards (ESRS) which provide companies with a framework for reporting on environmental, social and governance issues and on the basis of double materiality	The document reports on sustainability topics with the aim of improving the quality, consistency and comparability of sustainability reporting. It is based on the ESRS standards that introduce detailed information requirements for a wide range of sustainability topics.

Source Authors' elaboration from Persico and Rossi (2016) and Bortoli (2023)

reporting more specific and detailed information. The directive defines the principles and scope of the Sustainability Report. Alongside the GRI principles, new principles for sustainability reporting are outlined. In 2023, the EU published the European Sustainability Reporting Standards (ESRS), developed by EFRAG (European Financial Reporting Advisory Group), which will constitute the reference framework for companies required to prepare the document. EFRAG has played a key role in developing sustainability reporting standards, becoming the EU's standard-setting body in this area. On 31 July 2023, the European Commission officially adopted the ESRS in order to ensure a link between the topics covered by the CSRD and the ESG dimensions.

Compared to the NFRD, the CSRD presents some significant differences. With reference to reporting requirements and scopes, the NFRD focuses on environmental protection, social responsibility, employee relations and respect for human rights; the CSRD introduces more specific reporting obligations, presenting the concept of dual materiality, long-term ESG objectives, due diligence on operations and supply chains, disclosure of intangible information, alignment with sustainable finance regulations and mandatory external assurance.

One significant area of differentiation is associated with the reference reporting standards. While the NFRD allowed companies to choose between different reporting frameworks (including the GRI), the CSRD aligns with the ESRS, providing a common set of guidelines and requirements for sustainability reporting. An interoperability system between the GRI standards and the ESRS has also been developed (Biancone et al. 2024; Chalmers & Klingler-Vidra 2023). Furthermore, external assurance was optional in the NFRD. In the CRSD it is mandatory. With respect to the digital aspects of reporting, the NFRD does not require specific requirements. The CSRD requires companies to publish sustainability reports through a standardized digital format in order to improve comparability. The main purpose of the CSRD directive is to enhance sustainability information by correlating the ESG indicators of the sustainability report with those of the civil financial statements. Sustainability information and data are included in the management report. The sustainability report is divided into four parts: general information, environmental information (including information pursuant to Article 8 of Regulation (EU) 2020/852), social information and governance information. The implementation timeline for sustainability reporting is mandatory:

- from 1 January 2024 (publication date 2025 of the 2024 financial year) for large public interest enterprises (with more than 500 employees) already subject to the Non-Financial Rep—orting Directive—NFRD that have one of the following characteristics: assets of 20 million euros; net revenues exceeding 40 million euros.
- from 1 January 2025 (publication date 2026 of the 2025 financial year) for large enterprises (including unlisted ones) not yet subject to the Non-Financial Reporting Directive—NFRD that have two of the following criteria: number of employees equal to or greater than 250; net revenues exceeding 50 million euros; assets exceeding 25 million euros.
- from 1 January 2026 (publication date 2027 of the 2026 financial year) for listed SMEs and other listed companies that meet two of the following criteria: assets exceeding €450,000; net revenues exceeding €900,000; average number of employees greater than or equal to 10. SMEs may not apply the new regulation for two years (i.e. until 1 January 2028), except for the need to explain why the company has decided to avail itself of this option.
- from 1 January 2028 (publication date 2029 of the 2028 financial year) for companies with a non-EU parent company, which have generated net revenues exceeding €150 million through a subsidiary in the EU for each of the last two consecutive financial years, and which have at least one of these characteristics: a controlled company satisfies the CSRD size requirements; a branch generated net revenues exceeding EUR 40 million in the previous financial year.

The Directive will provide opportunities and impetus to stakeholders, who will have to reconsider internal processes and business models, directing management towards a more conscious vision connected to the areas of sustainability. The new European Sustainability Reporting Standards (ESRS), provided by the Corporate Sustainability Reporting Directive (CSRD), define challenges and opportunities by innovating the current sustainability reporting practices that were mainly based on the GRI principles. The main challenges, in fact, concern the transition between different standards and the creation of useful transition steps and processes for the application of the ESRS.

3.4 The Approach to Sustainability Through Double Materiality

With sustainability reports based on the European Sustainability Reporting Standards (ESRS) principles, the objectives of the reporting system are broadened, placing greater emphasis on stakeholder expectations and the norms of the social and cultural context. Through the entry into force of the CSRD, the company makes explicit its commitment to the environment and the territory and creates a means to communicate in a transparent way the actions undertaken by the company in the social and environmental field (Idowu 2023).

Companies within the scope of the mandatory reporting requirements are obliged to verify their alignment with the EU Taxonomy, which provides an essential reference framework for sustainable reporting. Literature, starting from the EU Taxonomy Regulation and the new European Sustainability Reporting Standards, has analyzed specific areas of measurement, such as emissions, biodiversity, resource use/circular economy and water-related measures (Velte 2024). Compliance with the taxonomy ensures that companies can demonstrate their commitment to sustainability in a clear and verifiable way, also facilitating regulatory compliance. The objective of the Taxonomy (Regulation (EU) 2020/852) is to make transparent and easily recognizable, for consumers and investors, the activities that are truly sustainable from an environmental, social and governance point of view. Economic activities are classified based on different actions and specifically: contributing to the achievement of the established environmental objectives; not causing harm to the environmental objectives (Do Not—Significant Harm, or DNSH) and respecting the criteria and technical thresholds (screening criteria) defined for each activity aimed at environmental objectives. An important aspect is the respect of the social safeguard guarantees (Minimum Governance and Social Safeguards—MSGS). These guarantees certify that the company is carrying out an economic activity in order to ensure that it is in line with the OECD (Organisation for Economic Co-operation and Development) Guidelines for Multinational Enterprises and the United Nations Guiding Principles on Business and Human Rights, including the principles and rights established by the fundamental conventions identified in the International Labour Organisation Declaration on Fundamental Principles and Rights at Work and the International Bill of Human Rights.

In addition to the adaptation to the EU taxonomy, the CSRD requires that sustainability reporting be based on a dual materiality (DM). Based on this approach

(Berlinger 2025; Driver & ElAlfy 2023), companies will have to provide sustainability information both on the impact of their activities affecting people and environment (inside-out approach), and on the sustainability aspects impacting their performance and results (outside-in approach).

The literature (Adam et al. 2021; De Cristofaro & Gulluscio 2023) has contributed to the evaluation of the contrast detected between the initial debate and the low level of empirical knowledge on *Double Materiality*, by carrying out an exploratory analysis on the non-financial reports of 58 companies, European and non-European, operating in different sectors in the period 2019–2021. The results reveal that DM in reports is found in few companies, highlighting variety and critical issues both in the assessments of double materiality and in the information methods (De Cristofaro & Gulluscio 2023).

Double materiality includes two dimensions of materiality:

- impact materiality, which concerns material information on the impacts of the company on people or the environment related to a sustainability issue;
- financial materiality, which concerns material information on risks and opportunities related to a sustainability issue that could have a material influence on the company's development, financial position and performance, cash flows, access to finance, or cost of capital in the short, medium, or long term.

With reference to the assessment of impacts, for actual negative impacts the relevance must be assessed based on their severity, while for potential impacts, in addition to the severity, the probability must also be assessed. The severity of the impact is based on the following factors: a) the entity; b) the scope; c) the irremediable nature of it. With reference to positive impacts: materiality is assessed based on the following aspects: a) the scale and scope of the impact with regard to actual impacts; b) the scale, scope and likelihood of the impact with regard to the potential ones.

In May 2024, EFRAG published a document entitled "Materiality assessment implementation guidance"(https://www.efrag.org/sites/default/files/sites/webpublishing/SiteAssets/IG%201%20Materiality%20Assessment_final.pdf). It provides suggestions on how to conduct the materiality analysis according to the following steps: phase A: analysis and understanding of the context; phase B: identification of current or potential impacts, risks and opportunities related to sustainability issues; phase C: assessment and determination of relevant impacts, risks and opportunities related to sustainability issues; phase D: Reporting activities.

With respect to phase A, it is necessary to consider the business activities and relationships and, to this end, the elements to be defined are: a) analysis of the business plan, strategy, financial statements and, where applicable, other information provided to investors; b) activities, products/services of the company and geographical location of these activities; c) mapping of the business relationships of the company upstream and downstream of the value chain, including the type and nature of the business relationships; d) identification of the scope of information to be reported outside of its operations: expansion of the scope to reflect the impacts, risks and opportunities arising from the business relationships at the beginning and end of the value chain.

The company outlines its business activities and relationships, and the context in which these take place and the identification of the main stakeholders. In order to identify the relevant stakeholders, it is necessary to direct the analysis especially towards those who could be interested in the company's own activities and in the upstream and downstream value chain. In this process, it will therefore be important to understand what their opinions and interests are towards the company's activities.

To identify the interested parties, the company can consider:

- an analysis of existing stakeholder engagement initiatives;
- a mapping of the stakeholders interested in the company's business activities and relationships;
- the definition of the moment in which to implement stakeholder engagement in the materiality assessment process.

Phase B focuses on identifying the impacts of current and potential risks and opportunities related to sustainability issues. In this phase, the company identifies the relevant impacts, risks and opportunities related to ESG factors considering both its own activities and the operations upstream and downstream of the value chain. The result will be a list that must consider both the elements deducible from the list in ESRS1 paragraph on Application Requirement RA16 and the sustainability issues specific to the sector in which the company operates. For each impact, risk or opportunity identified, the company should consider and determine what it refers to (i.e. its own operations or upstream/downstream value chain) and the time horizon (short, medium or long term).

Phase C represents the last phase of the materiality assessment process in which the list of impacts of the selected risks and opportunities will form the basis for drafting the sustainability statement. It is divided into: Assessment of Impact Relevance; Assessment of Financial Relevance; Consolidation of the results of impact relevance and financial relevance and consideration of their interaction. In this phase, it is necessary to assess the scale, i.e. how serious the impact is; the scope, i.e. how widespread the impact is; the irremediability, i.e. the extent to which the impact can be repaired. With regard to potential impacts and severity, the probability that the impact will occur must be added. In this phase, stakeholder engagement is of fundamental importance as interested parties could help evaluate, validate and ensure the completeness of the final list of relevant impacts. The assessment of financial relevance must consider the substantial risks and opportunities for the company that generally arise from impacts or dependencies. To assess materiality, appropriate quantitative and/or qualitative thresholds are used based on financial effects in terms of performance, financial situation, cash flows, access and cost of capital.

The last step consists in consolidating the results of the impact dimensions of financial materiality and their interaction.

The objective of the last step is to consolidate the results of the previous steps and obtain the list of material impacts, risks and opportunities that will form the basis for the preparation of the sustainability report.

Phase D represents the final result of the entire process that concludes with the Sustainability Report. The company must report, with a concise, clear and effective narrative, the evaluation process and its outcome, based on its sustainability policies indicating the strategies implemented, the main risks/opportunities generated or suffered and the results achieved, also representing them through the fundamental performance indicators adopted.

The ESRS standards do not impose a specific management method of the relevance (materiality) evaluation process, because each company has specificities and peculiarities. It is difficult to standardize the materiality evaluation process.

The reporting requirements under ESRS 2, the thematic ESRSs and the sector ESRSs are divided into the following reporting areas:

(a) governance (GOV): the governance processes, controls and procedures used to monitor, manage and control impacts, risks and opportunities;
(b) strategy (SBM): how the company's strategy and business model interact with material impacts, risks and opportunities, including how the company addresses those impacts, risks and opportunities;
(c) impact, risk and opportunity management (IRO): the processes by which company assesses their materiality and manages material sustainability issues through policies and actions;
(d) metrics and objectives/targets (MT): the company's performance, including progress towards its objectives.

In making the assessment of materiality, the company shall consider the list of sustainability issues covered in the thematic ESRSs. Where, following the assessment of the materiality of the company, a particular sustainability issue on this list is determined to be material, the company shall disclose information in accordance with the corresponding disclosure requirements of the relevant thematic ESRS. The use of this list does not replace the process of determining the material issues. The list is a tool to support the assessment of the materiality of firms. In determining the material issues, the company shall nevertheless consider its specific situation. Where necessary, the company shall also develop entity-specific disclosures regarding material impacts, risks and opportunities not covered by the ESRS.

The relevance analysis is a process that must be activated periodically according to the methodologies proposed by the ESRS. In short, the main steps to follow could be:

- identification of possible material topics (for example through the examination of the business model and market benchmark);
- identification of the reference stakeholders and their representatives;
- collection of the necessary information through data analysis, comparison with experts and scientific institutions and with the representatives of the stakeholders;
- identification of the actual and potential impacts and assessment of their relevance;
- development of the Materiality Matrix.

With reference to the scope of analysis, companies are called upon to conduct the relevance assessment taking inspiration from the sustainability issues contemplated in the thematic ESRS. The use of this list cannot, however, be a substitute for an internal process, tailored to the specific characteristics of the individual company;

where necessary, in fact, firms are called upon to include in the assessment additional aspects not contemplated by the ESRS.

3.5 Sustainability, Stakeholder Engagement and Social Inclusion

Corporate Social Responsibility (CSR) is the set of strategies, initiatives and behaviors adopted by the company towards all stakeholders (Nygren and Hallan 2024). The sustainability report represents a useful strategic tool for communicating social responsibility. In the sustainability report, the theme of social inclusion represents an important social challenge, which begins primarily with considering the individuals and groups who have an interest in the organization, are affected by its activities, or are involved in its interaction processes.

ESRS, in fact, define stakeholders as those who can exert an influence on the company or be influenced by it. Paragraph 24 of ESRS 1 highlights the involvement of relevant stakeholders as a central element for the assessment of materiality. Engagement with relevant stakeholders is a tool that supports the company's business processes as well as the management of sustainability issues. Stakeholders include: those involved in the business, whose interests are or could be affected (positively or negatively) by the activities of the company and its business partners (i.e. employees, suppliers, consumers, end customers, local communities, authorities, etc.); users of sustainability statements such as investors, financiers and other existing and potential creditors, business partners of the company, trade unions and social partners, civil society, non-governmental organizations and public administrations. ESRS standards consider stakeholder involvement a central element of the materiality assessment and dialogue with key stakeholder plays a prominent role in the acquisition of information. The practical application of double materiality, on the one hand, improves stakeholder engagement, on the other, in turn requires their broader and more direct involvement in order to acquire a complete understanding of what is really relevant for the company that operates in complex social contexts (EFRAG, Materiality assessment implementation guidance, May 2024).

Stakeholders are characterized by the heterogeneity of interests that have various (and sometimes conflicting) views on relevant sustainable issues. The stakeholder engagement required by the analysis of double materiality is the basis of a reciprocal relationship between companies, stakeholders and society as a whole. The engagement process is defined and regulated by the GRI guidelines and the ESRS standards. Furthermore, the AA1000SES standard (2015) is specific on stakeholder engagement. The ESRS does not impose a specific approach to stakeholder engagement, although it recognizes its central role in the materiality assessment. The ESRS take into account the interests and concerns of different stakeholder groups. Disclosure requirements and reporting mechanisms provide transparency to stakeholder groups on the impacts of companies (Scamans, 2024). The GRI (Global Reporting Initiative) standards propose a clearer and more concise definition of stakeholders, focused on the company's impacts (positive or negative) on them, i.e. "an individual or group that has an interest on which the company's activities have or could have an impact". Furthermore, the importance of involving stakeholders before starting the reporting process is underlined, to increase the effectiveness of prevention and mitigation actions. The "dialogue with stakeholders" is a continuous, documented and institutionalized process of interaction between an organization and its stakeholders with the aim of informing, creating a channel of dialogue, collaborating, co-designing and implementing mechanisms and changes in the engagement and participation processes. The AA1000SES (Stakeholder Engagement Standard—2015) standard was developed specifically to guide stakeholder engagement. It is a generally applicable framework for assessing, designing, implementing a stakeholder engagement system. It defines precise requirements for creating effective stakeholder engagement. According to this principle, stakeholder engagement is the process used by an organization to engage relevant stakeholders following a clear purpose. Engagement is a fundamental accountability mechanism, as it requires an organization to involve stakeholders in identifying, understanding and responding to sustainability issues and to report, explain, and respond to stakeholders regarding decisions, actions, and performance (Grushina 2017; Stocker et al. 2020).

There may be different criteria for classifying stakeholders with respect to sustainability issues and their perceptions (Alwaer et al. 2008; Block et al. 2023). With respect to the possession of specific attributes, stakeholders can be classified based on:

- dependence: groups or individuals who directly or indirectly depend on the organization's activities, products or services and associated performance, or on which the organization depends;
- tension: groups or individuals who require immediate attention from the organization regarding broader financial, economic, social or environmental issues.
- responsibilities: groups or individuals to whom the organization has, or may in the future have, legal, commercial, operational or ethical/moral responsibilities.
- influence: groups or individuals who may have an impact on the strategic or operational decision-making process of the organization or a stakeholder.
- different perspectives: groups or individuals whose different opinions may lead to a new understanding of the situation and the identification of different opportunities. Stakeholder engagement is a two-way process. However, there are different levels and methods of engagement associated with it, depending on the nature and extent of stakeholder engagement.

The study of Herremans et al. (2016) explains the diversity in sustainability disclosure by examining how it is used to engage stakeholders. Specifically, authors identify five characteristics of sustainability reporting that are associated with a company's stakeholder engagement strategy: immediacy of communication, clarity of stakeholder identity, intentionality in gathering feedback, breadth of stakeholder inclusiveness, and use of stakeholder engagement for learning purposes.

Stakeholder focus is the first fundamental step towards sharing, participation and inclusion. Social inclusion includes several elements, such as political participation, social rights, equal access, ethnicity and gender, access to social services and the labour market, diversity and disability. Based on these areas, indicators are built to help measure the multiple dimensions of social inclusion (Paraschiv et al., 2021). To measure social inclusion in the sustainability report, several quantitative and qualitative indicators can be used, such as classification of employees who represent groups or interests of other employees, assessment of the level of employee satisfaction, implementation of policies and initiatives that promote diversity and inclusion.

Social inclusion is linked to social and economic equality. Both are fundamental objectives to build a more equitable and ethical society. Measuring social inclusion is not simple because the social phenomena to be assessed are complex (Al-Hamdan 2024). The development of solid indicators and parameters are based on participatory approaches and continuous review of sharing mechanisms.

From a quantitative point of view, there are inclusion indicators that consider diversity. For example, assessing the composition of staff in terms of gender, age, education and other economic and social characteristics can be the basis for the creation of diversity reports.

Social inclusion indicators are based on measuring the impact of human activities on society, assessing aspects such as engagement, education, employment, health, inclusion, quality of life, safety and well-being of the community. These indicators are fundamental to assessing progress towards sustainable development goals that promote equity, justice and social cohesion.

Another element is gender equality and all the policies and actions that ensure non-imbalanced situations between men and women. In gender reports there are various areas of analysis, including evaluation and number of women in leadership positions, pay differences and presence of benefits to protect the role of mother. To improve the quality and quantity of gender information following the introduction of the ESRS, the literature has investigated the qualitative and quantitative differences between GRI standards and ESRS outlining the technical reasons for such differences (Paoloni et al. 2025).

The inclusion of disabled people or people with special needs is also an important element that aims to evaluate the presence of people with disabilities in the company, their accessibility and their participation in training and development programs (Baldarelli & Cardillo, 2022). Organizations aimed at social inclusion also monitor the presence of employees of different ethnic origins to support their integration, inclusion of young people to promote their professional growth and inclusion of elderly people to support their contribution even in old age.

Qualitative indicators evaluate employee satisfaction, collecting feedback through questionnaires, internal surveys and interviews to assess their level of satisfaction and inclusion. This involves measuring the degree of employee participation in training programs and initiatives on diversity and inclusion. The presence of social value and a corporate culture aimed at inclusiveness and respect are elements of evaluation of the degree of inclusion of an organization (Carnemolla et al. 2021). Elements to be evaluated and monitored are therefore participation in diversity and inclusion initiatives, commitment to the community, the implementation of social and inclusive projects, and the support offered to individuals with special needs. Even in relationships with suppliers, inclusive organizations are oriented towards choosing suppliers that promote inclusion and sharing.

Al-Hamdan (2024,150) identifies some main characteristics that should be considered in the measurement of social inclusion, such as: "Defining and Operationalizing Concepts:Social inclusion and economic equality are multifaceted concepts that can be challenging to define and operationalize in a way that is meaningful and measurable; Data Availability and Accessibility: Data on social inclusion and economic equality can be limited in many countries, particularly in developing contexts. Even when data exists, it may not be readily accessible or reliable; Cultural and Contextual Specificity: Indicators and metrics need to be sensitive to cultural and contextual differences, recognizing that social inclusion and economic equality mean different things in different societies". At country level author (Al-Hamdan 2024, 150–151) identifies some existing indicators and metrics (Table 3.2).

The indicators described above focus on a macro dimension of social inclusion defined to improve the overall management of public services, policies of involvement and support to vulnerable categories. With reference to the micro dimension of social inclusion, not widely developed in the literature (Fan, 2025), it generally refers to actions promoted by a single organization or individual. Social inclusion at the micro level is aimed at supporting social and work participation, essential needs of individuals such as health and education, personal skills and dignity. The contribution of Fan (2025)(Table 3.3) links the measurement of social inclusion to two areas: social sustainability and social capital. Social sustainability is defined as the economic, cultural and political inclusion of individuals and groups to strengthen their dignity and acceptance (Bafarasat 2023). Social capital is understood as networks, norms and relationships of trust that combine individual and collective dimensions (Schwitter 2022).

The axes and factors (Table 3.3) highlight the links in factors related to social inclusion that promote individual social capital and contribute to the pursuit of

Table 3.2 Existing indicators and metrics

Multidimensional poverty index (MPI): Developed by the Oxford poverty and human development initiative (OPHI), the MPI measures poverty based on three dimensions: Health, education, and living standards.
Social Progress index (SPI): This index, created by social Progress imperative, measures social progress across a range of factors, including basic human needs, foundations of Well-being, and opportunities
Human development index (HDI): The HDI, developed by the UNDP, combines indicators of life expectancy, education, and income to measure a country 's level of human development.
Gender inequality index (GII): The GII, also developed by the UNDP, measures gender inequalities in areas like reproductive health, educational attainment, and economic participation.

Source Al-Hamdan 2024, 150–151

Table 3.3 Main axes and factors of social inclusion

Category	Extracted factors	Extracted theme	Hierarchy of needs
Family and marriage	Acceptance, belongingness	Micro-social inclusion	Social needs
Friendship and relationship	Social network, cohesion	Individual social capital	
Trust and charity	Trust, reciprocity, sharing	Individual social capital	Security needs, social needs
Sharing	Security dependency		Esteem needs
Saving and money	Quality of life	Micro-social inclusion	Physiological needs
Wellbeing and health	Life related social resources	Individual social capital	Security needs
Rent, price, and housing	Sustainable living and working	Individual social sustainability	
Work-life balance	Sustainability community		
	Social wellbeing		
Job and retirement	Security protection	Micro-social inclusion	Physiological needs
Education	Life related social resources	Individual social capital	Social needs
	Sustainable living and working	Individual social sustainability	Self-actualization needs
	Secure future		
Fairness, equality	Diversity, cross-cultural	Multicultural background	Social needs
	Acceptance	Micro-social inclusion	Esteem needs
	Reciprocity	Individual social capital	Self-actualization needs
	Equal opportunity	Individual social sustainability	Esteem needs

Source Fan 2025, 16

social sustainability. This framework is important for defining areas and scopes of measurement and therefore provides practical ideas for implementing social inclusion assessment models.

The specific and measurable objectives for social inclusion are in line with sustainability objectives. Organizations have to measure social inclusion in the sustainability report through specific inclusion indicators, taking into account both quantitative and qualitative aspects, and actively involving employees and stakeholders.

3.6 Conclusions

The purpose of this chapter was to identify differences and similarities between the main social and environmental reporting tools. While the temporal evolution of government policies and operational approaches has led to the proliferation of tools, almost always voluntary, diversified in terminology and logic, this has often created confusion and lack of clarity in the formulation and categorization. Building on these premises, the chapter aims to identify an evolutionary path by tracing the main characteristics of the tools that share a common denominator: the responsibility to be socially responsible and sustainable.

The CSRD (Directive 2464/2022), acronym for Corporate Sustainability Reporting Directive, has defined more comprehensively rules, criteria and models for measuring and communicating impacts on environment, social sphere and governance. The sustainability report based on the ESRS principles makes explicit the company's commitment to sustainability through the measurement of Double Materiality. The sustainability report represents a useful strategic tool for communicating social responsibility and addressing the issue of social inclusion. Corporate Social Responsibility (CSR) is the set of strategies, initiatives and behaviors adopted by the company towards all stakeholders and, in this sense, the topic of social inclusion represents a significant social challenge.

Social inclusion includes different elements, such as political and social participation, equal access, ethnicity and gender, diversity and disability. To measure social inclusion in the sustainability report, it is possible to use different quantitative and qualitative indicators. Measuring social inclusion is not simple because the social phenomena to be assessed are complex. To this end, the chapter presents some macro indicators and possible micro evaluation factors that can evaluate the participatory approaches and sharing mechanisms underlying social inclusion.

References

Abeysekera, I. (2022). A framework for sustainability reporting. *Sustainability Accounting. Management and Policy Journal, 13*(6), 1386–1409.

Adams, C. A., Alhamood, A., He, X., Tian, J., Wang, L., & Wang, Y. (2021). The double-materiality concept. Application and issues. published by the Global Reporting Initiative.

Al-Hamdan, F. (2024). The importance of measuring social inclusion and economic equality: developing robust indicators and metrics. In *International Conference" Actual economy: local solutions for global challenges"* (pp. 149–152).

Al-Shaer, H., Albitar, K., & Hussainey, K. (2022). Creating sustainability reports that matter: An investigation of factors behind the narratives. *Journal of Applied Accounting Research, 23*(3), 738–763.

AlWaer, H., Sibley, M., & Lewis, J. (2008). Different stakeholder perceptions of sustainability assessment. *Architectural Science Review, 51*(1), 48–59.

Baldarelli, M. G., & Cardillo, E. (2022). Managerial paths, social inclusion, and NBS in tactile cultural products: Theory and practice. *Journal of Hospitality & Tourism Research, 46*(3), 544–582.

Baldarelli, M. G., Del Baldo, M. & Nesheva Kiosseva, N. (2017). Environmental accounting and reporting: Theory and practice, Cham: Springer. DOI https://doi.org/10.1007/978-3-319-50918-1.

Barbu, E. M., Ionescu-Feleagă, L., & Ferrat, Y. (2022). The evolution of environmental reporting in Europe: The role of financial and non-financial regulation. *The International Journal of Accounting, 57*(02), 2250008. https://doi.org/10.1142/S1094406022500081

Berlinger, F. (2025). Assessing the Early Adoption of Double Materiality: A Content Analysis of Sustainability Reporting Practices of Swiss Public Corporations (Doctoral dissertation, Technische Hochschule Nürnberg Georg Simon Ohm).

Beyne, J., Visser, W., & Allam, I. (2021). Sustainability reporting in the Antwep port ecosystem, understanding the relationship between reporting on the sustainable development goals and integrated thinking. *Frontiers in Sustainability. Belgium Article, 689739*, 2. https://doi.org/10.3389/frsus.2021.689739

Biancone, P. P., Chmet, F., & Demarchi, L. (2024). Analyzing non-financial reporting through GRI-ESRS interoperability. *Economia Aziendale Online, 15*(2), 375–394.

Block, C., Rennings, M., & Bröring, S. (2023). Selecting technologies to engage in sustainability transitions—A multi-stakeholder perspective. *Business Strategy and the Environment, 32*(6), 3569–3595.

Bortoli, C. (2023). *Il report di sostenibilità come strumento strategico di comunicazione della Corporate Social Responsibility nel settore moda in Italia.*-Tesi di laurea Magistrale-AA 2021–2022.

Cañibano, L., & Sánchez, P. (2004). Measurement, management and reporting on intangibles. *State of the art. Accounting and Business Review, 3*(1), 37–62.

Carnemolla, P., Robinson, S., & Lay, K. (2021). Towards inclusive cities and social sustainability: A scoping review of initiatives to support the inclusion of people with intellectual disability in civic and social activities. *City, Culture and Society, 25*, 100398.

Chalmers, W., & Klingler-Vidra, R. (2023). European Sustainability Reporting Standards (ESRS): Interoperability as innovation? *Global policy.* Available at: https://www.globalpolicyjournal.com

Contrafatto, M. (2014). The institutionalization of social and environmental reporting: An Italian narrative. *Accounting, Organizations and Society, 39*(6), 414–432.

De Cristofaro, T., & Gulluscio, C. (2023). In search of double materiality in non-financial reports: First empirical evidence. *Sustainability, 15*(2), 924.

Driver, T. R., & ElAlfy, A. (2023). Double materiality: Why does it matter for sustainability reporting?. In The Routledge handbook of green finance (pp. 41–56). London:Routledge.

Eckstein, C. (2004). The measurement and recognition of intangible assets: Then and now. *Accounting Forum, 28*(2), 139–158.

Elkington, J. (1999). The triple bottom line: Implications for the oil industry. *Oil and Gas Journal, 97*.

Fan, Q. (2025). The promotion of social sustainability by micro-level social inclusion in a multicultural context: Literature review and interview evidence. *Frontiers in Sociology, 10*, 1557463.

Global Reporting Initiative. (2016). GRI—Consolidated set of GRI Sustainability Reporting Standards. https://www.globalreporting.org/standards.

Grushina, S. V. (2017). Collaboration by design: Stakeholder engagement in GRI sustainability reporting guidelines. *Organization & Environment, 30*(4), 366–385.

Haniffa, R. M., & Cooke, T. E. (2005). The impact of culture and governance on corporate social reporting. *Journal of Accounting and Public Policy, 24*(5), 391–430.

Herremans, I. M., Nazari, J. A., & Mahmoudian, F. (2016). Stakeholder relationships, engagement, and sustainability reporting. *Journal of Business Ethics, 138*, 417–435.

Hess, D. (2007). Social reporting and new governance regulation: The prospects of achieving corporate accountability through transparency. *Business Ethics Quarterly, 17*(3), 453–476.

Hohnen, P. (2012). The future of sustainability reporting. EEDP Programme Paper. Chatham House, London.

Idowu, S. O. (2023). Democracy and sustainable development: Emerging links for effective citizenship development strategic implementations. *Humanities, Management and Social Sciences, 3*(2), 145.

Lev, B. (2000). Intangibles: Management, measurement, and reporting. Rowman & Littlefield.

Magnaghi, E. (2014). Primi passi nell'integrazione delle informazioni finanziarie e socio-ambientali: *l'Integrated Reporting dell'IIRC.*

Mongiello, M. (2017). Il punto di vista di Paul Druckman sul ruolo dell'IIRC e il futuro del corporate reporting. *L azienda Sostenibile, Venezia: I Libri di Ca Foscari, 4*, 31–39.

Nygren, O., & Hallan, R. L. (2024). Stakeholder Engagement Influence on CSRD-Reporting Readiness: A qualitative study of the Norwegian fishing and aquaculture industry (Master's thesis, NTNU).

Paoloni, P., Cosentino, A., & Venuti, M. (2025). Global reporting initiative (GRI) and European sustainability reporting standards (ESRS) in comparison: Critical analysis from a gender perspective. Shaping tomorrow: Gender perspectives in a sustainable world (pp. 35–47). Cham: Springer.

Paraschiv, D. M., Manea, D. I., Ţiţan, E., & Mihai, M. (2021). Development of an aggregated social inclusion indicator. Disparities in the European Union on inclusion/exclusion social determined with social inclusion index. *Technological and Economic Development of Economy, 27*(6), 1301–1324.

Persico, M.G., & Rossi, F., (2016). Comunicare la sostenibilità, Milano: Franco Angeli Editore.

Quilice, T. F., Cezarino, L. O., Fernandes, M., Alves, R., Liboni, L. B., & Caldana, A. C. F. (2018). Positive and negative aspects of GRI reporting as perceived by Brazilian organisations. *Environmental Quality Management, 27*, 19–30.

Rusconi, G. (2024). La rendicontazione sociale/di sostenibilità: terminologia e sostanza (editorial). *Impresa Progetto.Electronic. Journal of Management, 1*, 10.15167/1824-3576/IPEJM2024.1.1608.

Scamans, S. (2024). Corporate Sustainability Reporting Directive's (CSRD) impacts on stakeholders: an analysis of the European Sustainability Reporting Standards (ESRS).

Schwitter, N. (2022). Social capital in retirement villages: a literature review. *Ageing & Society, 42*(7), 1560–1588.

Siano, A. (2014). Management della comunicazione per la sostenibilità. Milano: Franco Angeli Editore.

Siano, A. (2020). La comunicazione per la sostenibilità nel management delle imprese. Milano: Sinergie.

Siew, R. Y. (2015). A review of corporate sustainability reporting tools (SRTs*). Journal of Environmental Management, 164*, 180–195.

Spence, C. (2009). Social and environmental reporting and the corporate ego. *Business Strategy and the Environment, 18*(4), 254–265.

Stocker, F., de Arruda, M. P., de Mascena, K. M., & Boaventura, J. M. (2020). Stakeholder engagement in sustainability reporting: A classification model. *Corporate Social Responsibility and Environmental Management, 27*(5), 2071–2080.

Unerman, J. (2000). Methodological issues-reflections on quantification in corporate social reporting content analysis. *Accounting, Auditing & Accountability Journal, 13*(5), 667–681.

Velte, P. (2024). A literature review concerning the non-carbon-related environmental goals of the EU Taxonomy Regulation and the European Sustainability Reporting Standards (ESRS). *Journal of Global Responsibility*, 16(3), 542–568. doi:https://doi.org/10.1108/JGR-02-2024-0032.

Vourvachis, P., & Woodward, T. (2015). Content analysis in social and environmental reporting research: Trends and challenges. *Journal of Applied Accounting Research, 16*(2), 166–195.

Maria-Gabriella Baldarelli PhD, CPA, is Associate Professor of Accounting, at University of Bologna, Department of Management—Rimini Campus. Full professor availability. Envited professor at Sophia University Institute. SIDREA board member until 2018. She is a member of international scientific networks: the Centre for Social and Environmental Accounting Research (CSEAR) and the European Business Ethics Network (EBEN). Key-note Speaker second International Conference on Economics, Business, Finance and Governance (ICEBFG) by Economics and Business Faculty of University of Bandar Lampung-Bali-Indonesia-Dic. 4–5, 2019. Research interests includes: accountability and gambling enterprises; corporate social responsibility; ethical, social and environmental accounting and accountability, sustainability in tourist enterprises; responsible and accessible tourism for blind people, economy of communion; gender accounting; accounting history, accounting education and Feminist Economics.

Eleonora Cardillo is Associate Professor of Business Economics—at the Department of Economics and Business of the University of Catania. She was Visiting Scholar at the CSEAR (Centre for social and environmental accounting research) School of Management of the University of St Andrews (Scotland) for the research project: "Study and analysis of the methodological and operational paths of environmental and social reporting in the evolution process of accounting information systems". Professor of Accounting and Financial Statements and Public accounting iin local administrations. She was Director and Scientific Coordinator of the Master in Accounting and Control in Local Authorities, organized by the Department of Economics and Business of the University of Catania. Her research topics are public accounting systems, performance measurement, socio-environmental reporting, social inclusion in tactile museums, sustainability and accountability.

Part II
Accounting and Accountability for Social Inclusion: Best Practices in Cultural Institutions, Leisure and Beyond

Chapter 4
Theoretical Perspectives and Approaches for Social Inclusion In Cultural Institutions

Maria-Gabriella Baldarelli and Eleonora Cardillo

Abstract Cultural institutions move in the perspective of realizing an inclusive action, through certain behaviors that can strengthen or discourage access and sharing. From an accounting and managerial perspective, paying attention to stakeholders—especially in institutions that fulfill a specific social role, such as cultural organizations or museums—requires acknowledging their interests and needs as a moral and ethical responsibility. This action should involve a closer link between individuals and their involvement. In the introduction, the chapter underscores the importance of generating and disseminating social value for users and the wider community, framing this objective within an accounting and accountability perspective that enables cultural institutions to assess, measure, and communicate their social impact. Several sections present some theoretical approaches and frameworks (Museum as agent of social inclusion; Nature Based Solutions Approach and Innovation technology in art institutions) that can be adopted in the context of cultural institutions. They provide logics and tools to improve management and social inclusion by supporting the attractiveness of the museum.

4.1 Measuring Social Value in Cultural Institutions

Measuring value in organizations involves not only accounting for economic value but also considering the lives of individuals, communities and society that generate social and cultural values (Klamer 2002; Salter et al. 2013). Accounting and accountability are two appropriate perspectives in measuring social value of organizations and institutions. Accounting, as an activity of recording and measuring the events

M.-G. Baldarelli
University of Bologna, Bologna, Italy
e-mail: maria.baldarelli@unibo.it

E. Cardillo (✉)
University of Catania, Catania, Italy
e-mail: cardillo@unict.it

M. Baldarelli et al. (eds.), *Accounting and Accountability for Social Inclusion*, CSR, Sustainability, Ethics & Governance, https://doi.org/10.1007/978-3-032-09271-7_4

of the organization, represents an essential information basis for evaluating performance and assets. However, many cultural institutions rely on a simplified cash-based accounting system, which records only monetary inflows and outflows and therefore fails to capture the broader economic effects of their activities. This limitation prevents the production of more analytical and meaningful data on specific accounting items and on the real impact generated by the institution. For example, the current regulation on reporting obligations for museums is inadequate to ensure the provision of useful information for the types of decision-making processes relevant to the needs of stakeholders. To pursue accountability as a theoretical approach that relies in the duty/obligation to report actions and activities carried out, it is necessary to develop a more complete reporting model for these organizations. Information reporting for stakeholders should include a series of ethical and organizational values and highlight cultural performance as well as mandatory financial data and information. For example, users' satisfaction, inclusive activities, reputation and social initiatives are relevant areas that should enrich traditional accounting (Wild, 2013).

Carnegie et al. (2022) highlights, as underlined in chap. 1, that traditional accounting systems neglect the social and moral aspects of accounting as a multidimensional phenomenon. In this sense, accounting and accountability contribute to a revised definition of accounting to be extended to all organizational and social contexts in which accounting is implemented. By acknowledging its capacity to reveal social impacts and guide responsible behavior, accounting becomes not only a technical tool but also a mechanism for supporting inclusivity, transparency, and the broader social mission of cultural institutions.

Literature of cultural institution consider the relevant role of disseminating and creating social value for users and community (Donato and Visser Travagli 2010; Zan 1999, 2003; Camarero and Garrido 2009). The definition of cultural institution is: "the set of legitimate material and symbolic relationships and practices through which individuals and organizations allow the maintenance and reproduction of a social order with not-utilitarian cultural purpose" (Sibilio and Donato 2015, 21). Contributions examined the processes of creating and measuring the value of museums and historical-artistic heritage (Ecchia 1998; Chirieleison 1998; Sibilio 2004; Magliacani 2008), also with reference to managerial profile (Zan 1999, 2003; Donato and Visser Travagli 2010). Value is associated with the "social" utility that derives from the enjoyment of artistic and cultural products, extending this perspective not only to cultural goods of public museums but also to cultural institutions of the private-sector; that, in any case, do not limit or should not limit the realisation of a social purpose. The value created by museums or cultural institutions comes from a variety of tangible and intangible activities. A quantitative evaluation of the benefits provided is associated with the qualitative one, even if the intangible nature of the activities prevails, depending on individual skills, ideas, creativity and rationalisation capacity (Chirieleison 1998).

The museum is an institution for society, fulfilling its essential role of transmitting culture as well as the historical and artistic significance of the heritage it preserves. The process of knowledge transfer and value creation plays a particularly complex role in museums and in the management of cultural products. Accessible museums and accessible cultural products create value for the community. Accessibility to heritage, inclusive processes and physical and cultural modalities become essential prerogatives for the pursuit of their objectives (Magistrali 2008; Baldarelli and Cardillo 2012). Museums, as institutions at the service of society and its cultural development, exhibit works that constitute tangible and intangible testimonies of humanity and its historical evolution. One of the distinctive features of museums and cultural institutions is certainly their accessibility and inclusion initiatives, with the aim of transferring culture and historical-artistic meanings to stakeholders (Freeman 2017; Jones et al. 2018).

4.2 Social inclusion and Vulnerability in Cultural Institutions: Literature Review

Sustainability becomes complete only when it is able to actively engage all the subjects in the social and economic processes, even those with different abilities (Nussbaum 2007). Creating an economic system that fosters human well-being (Bruni and Zamagni 2004) depends on the active inclusion of people with diverse abilities, guaranteeing them equal dignity in the workplace and meaningful participation in social and economic life.

From a managerial point of view, these goals are pursued through the actions of management and the behavior of individuals operating within the organization. The perspective adopted for the purpose of identifying the relationships between organisation and stakeholders in value creation processes, is that of Carroll (1991, 2000), who highlights the principles of ethics and morality, that are even more essential in managing relationships with people with disabilities. The author highlights several facets of social responsibility, including those related to philanthropic activities. These encompass acting in accordance with society's philanthropic expectations, encouraging management and staff to participate in community volunteering, and supporting projects that aim to improve quality of life (Carroll 1991). The same author identifies three different ethical approaches such as amoral management, immoral management, and moral management, based on which, various relationships between business management and stakeholder groups can be drawn. The first approach is that of immoral management, which outlines egoistic behaviour of the manager oriented essentially to achieving adaptable economic performance. These behaviors are reflected in managerial conduct and decision-making, which can be difficult to navigate and may sometimes conflict with ethical values and the principles of fairness. However, amoral management is characterised by a kind of indifference and insensitivity to the effects and impacts of corporate choices on the community, thus neglecting respect for ethical values. Depending on the intentional nature of their actions, amoral managers, on the one hand, consider ethics as an element to be neglected in the professional context, connecting only to the sphere of private relations (intentional managers); whereas, on the other, they focus exclusively on their activity without ethically reflecting on the fact that their behaviour may be affecting the community in general (unintentional managers). However, these categories are more sensitive to changes and therefore less rigid in maintaining certain positions. Finally, moral principles, while respecting certain rules and values, bring about ethical behaviour; while not disregarding the importance of the economic result, this kind of manager attributes a profound value to the rules, ethics and honesty of actions.

The theme of social inclusion is connected to that of exclusion and vulnerability (Pelligra 2008). Contractual relations, according to Pelligra (2008), make our lives more individualistic and less relational. The contract is based on mutual benefit. However, when it fails to uphold the principles inherent in it, "exclusion" occurs, as vulnerable individuals are unable to participate in the contractual framework. In such cases, it is assumed that, without an exchange, these individuals have nothing to offer. Vulnerability and dependence seem to be at the core of the social link. That goes beyond the contract and develops the logic of "taking care" and that is the logic of responsibility.

This consideration adds to the traditional characteristics of the production of goods and services the possibility for institutions and organizations to exercise a high degree of autonomy in strengthening supply processes and dynamics. A direct effect of this action could involve the inclusion of "vulnerable" workers, while indirect effects could be the ability to generate relational networks both within and outside the institution. Organizations often have a strong link with the territory in which they operate, aiming to strengthen and improve democracy. The presence of social ties within the market and the logic of true sustainability, as understood by Nussbaum (2002), lead to considering vulnerability, hence "different ability", not a negative aspect to sustainable development, but a constructive aspect, relating to vulnerable subjects who feel more liable to "do" something that can improve the relationship. These reflections connect to the theory of the museum as a tool for social inclusion and an agent of cultural change. This is because, through museum activity, vulnerable individuals appreciate the social connections (Pelligra 2008) that can regenerate culture, viewing vulnerability not as a negative aspect, but as an opportunity for new creativity and relationships.

A relevant consideration, regarding cultural institutions and cultural products in general, is to understand the nature of the museum's action towards such categories. Specifically, cultural institutions can generate exclusion processes or activate inclusion mechanisms.

Literature highlights the role of the museum as a social inclusion agent (Sandell 2000, 2002, 2003, 2007; Kotler 2001; Coffee 2008; McMillen and Alter 2017). "Inclusion may be derived by combining both a functional and a social approach to creating inclusive groups" (Fredette et al. 2015, 31).

Within the UK government, particularly the Department for Digital, Culture, Media & Sport (DCMS, 1999), social inclusion work should: "promote the involvement in culture and leisure activities of those at risk of social disadvantage or marginalisation, particularly by virtue of the theatre they live in; their disability, poverty, age, racial or ethnic origin" (Social Exclusion Unit, DCMS 1999). In order to understand social inclusion, social exclusion aspects (Belfiore 2002; Bradshaw et al. 2004; Barnes et al. 2006) are defined.

Based on the theme of scarcity and under-development, Haan (1998) suggests three important elements of social exclusion. It represents the opposite of social integration; it refers to both a state and a process and finally the concept is multi-dimensional. Exclusion creates an alienation from society as expressed by Daffy (1995): "Social exclusion is a broader concept than poverty, encompassing not only low material means but the inability to participate effectively in economic, social, political and cultural life and in some characterizations alienation and distance from mainstream society". Bhalla and Lapeyre (1997) analyze three dimensions of social exclusion: economic, social and political and the interrelationships between these different dimensions.

The issue of social exclusion in relation to cultural contexts is linked to the possibility that cultural heritage and products refuse or limit accessibility and enjoyment.

As explained by Sandell (1998), the cultural institutions and museums have been usually considered as an exclusive environment as they are: "products of the establishment and authenticate the established or official values and image of a society in several ways, directly, by promoting and affirming the dominant values, and indirectly, by subordinating or rejecting alternate values" (Sandell 1998, 407–408). Author indicates three fundamental topics in order to consider cultural institutions and museums agents of social exclusion: access, representation and participation. The problem of access to cultural institutions is crucial, as it is not only a question of physical access, but to be able to enjoy the products. The issue of representation relies on their history and collections and sometimes the museum presents itself as an exclusive institution, which is not entirely open. Participation in the process of creating cultural production may generate social exclusion when the product is not accessible to the different abilities of the public. However, if the action of the museum or cultural institutions is activated to curb these barriers, the museum becomes social inclusion agent and activator of a new culture of social inclusion.

The contribution of Sandell (1998) suggests a possible framework (Fig. 4.1) in which the museum expresses its potential with recourse to social inclusion, exploring the relevance and implications for the museum sector. In this sense "culture might possess the potential to bring about social cohesion or to reduce social inequalities" (Sandell 1998).

Sandell's model highlights a process for change in the museum that is qualified in three ways: "the inclusive museum", "the museum as an agent of social regeneration" and "the museum as a vehicle for broad social change". Each type of museum has different objectives, tools and actions. Specifically, the inclusive museum aims to represent excluded groups and ensure access to marginalized groups in order to strengthen participation and inclusion.

The second category of the socially inclusive museum is the museum as an agent of social regeneration. In this case the museum has a strong interaction with the community and promotes initiatives aimed at improving the lives of individuals.

416 *Museums as Agents of Social Inclusion*

Table 1. Museums as agents of social inclusion—a typology

	The Inclusive Museum	The Museum as Agent of Social Regeneration	The Museum as Vehicle for Broad Social Change
Goal	To achieve cultural inclusion	To improve individuals' quality of life (e.g. increase self-esteem)	To influence society/instigate positive social change (e.g. promote greater tolerance towards minorities)
Achieved through—	Representation of, and participation and access for, those excluded	Initiatives which seek to alleviate disadvantage/ encourage personal development (with individuals and small groups)	Providing a forum for public debate, education and persuasion
Exclusion is tackled within—	The cultural dimension	The economic, social, political and cultural dimensions	
Social problems associated with exclusion—	Might be addressed indirectly	—provide the rationale behind initiatives —might be directly expressed within the museum's goals	

Fig. 4.1 The Sandell model. *Source* Sandell 1998, *416*

The third type is the museum as a vehicle for broad social change. The museum takes on a social role because it influences society and individuals by increasing their awareness of the value of social inclusion. Sandell's model (1998) offers a theoretical framework to measure social inclusion in museums.

4.3 Nature Based Solution Approach and Social Inclusion

Nature Based Solution (NBS) approach represents an idea that takes nature as a crucial element in evaluating and implementing processes. Everything revolves around nature; therefore, to study how human actions and choices interface with nature represents a way to interpret the impact of some managerial paths, considering nature as a resource that contributes to producing social benefits.

Solutions that consciously use nature can help satisfy different ethical and social aspects with reference to different contexts. NBS has been applied in a wide variety of sectors in order to address societal issues, such as developing green infrastructure in urban environments (Hall and Robertson 2001; Sharp et al. 2005, Cohen-Shacham et al. 2016). Scientific contributions regarding the NBS approach, underlined that an important issue is to evaluate the impact of NBS with regard to different social challenges. Raymond et al. (2017) proposed a framework to identify how NBS can produce both synergies through ecosystem services and co-benefits deriving from different contexts. The framework includes four dimensions that are considered: "when implementing NBS in urban areas: 1) co-benefits for human health and well-being; 2) integrated environmental performance (e.g., the provision of ecosystem services); 3) trade-offs and synergies to biodiversity, health or economy; and 4) potential for citizen's involvement in governance and monitoring" (Raymond et al. 2017, 16). The authors consider costs and benefits in different areas, such as: climate and physical environment, socio-economic and socio-cultural systems, ecosystems and biodiversity. They highlight ten key societal challenges: "climate adaptation and mitigation, water management, coastal resilience, green space management, air quality, urban regeneration, participatory planning and governance, social justice and social cohesion, public health and well-being, economics opps. and green jobs" (Raymond et al. 2017, 17).

Several studies address the issue of social benefits that can generate solutions based on nature (Farrington and Farrington 2005; Keniger et al. 2013). Accessing the green space may overcome certain social challenges and improve social cohesion (Kingsley and Townsend 2006). Moreover, interaction with nature can facilitate interaction among subjects, reinforcing social participation. Nature therefore becomes a resource for creating a social context and a place for interaction and sharing (Briot et al. 2007).

NBS "produces societal benefits in a fair and equitable way, in a manner that promotes transparency and broad participation" (Cohen-Shacham et al. 2016, 6). This approach requires planning approaches and governance architectures to support accessibility to green spaces or institutional spaces for dialogue and interactions of different stakeholders (Dennis and James, 2016). The concept of inclusion of disadvantaged subjects is considered in term of social cohesion and inclusion as relevant challenges of NBS. NBS activate paths of participation and promotes social inclusion. Indeed, it is highlighted that "green care and nature-based services can be a very important supplement to traditional health- and welfare services" (Kogstad et al. 2014, 6065), helping the community to have a more satisfying life and a more significant role in society.

This approach can be a tool to improve social inclusion in cultural institutions and museums (Baldarelli and Cardillo 2012, 2022). Studies (Panaro et al. 2025) have linked the Cultural Ecosystem Services (CES) framework to the NBS approach in the UK context. This approach is increasingly being applied in research, policy and planning to achieve sustainable change benefits.

The contribution of Privitera and Jelo (2025) studies the NBS approach in the context of historic cities that host architectural and cultural heritage and that sometimes have a poor provision of green spaces. In this context, the NBS approach has allowed to identify open spaces suitable for improving the conservation of the built heritage in historic cities. The integration of NBS into cultural contexts can enhance visitor enjoyment and experience, adding a cultural dimension to the benefits offered by NBS. These solutions offer the opportunity to "collaborate" with nature to preserve cultural sites and assets (Richards et al. 2024). For museums, NBS can enhance both environmental sustainability and visitor experience. Integrating green spaces, natural light, and outdoor exhibition areas can reduce energy consumption and improve the ecological footprint of museum operations. For example, museum gardens, green roofs, and natural ventilation systems not only support sustainability goals but also create immersive and restorative environments for visitors. Such spaces can foster engagement, education, and social inclusion, particularly for audiences seeking accessible and multisensory experiences. Moreover, NBS can support museums in community engagement and educational programming. By linking exhibits to nature-based practices or environmental awareness initiatives, museums can create interdisciplinary learning opportunities that combine art, history, and ecology. This approach encourages visitors to consider broader societal and environmental issues, positioning museums as active contributors to sustainable development. Finally, NBS can enhance the social role of museums by creating inclusive, multi-functional spaces where diverse communities interact. Outdoor and nature-integrated areas can facilitate social gatherings, workshops, and participatory projects, increasing accessibility and promoting well-being among vulnerable or differently-abled visitors. In summary, adopting an NBS approach allows museums to align sustainability with social and educational missions, creating environments that are ecologically responsible, inclusive, and engaging. It transforms museums from static cultural repositories into dynamic spaces that connect art, nature, and community.

4.4 The Impact of Technology on Culture Institutions

Literature (Bakhshi and Throsby 2012) presents research areas on new technologies and their impact on cultural institutions, highlighting the phenomenon of art sharing and the managerial implications linked to the evaluation of the effects of technological innovation on inclusion and accessibility. The impact of new technologies in cultural institutions mainly concerns the ways of the services providing and their usability and accessibility.

In the context of cultural technological innovations, the phenomenon of art sharing is developing. This term represents an application of the sharing economy to art and falls within the scope of the circular economy of society. Art sharing constitutes an opportunity to enjoy cultural, historical, pictorial and artistic works and products of different forms of the current digital artistic world. Some studies address knowledge sharing through digital tools that share information and skills between people, communities or organizations (Charband and Jafari Navimipour 2016). In general, the sharing economy represents a new economic and cultural model capable of rationalizing the use of resources based on the exchange or sharing of goods and services rather than their purchase. In this context, accessibility becomes an element that surpasses possession or ownership. Even if the concept is not new, digital technologies have strengthened this economic model which also concerns the cultural sector. In fact, art sharing creates new relationships between artists and those who wish to use artistic works for various reasons (Mondal and Samaddar 2021). Through this system which adopts digital platforms, anyone who wishes can use the cultural product even by renting it at low costs. This new modality raises questions related to the concept of accessibility. If on the one hand, this system allows people to improve the use and possibility of valorizing artistic works, on the other hand, we wonder whether even the most disadvantaged people benefit from an improvement in terms of access to culture and inclusion. The areas of the sharing economy are not always clear and the practical aspects linked to its implementation present some critical issues (Mondal and Samaddar 2021). For example, passive engagement may occur, as sharing artworks online does not always provide meaningful interaction or participation. Users may view or download works but lack opportunities for dialogue, interpretation, or co-creation, which are essential elements of inclusive cultural experiences. Furthermore, art-sharing platforms often decontextualize artworks from their original cultural or historical context. This can create misunderstandings or reduce the richness of the experience for audiences and users from diverse backgrounds. Digital transformation process underlying the sharing economy determines the creation of new roles and functions among the actors (Massi et al. 2021). This requires greater clarity in defining areas and opportunities for cultural users in using the potential of digital technology, trying to find, in the new system of intermediation and exchange, an opportunity for socialization (Navarrete 2013; Massi et al. 2021).

The topic of the impact of technology in cultural institutions was treated in depth by Bakhshi and Throsby (2012), who give a definition of innovation technology in art institutions and consider innovation to be truly important for solving various problems relating to cultural institutions management. According to these authors, in fact, "although the term 'new technologies' in the cultural field could be used to describe any form of technical advance affecting cultural production from the invention of the printing press onwards, it is used nowadays as shorthand for new information and communication technologies arising from two related late twentieth century sources: the explosion in computational speed and capacity that has transformed day-to-day life in countless ways, and the advent of the Internet" (Bakhshi and Throsby 2012, 208). Technology has increasingly become a transformative force in museums, reshaping how cultural institutions engage with audiences, manage collections, and generate value. According to Bakhshi and Throsby (2012), digital technologies provide museums with the tools to expand access to cultural content, enabling new forms of participation and interaction that transcend physical boundaries. Online collections, virtual tours, and interactive exhibits allow museums to reach a wider and more diverse audience, including those who may face barriers to physical attendance. This democratization of access aligns with broader social objectives, enhancing inclusion and fostering public engagement with cultural heritage.

Lazzeretti and Sartori (2016) focused on the analysis of the progressive digitization of the works and processes of the Uffizi Museum in Florence. Furthermore, they analyzed the impact on the production and communication process of new technologies, demonstrating their potential. Alongside the potential of new technologies, the authors also underlined their ability to create public-private collaboration networks, which have facilitated—and will continue to facilitate—the ongoing transformation toward digitalization. Lazzeretti and Sartori (2016) further emphasize that technology is not merely a means of dissemination but also a driver of innovation in museum management. Digital platforms facilitate the development of public-private partnerships, the collection and analysis of visitor data, and the creation of personalized experiences. Through these mechanisms, museums can tailor services to meet the specific needs of different audiences, thereby improving both educational outcomes and visitor satisfaction. However, the authors also caution that the integration of technology requires careful consideration of accessibility and equity. While digital tools have the potential to broaden participation, they may inadvertently exclude individuals who lack digital literacy or access to necessary devices, highlighting the ongoing challenge of ensuring inclusivity. Moreover, the effective use of technology demands investment in skills and infrastructure, raising managerial and financial considerations that museums must address. Recent research by Esposito et al. (2023) traces an analysis of the impact of the digitalisation of five Italian museums on the governance structure and on the relationship with stakeholders. At the end of this research, it is underlined that the process of applying new technologies is strongly influenced, at least for public management institutions, by the institutional and cultural characteristics of the regulatory context of reference. This generates limitations on the potential that new technologies could offer (Esposito et al. 2023).

Technological innovations are supporting museums and cultural institutions in carrying out their mission (Navarrete 2013), impacting inclusion and accessibility (McMillen 2015). In museums, different platforms are implemented (for example, video mapping, projection mapping, virtual tours and Internet of Things operations) that expand the experience and enjoyment of visitors (Suroto et al. 2020), increasing attraction and inclusive value. In summary, literature (Bakhshi and Throsby 2012; Lazzaretti and Sartori 2016) suggests that technology serves a dual role in museums: as a facilitator of access and social engagement, and as a strategic tool for organizational innovation. When implemented thoughtfully, digital technologies can enhance both the educational mission and the social impact of museums, while also introducing new challenges related to equity and resource allocation.

4.5 Conclusions

This chapter has examined the issue of measuring social value in cultural institutions. This involves reporting not only economic value but also the actions of individuals, communities, and society that generate social and cultural value. In this context, accounting and accountability represent two perspectives to be revisited and expanded to detect ethical, social and inclusive values. The chapter presents several frameworks and conceptual approaches to evaluate the impact of some elements such as nature and technology on the management and fruition of museums. Specifically, the first framework proposed is that of the inclusive museum. Museums are institutions at the service of society and exhibit works that constitute tangible and intangible testimonies of the historical evolution of humanity. In this context, accessibility and inclusion are important, with the aim of transferring culture and historical-artistic meanings to stakeholders. Another approach highlighted is the Nature Based Solution

(NBS). It considers nature as a crucial element in the evaluation and implementation of processes. This approach is also important in the cultural institutions sector, where it can improve the enjoyment and experience of visitors. Finally, technological innovations are supporting museums and cultural institutions in carrying out their mission and in strengthening accessibility and inclusive paths. In this context, digital transformation process and sharing economy create new roles and functions among key actors and cultural institutions.

References

Bakhshi, H., & Throsby, D. (2012). New technologies in cultural institutions: Theory, evidence and policy implications. *International Journal of Cultural Policy, 18*(2), 205–222.

Baldarelli, M.G., Cardillo, E. (2012). Viaggio ad occhi chiusi: creazione e misurazione del valore nel prodotto culturale accessibile a tutti tra percorsi teorici ed evidenze empiriche, E., Cardillo, G. D., Caruso, A., Leotta (eds), *Sistemi manageriali nelle aziende ad elevata socialità. Processi innovativi e rilevanza degli stakeholder*, Book series: Quaderni di ricerca economico-aziendale: teoria e casi, (pp. 165–196). Aracne.

Baldarelli, M. G., & Cardillo, E. (2022). Managerial paths, social inclusion, and NBS in tactile cultural products: Theory and practice. *Journal of Hospitality & Tourism Research, 46*(3), 544–582.

Barnes, M., Evans, R., Plumridge, G., & McCabe, A. (2006). *Preventative Services for Disabled Children: A final report of the National Evaluation of the children's fund*. DfES.Google Scholar.

Belfiore, E. (2002). Art as a means of alleviating social exclusion: Does it really work? A critique of instrumental cultural policies and social impact studies in the UK. *International Journal of Cultural Policy, 8*(1), 91–106.

Bhalla, A., & Lapeyre, F. (1997). Social exclusion: Towards an analytical and operational framework. *Development and Change, 28*(3), 413–433.

Bradshaw, J., Kemp, P., Baldwin, S., & Rowe, A. (2004). *The drivers of social exclusion. A review of the literature for the social exclusion unit in the breaking the cycle series*. The Office of the Deputy Prime Minister Pubblication.

Briot J.P., Guyot, P., & Irving, M. (2007). Participatory simulation for collective management of protected areas for biodiversity conservation and social inclusion. F. Barros, C. Frydman, N. Giambiasi & B. Ziegler (Eds.), AIS-CMS 2007 *international Modeling and simulation multi-conference* (IMSM 2007), Buenos Aires, Argentina (183–188). San Diego, CA: The Society for Modeling and Simulation International (SCS).

Bruni, L., & Zamagni, S. (2004). The economy of communion: Inspirations and achievements. *Finance & Bien Commun, 20*(3), 91–97.

Camarero, C., & Garrido, M. J. (2009). Improving museums' performance through custodial sales and customer orientations. *Non-Profit and voluntary sector quarterly, 38*(5), 846–868.

Carnegie, G. D., Ferri, P., Parker, L. D., Sidaway, S. I., & Tsahuridu, E. E. (2022). Accounting as technical, social and moral practice: The monetary valuation of public cultural, heritage and scientific collections in financial reports. *Australian Accounting Review, 32*(4), 460–472.

Carroll, A. B. (1991). The pyramid of corporate social responsibility: Toward the moral Management of Organizational Stakeholders. *Business Horizons, 34*(4), 39–48.

Carroll, A. B. (2000). Ethical challenges for business in the new millennium: Corporate social responsibility and models of management morality. *Business Ethics Quarterly, 10*, 1.

Charband, Y., & Jafari Navimipour, N. (2016). Online knowledge sharing mechanisms: A systematic review of the state of the art literature and recommendations for future research. *Information Systems Frontiers, 18*, 1131–1151.

Chirieleison, C. (1998). Le problematiche legate alla misurazione della performance nelle gestioni museali. in Misc,. *La gestione e la valorizzazione dei beni artistici e culturali nella prospettiva aziendale - Conference proceedings* - 30th/31st October (451–503). CLUEB.
Coffee, K. (2008). Cultural inclusion, exclusion and the formative roles of muse- ums. *Museum Management and Curatorship, 23*(3), 261–279.
Cohen-Shacham, E., Walters, G., Janzen, C., & Maginnis, S. (2016). *Nature-based solutions to address global societal challenges.* IUCN.
Dennis, M., & James, P. (2016). User participation in urban green commons: Exploring the links between access, voluntarism, biodiversity and well being. *Urban Forestry & Urban Greening, 15*, 22–31.
Donato F., Visser Travagli, A. M. (2010). Il museo oltre la crisi. Dialogo tra museologia e management. Electa.
Ecchia, S. (1998). La valorizzazione dei beni artistici e culturali nelle prospettive socio-culturale. economica ed aziendale. in Misc. *La gestione e la valorizzazione dei beni artistici e culturali nella prospettiva aziendale- Conference Proceedings*—30th/31st October (61–88). CLUEB.
Esposito, P., Braga, A., Sancino, A., & Ricci, P. (2023). The strategic governance of the digital accounting environment: Insights from virtual museums. *Meditari Accountancy Research, 31*(2), 366–380.
Farrington, J., & Farrington, C. (2005). Rural accessibility, social inclusion and social justice: Towards conceptualisation. *Journal of Transport Geography, 13*(1), 1–12.
Fredette, C., Bradshaw, P., & Krause, H. (2015). From diversity to inclusion. A multi- method study of diverse governing groups. *Nonprofit and Voluntary Sector Quarterly, 45*(1), 28–51.
Freeman, R. E. (2017). Five challenges to stakeholder theory: A report on research in progress. In *Stakeholder management* (pp. 1–20). Emerald Publishing Limited.
Hall, T., & Robertson, I. (2001). Public art and urban regeneration: Advocacy, claims and critical debates. *Landscape Research, 26*(1), 5–26.
Jones, T. M., Harrison, J. S., & Felps, W. (2018). How applying instrumental stakeholder theory can provide sustainable competitive advantage. *Academy of Management Review, 43*(3), 371–391.
Keniger, L. E., Gaston, K. J., Irvine, K. N., & Fuller, R. A. (2013). What are the benefits of interacting with nature? *International Journal of Environmental Research and Public Health, 10*(3), 913–935.
Kingsley, J.Y., & Townsend, M. (2006). dig in to social capital: Community gardens as mechanisms for growing urban social connectedness. Urban Policy and Research, 24(4), 525–537.
Klamer, A. (2002). Accounting for social and cultural values. *De Economist, 150*(4), 453–473.
Kogstad, R. E., Agdal, R., & Hopfenbeck, M. S. (2014). Narratives of natural recovery: Youth experience of social inclusion through green care. *International Journal of Environmental Research and Public Health, 11*(6), 6052–6068.
Kotler, N. (2001). New ways of experiencing culture: The role of museums and marketing implications. *Museum Management and Curatorship, 19*(4), 417–425.
Lazzeretti L. & Sartori A. (2016). Digitization of Cultural Heritage and Business Model Innovation: the case of the Uffizi Gallery in Florence. *Capitale Culturale, XIV*, 945–970.
Magistrali, G. (2008). *Turismo Sociale.* Maggioli.
Magliacani, M. (2008). *L'approccio etnografico all'attività dei musei.* Aracne.
Massi, M., Vecco, M., & Lin, Y. (2021). Digital transformation in the cultural and creative industries. Production, consumption and entrepreneurship in the digital and sharing econom. In *Routledge research in the creative and cultural industries.* Taylor & Francis Group.
McMillen, R. (2015). Museum disability access: Social inclusion opportunities through innovative new media practices. *Pacific Journal, 10*, 95–107.
McMillen, R., & Alter, F. (2017). Social media, social inclusion, and museum disability access. *Museums & Social Issues, 12*(2), 115–125.
Mondal, S., & Samaddar, K. (2021). Issues and challenges in implementing sharing economy in tourism: A triangulation study. *Management of Environmental Quality, 32*(1), 64–81.

Navarrete, T. (2013). *Digital cultural heritage. Handbook on the economics of cultural heritage.* Edward Elgar Publishing.

Nussbaum, M. (2002). Capabilities and human rights. In P. De Greiff & C. Cronin (Eds.), *Global justice and transnational politics: Essays on the moral and political challenges of globalization* (pp. 117–149). MIT Press.

Nussbaum, M.N. (2007). *Le nuove frontiere della giustizia.* Bologna:Il Mulino. (or. ed.: Frontiers of Justice. Harvard University Press. Cambridge).

Panaro, S., Delabre, I., & Marshall, F. (2025). Cultural ecosystem services and opportunities for inclusive and effective nature-based solutions. *Ecological Economics, 230*, 108525.

Pelligra, V. (2008). Vulnerabilità e dipendenza. Dal contratto alla responsabilità…e ritorno. In V. Pelligra (Ed.), *Imprese sociali. Scelte individuali e interessi comuni* (pp. 1–15). Mondadori.

Privitera, R., & Jelo, G. (2025). Built heritage preservation and climate change adaptation in historic cities: Facing challenges posed by nature-based solutions. *Sustainability, 17*(13), 5693.

Raymond, C. M., Frantzeskaki, N., Kabisch, N., Berry, P., Breil, M., Nita, M. R., & Calfapietra, C. (2017). A framework for assessing and implementing the co-benefits of nature-based solutions in urban areas. *Environmental Science & Policy, 77*, 15–24.

Richards, J., Cooke, E. L., Coombes, M., Jones, J., & Viles, H. (2024). Are nature-based solutions for built heritage conservation resilient to climate change? The response of grass-based soft caps in Britain and Ireland to future climate scenarios. *Studies in Conservation*, 1–12.

Salter, S. B., Kang, T., Gotti, G., & Doupnik, T. S. (2013). The role of social values, accounting values and institutions in determining accounting conservatism. *Management International Review, 53*, 607–632.

Sandell, R. (1998). Museums as agents of social inclusion. *Museum Management and Curatorship, 17*, 401–418.

Sandell, R. (2000). The strategic significance of workforce diversity in museums. *International Journal of Heritage Studies, 6*(3), 213–230.

Sandell, R. (2002). *Museums. Society*. Routledge.

Sandell, R. (2003). Social inclusion, the museum and the dynamics of sectoral change. *Museum & Society, 1*(1), 45–62.

Sandell, R, Janes, R.R., (eds.). (2007). Museum management and marketing, Routledge.

Sharp, J., Pollock, V., & Paddison, R. (2005). Just art for a just City: Public art and social inclusion in urban regeneration. *Urban Studies, 42*(5–6), 1001–1023.

Sibilio, B. (2004). *Creare e valorizzare i distretti museali.* Franco Angeli.

Sibilio, B., & Donato, F. (Eds.). (2015). *Governare e gestire le aziende culturali.* Franco Angeli.

Suroto, P. Z., Dewantara, M. H., & Wiradarmo, A. A. (2020). The application of technology in museums. *International Journal of Applied Sciences in Tourism and Events, 4*(2), 170–181.

Wild, S. (2013). Accounting for heritage, cultural and community assets-alternative metrics from a New Zealand Maori educational institution. *Australasian Accounting Business & Finance Journal, 7*(1), 1.

Zan, L. (1999). *Conservazione e innovazione nei musei italiani. management e processi di cambiamento.* Etas.

Zan, L. (2003). *Economia dei musei e retorica del management.* Electa.

Maria-Gabriella Baldarelli PhD, CPA, is Associate Professor of Accounting, at University of Bologna, Department of Management-Rimini Campus. Full professor availability. Envited professor at Sophia University Institute. SIDREA board member until 2018. She is a member of international scientific networks: the Centre for Social and Environmental Accounting Research (CSEAR) and the European Business Ethics Network (EBEN). Key-note Speaker second International Conference on Economics, Business, Finance and Governance (ICEBFG) by Economics and Business Faculty of University of Bandar Lampung-Bali-Indonesia- Dic. 4–5, 2019. Research interests includes: accountability and gambling enterprises; corporate social responsibility; ethical, social and environmental accounting and accountability, sustainability in tourist enterprises;

responsible and accessible tourism for blind people, economy of communion; gender accounting; accounting history, accounting education and Feminist Economics.

Eleonora Cardillo is Associate Professor of Business Economics at the Department of Economics and Business of the University of Catania. She was Visiting Scholar at the CSEAR (Centre for social and environmental accounting research) School of Management of the University of St Andrews (Scotland) for the research project: "Study and analysis of the methodological and operational paths of environmental and social reporting in the evolution process of accounting information systems". Professor of Accounting and Financial Statements and Public accounting iin local administrations. She was Director and Scientific Coordinator of the Master in Accounting and Control in Local Authorities, organized by the Department of Economics and Business of the University of Catania. Her research topics are public accounting systems, performance measurement, socio-environmental reporting, social inclusion in tactile museums, sustainability and accountability.

Chapter 5
Nature Based-Solutions to Evaluate Social Inclusion in Tactile Museum

Maria-Gabriella Baldarelli and Eleonora Cardillo

Abstract The chapter examines the theme of social inclusion in the context of a specific type of cultural institution: the tactile museum. This type of museum is dedicated to people with visual impairments, but is appreciated by all visitors. The tactile museum is a museum typology designed and structured to offer sensorial experiences through the use of touch and takes on particular relevance in the activation of inclusive paths. The aim of this contribution is to combine two theoretical frameworks, such as Sandell's (*Museum Management and Curatorship 17*:401–418, 1998) inclusive museum and the Nature-Based Solution approach, to evaluate accounting and managerial tools and actions aimed at strengthening social inclusion. The chapter describes the qualitative case of the Multimedia Tactile Museum of Catania and describes how the museum develops social inclusion through an innovative management model. The contribution of the work is to provide a theoretical framework for evaluating social inclusion in tactile museums and the role that nature can play in strengthening this function.

5.1 Introduction to Social Inclusion in Tactile Museum

The activities carried out in the special tactile museum are consistent with the aims of any museum institution, that is, to "allow people to experience the quality of beautiful and rare objects that would otherwise be excluded to them and thereby enrich their knowledge and experience in an appropriate and dignified environment where visitors and art can meet" (Kotler and Kotler 1999, 42). The artistic productions

M.-G. Baldarelli
University of Bologna, Bologna, Italy
e-mail: cardillo@unict.it

M.-G. Baldarelli
e-mail: maria.baldarelli@unibo.it

E. Cardillo
University of Catania, Catania, Italy

M. Baldarelli et al. (eds.), *Accounting and Accountability for Social Inclusion*, CSR, Sustainability, Ethics & Governance, https://doi.org/10.1007/978-3-032-09271-7_5

contained are designed to be touched and/or accompanied by descriptions in Braille or by audio devices that allow the enjoyment of the historical and artistic work.

These institutions address the issue of social inclusion with great care, seeking to foster a logic of sharing and participation. Sometimes in some cultural organisations, there are still barriers, especially for blind people, that do not allow people with disabilities to enjoy cultural products or to appreciate museums in a comprehensive way. There are types of "vulnerable" users of cultural institutions. In this context, vulnerability can be understood as one of the driving factors behind trust and reciprocity (Bruni and Tufano 2015; Pelligra 2008).

The present research on this topic contributes to supporting studies and actions for the pursuit of two important goals of the 2030 Agenda: SDG 10 and SDG 11. Sustainable Development Goal (SDG) 10, *Reduce inequality within and among countries*, aims to remove those factors that prevent people from having a fair chance of achieving prosperity and development (Oestreich 2018; Kuhn 2020). It is about limiting, or rather eliminating, political, economic and social factors, such as discrimination, abuse and exclusion, which prevent people from carrying out personal projects and initiatives. Sustainable Development Goal (SDG) 11, *Make cities and human settlements inclusive, safe, resilient and sustainable* aims to strengthen accessibility to essential services to improve the quality of life. Specifically, Goal 11.4 highlights the need to preserve, protect and conserve cultural and natural heritage, an expression of the collective identity of a society. This implies actions to improve the enjoyment of heritage also through the creation of green spaces and other infrastructures that bring benefits not only to the environment and health but to the participation and enjoyment of communities (McCullough et al. 2022).

Contributions highlight the relevance of accountability in cultural institutions or museums as social inclusion agents (Sandell 2000, 2003; Sandell and Janes 2007; Coffee 2008; Belfiore 2002; Kotler 2001), facing the theme of vulnerability (Pelligra 2008). If an inclusion path is implemented, it is necessary to evaluate the possible benefit for excluded people and also for those who acquire a new vision of inclusion (Tang et al. 2009; Fredette et al. 2016). There is a link between vulnerability, dependence, trust and responsibility that is important to promote trust and create interdependence between agents (Nussbaum 2002). The satisfaction of the vulnerable agents gives meaning to the action and life of other subjects who develop their own social responsibility. There is a moral and ethical duty that motivates people to care for those who are excluded from the normal use of cultural services and activities (Magliacani 2008).

This study, starting from the analysis of two theoretical frameworks, the inclusive museum model by Sandell (1998) and the Nature Based Solution (NBS) approach (Raymond et al. 2017), aims to identify an evaluation tool to activate management actions and paths to strengthen social inclusion. Sandell's model highlights the process of change in the museum that aims to represent certain users and guarantee access to marginalized groups in order to strengthen participation and inclusion. The nature-based NBS approach is the basis for the creation of an accountability model for the evaluation of actions, initiatives and resources dedicated to social inclusion.

The Multimedia Tactile Museum of Catania will be analyzed according to a qualitative approach, as it plays an important role in the community and constitutes a meeting and sharing point for diverse communities and groups. The management of cultural heritage for blind and/or visually impaired people is particularly complex to achieve from the point of view of usability and accessibility, despite its importance for the education and development of all subjects.

5.2 Empirical Evidence: The Case of the Multimedia Tactile Museum in Sicily

5.2.1 Methodology

The contribution of Baldarelli and Cardillo (2022) analysed the case of the Multimedia Tactile Museum (MTM) of Catania (Sicily) trying to understand the logic of use of the museum and how management is oriented to social inclusion. The research contributed to provide an accountability framework for measuring social inclusion through the NBS approach, the results of which are presented in section (5.3). The methodology used is qualitative (Scapens 2011) and is based on interviews with the museum managers and on documentary analysis. The qualitative studies conducted (Baldarelli and Cardillo 2022) were based on interviews with the Director of the museum, in order to stimulate an informal dialogue to reconstruct the profile and the objective of the inclusive action carried out by the museum. General information on the museum, the accounting system, the projects and initiatives carried out also constituted a basis for grasping the aspects of inclusion in its various articulations. Interpretive approach (Scapens 2004) was very useful for understanding the subjects' perceptions, evaluating their points of view.

The following sub-sections report and comment the results of this contribution, highlights the managerial processes that have favoured social inclusion. Multimedia Tactile Museum of Catania was chosen because it is one of the very few tactile museum in Italy that produces artistic works for the blind or visually impaired. The use of the two frameworks (Sandell 1998; Raymond 2017) lies in the union of inclusive action and nature-inspired approach. The two basic elements, inclusion and nature, fall within the broader logic of sustainability. Furthermore, it is significant to understand how nature and solutions inspired by nature can be a means to foster inclusion and improve fruition in the tactile museum. Specifically, Sandell's model (1988) highlights the process of change within the museum, which aims to represent special users and ensure access to marginalized groups, in order to strengthen participation and inclusion. The NBS approach is the basis for the creation of an accountability model for evaluating actions, initiatives and resources dedicated to social inclusion.

5.2.2 *The Tactile Museum Social Mission and Reporting*

The MTM is conceived for blind and/or visually impaired people but its impacts in terms of transfer of values and meanings influence the whole community. It is a cultural institution of high social value whose purpose is to enable the enjoyment of artworks through touch and to provide meaningful sensory experiences. The museum represents an example of knowledge transfer that aims to overcome prejudices and phenomena of marginalization.

The reporting and governance processes of MTM promote social inclusion of vulnerable people and the social awareness of the community. The framework of Sandell (1998), presented and described in the previous chapter, is useful for interpreting the desire to respond to specific needs through the development of accessibility and limiting marginalization and exclusion.

The MTM is a first poly-functional tactile cultural institution in Europe devoted to the integration of blind and visually impaired people, promoted and realised by the "Regional Braille Stamperia" located in Catania. In Italy there are several structures that offer services to the blind, including the tactile museum of Ancona (Omero Museum). The MTM however offers, in the same structure, various types of services including cultural services through tactile "museum" path and playful services such as "Sensory Garden" and "Dark Café". These elements attract a certain number of visitors annually, not just blind people, especially students, families and groups.

Museum services are aimed at the blind and all people who are intent on experiencing a new way of appreciating art by touching it. It offers copies of original art works and historical and artistic monuments, and for this reason, it is not considered a museum in the usual sense. However, it tends to be regarded as a "special museum" because it makes cultural products—whose historical and artistic value is already recognized—accessible and enjoyable, seeking to transfer this value to individuals who are partially or totally impaired and therefore vulnerable. A key role in the establishment of the Tactile Pole was played by the Italian Union of the Blind, a moral entity with legal personality under private law. According to its statute and the law, it is entrusted with representing and protecting the moral and material interests of blind people. Its primary purpose is, in fact, to facilitate the integration of blind people into society.

The tactile structure exhibits copies of Greek and Renaissance sculptures and various monuments and architectural and natural landmarks of Sicily, including: the Agrigento Temples, the Etna Volcano, the Ursino Castle, the Church of San Giuliano, the Church and Palace of the Minorite, the Massimo "Bellini" Theatre, the Cathedral of S. Agata, the Chierici Palace, the "Liotro" Fountain. Even famous Italian and foreign works have been featured including: the Eiffel Tower, the United Kingdom's Stonehenge megalithic complex and the Basilica and Square of St. Peter in Rome. The creation of a gallery of Sicilian monuments has the function of allowing Sicilian blind people to be aware of and enjoy the artistic heritage of the region in which they reside. It also provides the opportunity for the visually impaired tourist to visit the places and appreciate cultural products.With reference to the artistic and cultural aspect, it is useful to name some of the masterpieces reproduced in the category of architectural and optical works: the "Venus of Milo", the "Discobolo" by Myron of Eleutherae, the bust of "Christ Crucified" by Donatello, the "Abandoned Psyche" by Pietro Tenerani, the "Venus of Doctors" and the "Medusa Head" by Caravaggio and "Les demoiselles de Avignon" by Pablo Picasso. A large space is devoted to "The Creation of Adam" by Michelangelo. In this case, the work has been deconstructed and reproduced in relief, enabling visually impaired individuals to explore it not only as a whole but also at different levels, allowing for an in-depth analysis as the surfaces overlap.

An articulated governance system characterises the MTM, the Braille Printing House is the central core; it has contributed greatly to the creation of the Tactile structure. Several organisations support and sustain such structures, like: the Italian Union of the Blind (UIC), the Ministry of Cultural Heritage, the Sicily Region and the Regional Province. Over time, the Museum Director sought to increase financial resources in order to better support the planning and implementation of activities, which require significant human and financial investment. The management of the Braille Regional Printing House is attributed to the board of directors, which consists of 5 members: four of which are designated by the UIC and one designated by the Regional Council for Cultural and Environmental Heritage. The board holds the office for 3 years with the possibility of being reconfirmed once.

Within the Stamperia, research and design activities are carried out. In fact, each work is a detailed study, in which experts evaluate its feasibility and the ways in which blind people can use it. The MTM is becoming a point of reference for subjects with visual impairment and, at the same time, a place where creative and innovative action is generated. It realizes the integration of "vulnerable" people (Bruni and Tufano 2015; Pelligra 2008) through accessibility and education. Undoubtedly, in the reality examined, it is not possible to refer to the acquisition and display of original artistic works, but rather of "special and simulated" works, since it is not original goods but reproductions studied and produced to be enjoyed by visitors with disabilities. This entails a remarkable commitment from the museum and specifically of the Stamperia, which deals with the design and production phase, and the development of high-value social activities. Managerial action is related to value generation processes, in which the analysis of the relationship between the institution and stakeholders is relevant. To this end, it is essential to identify the main users as if "you do not understand how the museum is run, it is not even possible to orient the evaluation system in order to verify how it is managed" (Chirieleison 1998, 473). Several interviews with managers and administrators of the Printing House (Regional Braille Stamperia) and the tactile museum have brought out some ethical principles and values that justify the dedication, the deep respect and the will to make the blind and visually impaired an integral part of a community. These elements could not emerge from the aseptic reading of the documents or from the detached observation of the economic-financial performances. The process of listening to the subjects, conducted by this study, has created a close proximity with the subjects interviewed, managing to grasp essential values such as respect, ethics and correctness of actions.

Starting from 2022, an important aspect developed by the museum is the *Social report* which expresses the commitment to communities and inclusive paths.

The document was developed to contribute to the well-being of the community and the integration of the blind and visually impaired. The *Social report*, in addition to reporting on the activity carried out by the tactile museum in line with its mission, aims to inform the territory of the potential and the role of social growth that the structure carries out.

The document presents the guiding principles and its purposes which are summarised below:

- provide all stakeholders with an overall picture of the activities;
- give useful information on the quality of the activity also from an ethical-social perspective;
- analyse the role played in civil society, highlighting and disseminating value and cultural approach;
- demonstrate and inform on the added value that the activities produce;
- implement a reporting of the social impacts in terms of usefulness, legitimacy and efficiency of the activities carried out;
- be a tool for reflection for all actors involved in the organization for the improvement of services, products, safety, respect for the environment and relations with all stakeholders (Regional Braille Stamperia Social Report, 2022).

For the tactile pole, the social report represents a tool for social inclusion both because it measures the social impact and highlights the commitment to creating a more equitable society, spreading an inclusive culture.

5.2.3 The Sandell's Perspective to Create Inclusive Paths

Moving from Sandell approach (1998), it is possible to identify elements of social inclusion carried out by the museum relating to three areas: the Inclusive Museum, the Museum as Agent of Social Regeneration and the Museum as Vehicle for Broad Social Change. Each dimension is represented on the basis of various information related to mission, initiatives to activate virtuous cycles, action limiting the exclusion and modes by which the museum is able to manage some issues associated with the exclusion. Baldarelli and Cardillo (2022) adapts the framework to the MTM, seeking to identify some managerial areas with respect to social exclusion.

The first area of the framework is about the *Inclusive cultural institution.* Sandell's framework assumes cultural inclusion as the relevant goal of an inclusive museum. Director expresses the mission of MTM that is "to offer blind and/or visually impaired people the opportunity to know the characteristics and value of historical and artistic goods through the creation of works for them studied and designed in order to make them take part in an important moment for their human and social growth" (Interview to General Director of the Tactile pole, June 2017). MTM was formed in 2008, after thirty years from the establishment of the Stamperia Braille, with the aim of completing the cultural offer. The mission is connected to the desire to make local and Italian cultural heritage accessible and appreciated even by those with visual impairments, through the creation of three-dimensional works that can be touched and experienced by them as well. The museum manager (July, 2017) states: "The museum does not promote inclusion because inclusion is the reason for its existence, so the museum exists as it integrates, it includes; if it does not accomplish this purpose, it does not exist".

The ways in which this dimension is realised relate to all actions that enable representation, participation and access to categories that are usually excluded from certain processes (Sandell 1998, 2000). The actions carried out by the Tactile Pole management are central to achieving the social goal of integration. For example, the purpose of integration also involves testing plastics produced in the Stamperia by blind individuals who have an average ability to perceive both the physical and historical aspects, as well as the artistic significance of the works. Selecting testers with an average capacity ensures that, in terms of the ability to enjoy and understand the work, a substantial portion of individuals with this type of disability is represented. The works are built in scale and details are emphasised and the use of strong colours also serves to affect the visually impaired person to perceive certain characteristics of the work. The facilities of the museum, in terms of accessibility are extraordinary. Behind them, there is a strong desire expressed by the general manager, who is an expert in the study of the conditions and issues of the blind, to identify himself in the condition of the blind and/or visually impaired people. Accessibility is developed in detail: at the entrance, there is a smart button that guides the blind visitor to access the museum describing his current location and access modes. The structure also features a yellow path designed with state-of-the-art elements and materials that allow a safe path for the blind visitor.

In this context the factors that limit exclusion take on a cultural connotation. First, the aim is to reduce the barriers that prevent blind individuals from enjoying historical and artistic works, by creating special services that help foster an understanding of the relationship between those with this disability and those who interact with them.

Continuous enrichment of collections implies a management action aimed at obtaining funds to improve cultural offerings. Thanks to the special fund for publishing of the Ministry for Cultural Heritage, the Stamperia has made further projects for the creation of new editorial products for the blind and visually impaired, including a series of tactile polymath books called "Wonders Under the Fingers". In addition, a convention with the Province of Catania for the implementation of a project called "From the eyes to the hands", has made it possible to realise many three-dimensional architectural plastics, that have enriched the Tactile pole. Further funding from the Ministry of Cultural Heritage in 2014 has allowed the Tactile pole to be expanded, creating another exhibition area and enhancing the realisation of architectural works.

The second area, that is examined, is *Social regeneration*. If a cultural institution assumes the goal of improving quality of life and the growth of self-esteem, then it assumes the features of an inclusive museum. In this regard, manager of the Tactile pole states that "inclusion is a process of continuous improvement. Actions should be studied first with respect to the objective that is intended. This is to avoid the failure of inclusion". There are several initiatives that aim to alleviate the disadvantage and increase self-esteem. For example, in the Braille Café Internet Room, there are pc-connected PCs, equipped with a Braille displays and screen readers, which are made available to the blind and visually impaired. Voice synthesis installed on PCs converts what appears on the screen in voice form. The goal of this area is that the Internet is perceived, as a socialisation and integration tool, and the blind can have access to this tool. The blind and the visually impaired can contact the Tactile pole for this service whenever they wish. The urge to make use of the Internet for the visually impaired was born with the constitution, by the Italian Union of the Blind, of the Observatory of the Internet, which assesses the degree of Internet accessibility for the disabled with visual rights. The right to surf the web and access the information was dictated by the Stanca Act (4/2004), which obliges public statements to render their sites accessible.

Museum therefore assumes an inclusive dimension when it manages to improve the lives of such disadvantaged and vulnerable people. On the issue of vulnerability, during the interviews, the general manager of MTM and the showroom manager have defined the vulnerability differently. While the general manager has correlated vulnerability to physical disadvantage that can indeed create situations of weakness and impotence in responding to the subject, the showroom manager, who is a blind person, has expressed a different idea, affirming that vulnerability does not necessarily derive from external agents but it is a mental setting. "Vulnerability is linked to our mind; it is not related to physicality. We can be healthy and very vulnerable, but also disabled and not easily vulnerable. Subjects or actions can condition vulnerability but it always depends on our minds. It is also not stable; it can be momentary or linked to a specific moment of life" (Showroom Manager). The issue of vulnerability takes on a peculiar connotation within the Tactile pole. The structure is also intended for non-blind people, who can experience blindness through specific areas (i.e. Bar in the Dark). It often happens that the non-blind person increases his/her vulnerability, such as getting himself/herself into such situation that he/she increases his/her level of awareness and anxiety.

Exclusion is therefore limited if the subject finds in the museum a dimension of growth and valorisation of his/her existence, giving himself/herself part of the life of the other subjects and feeling part of a moment of growth. The development of tactile works, thanks to the financial and political commitment of management, is tied to the desire to expand the opportunities for the blind to discover historical and artistic works. The initiatives promoted are designed to make blind people active participants in a world that considers their specific needs. These considerations highlight that any parameter or method used to assess value and managerial action must take into account the concerns of the intended audience and the activities being undertaken in pursuit of social improvement.

The third area, that is analysed, is about *Broad social change*. In fact, one goal of the Tactile pole's managerial processes is to influence society, raising awareness not just of understanding the status of certain categories, but also of enhancing the sharing of values and ethical principles. The MTM seeks to play a social action and to be a vehicle for a community change. An essential aspect of this change is consciousness. The visit of Pole is in fact a formative experience perhaps even more for non-blind people (about 40% of annual visitors are blind). At a first stage, the visit of the non-blind visitor is characterised by curiosity, from the interest of observing a place created for those who cannot see; afterwards, the visit triggers the visually impaired sensation. This visitor immerses in the condition of those who don' t see and, in that case, the blind person becomes the guide, the reference for non-blind people. This journey allows one to experience deep emotion, foster personal growth, and gain a better understanding and awareness of the condition of people with such disabilities. The structure that is stimulating in this sense, especially for the non-blind, is the "Bar in the dark", undoubtedly a successful experiment for the integration of the blind and non-blind through a reversal of roles. The visit consists of a tour of the bar and the furniture is also shown, for example, by touching the visitor with the relief paintings hanging on the wall in the dark. The non-blind person, after a first uncomfortable situation, becomes captivated and gets used to the darkness and begins to experience "with a different eye". For these people, this is a living experience that leads to profound reflections on the value of light and on the way of life in the blind world. This type of experience not only reduces the distance between the blind and non-blind people but allows the latter group to better understand the situation and the disadvantages of visual impairments because only through awareness can the blind be further integrated into society. In this context, indeed, the blind guiding the non-blind, who fully lives this experience, in the dark, leaves him/her perhaps a bit shaken but profoundly enriched. "The experience of the bar in the dark I consider it unique... an important moment for both the non-blind and the blind... maybe more for the non-blind... many times I have seen mothers of sightless children walk the path and cry afterwards... as if they had acquired a full awareness of the condition of their children" (General Director of the Tactile pole, 2018).

Education is an essential effect of the managerial action of the tactile museum. Related activities are connected to the creation of evaluation processes, meetings and initiatives to educate society, families, school children and the youth. At the end of the visit, visitors are given a questionnaire to help identify the feelings they experienced and which senses were most stimulated in the absence of sight. Beyond its role as a cultural institution, the tactile museum acts as an educational catalyst, promoting social awareness and inclusion. Its programs—ranging from interactive workshops to community outreach—aim to engage not only schools and families but society as a whole, encouraging a deeper appreciation of art, accessibility, and the shared responsibility to make cultural experiences meaningful for everyone, regardless of their abilities.

The MTM, in order to become a vehicle for educating society, tries to make its works and, consequently, the efforts made in their implementation known to the whole community. However, the dissemination should be further developed as stated by the museum director and the general manager. Efforts have been made to increase communication channels, by the website and the Facebook page, and to activate initiatives and projects that showcase Tactile pole activities, such as the National Day of Braille and the Dark Dinners. The MTM provides for the display of some works and items for the visually impaired, on a specially equipped bus, for the purpose of disseminating its activities and services. Visiting museum are particularly important by national and foreign schools, which may visit the museum many times during the year. The teaching staff of these structures feel that the visit to the museum is a moment of absolute human growth for the youths. To this end, the MTM develops a number of external social activities linked, for example, to the activation of manipulation workshops for students and pupils in schools. All of these activities serve as a vital tool in reducing exclusion, not only by providing direct access to cultural experiences but also by fostering awareness, empathy, and social participation. Through engagement with diverse audiences, the museum creates opportunities for interaction, understanding, and inclusion, helping to bridge gaps between individuals with disabilities and the broader community.

The president of the Braille Stamperia considers the tactile museum an example that can give everyone a "better conscience, the awareness that people who for whatever reason have a disadvantage are the same as those who are more fortunate, and the fortune is neither capacity nor conquest, therefore consciousness must enrich with knowledge and values, the true greatness of each individual and of mankind".

5.3 Nature-Based Solution Approach in Tactile Museum

Nature-based Solutions (NBS) involves the use of interventions and actions that use nature to solve environmental, social and economic problems (Cohen-Shacham et al. 2019; Raymond et al. 2017). This approach offers benefits for biodiversity protection and human well-being. NBS is linked to environmental protection and sustainable management and focuses on restoring natural ecosystems or using them to address social challenges. The choices of companies and institutions can follow this approach through an improvement and valorisation of green areas, in order to generate a series of benefits for users and community. Museums can also follow this logic, in fact they are often conceived and designed by redeveloping green areas or abandoned green structures or in any case by adopting solutions inspired by nature (Raymond et al. 2017, 1).

The contribution of Baldarelli and Cardillo (2022) adopted the NBS framework considering social inclusion as a challenge of the NBS approach in the context of the MTM. An example of a structure built according to this approach is the Sensory Garden situated in the MTM. The garden has 250 different species of plants including olive-, almond-, orange-, lemon- and palm-trees and laurel bushes, many types of fragrant flowers and fragrances: mint, sage, thyme and Melissa plant. Each plant is accompanied by a black/Braille label, which shows the name, species and type of vegetation. The garden, open to visitors, is meant to be a meeting place for blind, visually impaired, and sighted people—a space for socializing where the goal of increasing sighted visitors' awareness of blindness is clearly expressed. The non-blind, in fact, have the opportunity of visiting the garden blindfolded following tactile-plantar tiles arranged to trace a path. This path has been studied and based on the "non-rest state" because the tiles are made in such a way that they do not allow perfect balance. The visitor does not run the risk of going outside the pathway by mistake and the trail can still be abandoned by the blind, who can choose to go to the lawn following special attention signals.

After linking the NBS approach to Sandell's inclusive logic, the study (Baldarelli and Cardillo, 2022) developed an accountability framework that contains measures and indicators to measure inclusion paths and NBS contribution in supporting it.

The indicators (Tables 5.1, 5.2 and 5.3) represent a possible measurement of social inclusion as a relevant impact of NBS, considering costs, investments, benefits, initiatives and perceptions of stakeholders involved in the process.

The tables presented above offer some measures for evaluating and representing the characteristics of museum inclusion activity and, then, express how measurement and reporting systems can contribute to assess inclusion.

The accountability framework seeks to identify possible areas and themes of analysis to assess social inclusion, identifying certain characteristics of the museum which moves in the perspective of achieving inclusive action for disadvantaged subjects. Museums can positively affect the lives of marginalized people, since they can act as catalysts for social regeneration, creating a fairer society (Sandell 2003). This virtuous process starts with the purpose not only of giving the opportunity of fruition to the disabled, but also of developing a series of positive circuits for the human growth.

The definition of an accountability model, based on a set of indicators for representation and measurement of the qualitative and quantitative aspects of inclusion, represents a first approach towards the creation of a managerial tool to evaluate aspects of social inclusion and the effects of implementing NBS approach.

5.4 Conclusions

In some cultural organizations, barriers may exist—particularly those that prevent museums from being fully appreciated, especially by more "vulnerable" users. However, vulnerability can be an important factor for trust and reciprocity. The issue of accessibility and inclusion is linked to two important SDGs. SDG 10, *Reduce inequalities within and among countries* and SDG 11, *Make cities and human settlements inclusive, safe, resilient and sustainable*, which aim to strengthen accessibility and make the social context more equitable and ethical. The chapter addressed the issue of social inclusion with respect to a special type of cultural institutions, such as tactile museums.

This contribution, starting from the analysis of two theoretical frameworks, the inclusive museum model of Sandell (1998) and the Nature Based Solution (NBS) approach (Raymond et al. 2017), aims to identify factors that characterize inclusive museum, defining an evaluation framework to measure social inclusion. The chapter presents the qualitative case study of the Multimedia Tactile Museum of Catania in

Table 5.1 Social inclusion evaluation in museum: Inclusive Museum

The Inclusive Museum: description and accountability and performance measurement system		
Finalistic	Cultural inclusion	● measuring of social impact of museum activities (sustainability reporting, social reporting systems, accountability tools, etc.) ● measurement of social benefit produced by investments in usability and accessibility ● cost incurred for use and accessibility ● investments in the creation of accessible cultural works and products ● investments in social inclusion through NBS ● evaluation of human resources dedicated to the structure and achievement of objectives
	Fruition of cultural products	
	Accessibility to the museum	
	Increase quality and degree of involvement of disadvantaged people	
	Knowledge of the artistic and cultural heritage	
Instrumental	Development of access and usability activities	● % costs/ incurred for use and accessibility ● % Costs of engagement and participative actions ● % Costs of dissemination activities ● % Costs for events and initiatives for the dissemination of the museum ● % financial resources provided for the inclusive activities ● % financial resources planned for the increase of collections ● product and process innovations ● organisational innovations
	Engagement and participative actions	
	Dissemination activities	
	Events and initiatives for the dissemination of the museum in the territory	
	Creativity and innovation in "inclusive" activities	

(continued)

Table 5.1 (continued)

The Inclusive Museum: description and accountability and performance measurement system		
Motivational (which limits exclusion)	Removal of cultural obstacles and physical barriers	● cost/benefits ratio incurred for use and accessibility ● % financial resources planned for the increase of collections ● cost/benefits ratio incurred for social integration ● stakeholder mapping and perception of inclusive aspects ● stakeholder mapping and perception of NBS idea ● detection of perceptions of users' museum experience ● level of education of human capital both of top management bodies and of employees ● presence of participative governance mechanisms ● staff perception detection systems with respect to inclusive mechanisms
	Development of artistic works and collections	
	Social integration initiatives	
	Perception of "non-exclusion" by internal and external stakeholders	
	Inclusiveness of governance and staff motivation	
Critical	Gratuity/non-gratuity of visit	● economic impact of revenue from museum entries on operating result ● mapping of stakeholders and perception of motivational aspects ● detection of the motivational aspects of museum users ● estimate of revenues and expenditures to expand the museum offer to other disadvantaged groups ● ability to attract funding sources (for inclusive activities) ● % costs for the promotion and dissemination of the role of the museum ● % people of the organisation who perceive the museum's opportunities ● % people of the organisation with expertise and experience on specific disabilities ● % people of the organisation that develop inclusion ideas
	Motivations that drive visitors to fruition	
	Fruition by subjects who have other forms of disability	

(continued)

Table 5.1 (continued)

The Inclusive Museum: description and accountability and performance measurement system		
	Sharing with the community of the museum's purposes	
	Awareness of the importance and the role played by the museum	
	Acquisition and management of financial resources for "inclusive" activities	
	Managerial skills and inclination towards the development of "inclusive" ideas	

Source Baldarelli and Cardillo, 2022

Table 5.2 Social inclusion evaluation in museum: Social Regeneration Museum

The Museum as Agent of Social Regeneration: description and accountability and performance measurement system		
Finalistic	Cultural inclusion	● measurement of social impact of museum activities (sustainability reporting, social reporting systems, accountability tools, etc.) ● measurement of social benefit produced by investments in usability and accessibility ● evaluation of the objectives achieved for the disadvantaged ● measurement of social benefit produced by investments in NBS ● % financial resources provided for "inclusive" activities ● measurement systems for detecting the perception of the museum experience
	Self-esteem growth of disadvantaged users	
	Improvement of the quality of life of users	
	Increase quality and degree of involvement of disadvantaged people	
	Ability to appreciate the artistic and cultural heritage	

(continued)

Table 5.2 (continued)

The Museum as Agent of Social Regeneration: description and accountability and performance measurement system		
Instrumental	Development of access and usability activities	● cost/benefit ratio incurred for use and accessibility
	Engagement and participative actions	● cost/benefit ratio of engagement and participative actions
	Dissemination activities	● cost/benefit ratio of dissemination activities
	Events and initiatives for the dissemination of the museum in the territory	● cost/benefit ratio for events and dissemination initiatives of the museum
	Tools to alleviate the status of disadvantaged people	● % of financial resources provided for the inclusive activities
	Ability to generate employment and job attraction	● measurement of the effectiveness of tools to alleviate the status of disadvantaged people ● number of employees and relative % of people of vulnerable categories ● % increase number occupied workers ● composition and skills of the staff employed ● training activities on inclusive activities aimed at employees ● training activities on knowledge of NBS to improve social inclusion ● number of volunteers and interns

(continued)

Table 5.2 (continued)

The Museum as Agent of Social Regeneration: description and accountability and performance measurement system		
Motivational (which limits exclusion)	Removal of cultural obstacles and physical barriers	● cost/benefit ratio incurred for use and accessibility ● % of financial resources planned for the increase of accessible collections ● social integration activities ● stakeholder mapping and perceived improvement of disadvantage ● detection of the perceptions of the museum experience of museum users ● level of education of human capital both of top management bodies and of employees ● measurement of the effectiveness of integration initiatives (creation of groups, meetings, shared experiences, etc.)
	Development of accessible artistic works and collections	
	Social integration initiatives	
	Perception of the improvement of the quality of life by internal and external stakeholders	
	Quality and degree of involvement of disadvantaged people	
Critical	Gratuity/non-gratuity of the visit	● economic impact of revenue from museum admissions on the operating result and social reflections of non-gratuity ● mapping of stakeholders and perception of “motivational” aspects ● detection of vulnerability aspects of museum users ● estimate of revenues and expenditures to expand the museum offer to other disadvantaged groups ● management and development of funding sources for social integration initiatives ● % of costs for the promotion and dissemination of the role of the museum ● % of disadvantaged users who repeat the experience ● % of people of the organisation with expertise and experience on specific disabilities
	Motivations that drive visitors to fruition	
	Fruition by subjects who have other forms of disability	
	Awareness of the importance and the role played by the museum	
	Acquisition and management of financial resources for “socialising” activities	
	Correlation between the museum experience and the improvement of the state of disadvantage/vulnerability	

Source Baldarelli and Cardillo, 2022

Table 5.3 Social inclusion evaluation in museum: Broad Social Change Museum

The Museum as Vehicle for Broad Social Change: description and accountability and performance measurement system		
Finalistic	Positive cultural and social change	● measuring of social impact of museum activities (sustainability reporting, social reporting systems, accountability tools, etc.) ● measurement of social benefit produced by investments in usability and accessibility ● measurement of social benefit produced by investments in NBS ● % of financial resources provided for inclusive activities ● systems for detecting the perception of the museum experience ● research activity of private and public funds ● voluntary activities and external support
	Self-esteem growth of disadvantaged users	
	Improvement in the quality of life of users	
	Involvement of public and private subjects and institutions	
	Stimulate greater awareness and tolerance towards vulnerable people	

(continued)

Table 5.3 (continued)

The Museum as Vehicle for Broad Social Change: description and accountability and performance measurement system		
Instrumental	Sharing and interaction processes	● cost/benefit ratio of sharing/interaction processes
	Engagement and participative actions	● cost/benefit ratio of engagement and participative actions
	Dissemination activities	● cost/benefit ratio of dissemination activities
	Events and initiatives for spreading of museum activities over the territory	● cost/benefit ratio for events and dissemination initiatives of the museum ● % of financial resources provided for dissemination and educational activities (forums, meetings, groups, etc.) ● public or private initiatives or funds to start NBS projects
	Tools to alleviate the status of disadvantaged people	● measurement of the effectiveness of tools to alleviate the status of disadvantaged people
	Ability to generate employment and job attraction	● number of employees and relative % of people of vulnerable categories ● increase of number of employees ● composition and skills of the staff employed ● training activities on inclusive activities aimed at employees ● number of volunteers and interns

(continued)

Table 5.3 (continued)

The Museum as Vehicle for Broad Social Change: description and accountability and performance measurement system		
Motivational (which limits exclusion)	Removal of cultural obstacles and physical barriers	● cost/benefit ratio incurred for use and accessibility ● % of financial resources planned for the increase of accessible collections ● cost/benefit ratio incurred for social integration ● mapping of stakeholders and perception of awareness of the role of the museum and of the state of vulnerability ● detection of the perceptions of the museum experience of museum users ● economic sustainability of networks with public and private subjects ● measurement of effectiveness of integration initiatives (creation of groups, meetings, shared experiences, etc.) ● measurement of effectiveness of initiatives and support from the public and private sectors
	Development of accessible works and collections	
	Social integration initiatives	
	Perception of the role of the museum by internal and external stakeholders	
	Involvement of public and private institutions in limiting exclusion	
Critical	Management of fruition	● mapping of stakeholders and perception of consciousness and awareness issues ● number of collaborations with other institutions and changes in the managerial practices of these partners derived from this collaboration ● estimate of revenues and expenditures to expand the museum offer to other disadvantaged groups ● sources of financing for social interest and awareness initiatives ● % of costs for the promotion and dissemination of the role of the museum ● % of subjects of the organisation with expertise and experience on specific disabilities ● % of non-disadvantaged users who repeat the experience
	Motivations that drive visitors to fruition	
	Nature and areas of external collaboration	
	Sharing with the community of the museum's purposes	
	Awareness of the role played by the museum	
	Acquisition and management of financial resources for "awareness" activities	

Source Baldarelli and Cardillo, 2022

Sicily. The Tactile Pole plays a significant role in the community, fostering awareness and sensitivity toward critical social issues. The investigation has highlighted that management of cultural heritage for blind and/or visually impaired people is particularly complex. The analysis has first identified the areas of inclusive management of the museum through three different meanings such as: Inclusive Museum, Museum for Social Regeneration, and Museum for Broad Social Change, trying to understand the patterns of museum use and the management of social inclusion. The research then provided an accountability framework for measuring social inclusion through the NBS approach based on environmental protection and restoration of natural ecosystems. The proposed indicators represent a possible measurement of social inclusion as a relevant impact of NBS. The contribution of research lies in strengthening reporting and governance processes that promote social inclusion of vulnerable people and social awareness of community.

References

Baldarelli, M. G., & Cardillo, E. (2022). Managerial paths, social inclusion, and NBS in tactile cultural products: Theory and practice. *Journal of Hospitality & Tourism Research, 46*(3), 544–582. https://doi.org/10.1177/1096348020944440

Belfiore, E. (2002). Art as a means of alleviating social exclusion: Does it really work? A critique of instrumental cultural policy and social impact studies in the UK. *International Journal of Cultural Policy, 8*(1), 91–106.

Bruni, L., & Tufano, F. (2015). The value of vulnerability. The transformative capacity of risky trust. *CeDEx discussion paper series* ISSN 1749-3293.

Chirieleison, C. (1998). Le problematiche legate alla misurazione della performance nelle gestioni museali. in Misc,. *La gestione e la valorizzazione dei beni artistici e culturali nella prospettiva aziendale - Conference proceedings* - 30th/31st October (451–503). Bologna: CLUEB.

Coffee, K. (2008). Cultural inclusion. Exclusion and the formative roles of museums. *Museum Management and Curatorship., 23*(3), 261–279.

Cohen-Shacham, E., Andrade, A., Dalton, J., Dudley, N., Jones, M., Kumar, C., & Walters, G. (2019). Core principles for successfully implementing and upscaling nature-based solutions. *Environmental Science & Policy, 98*, 20–29.

Fredette, C., Bradshaw, P., Krause, H. (2016). From diversity to inclusion. A multimethod study of diverse governing groups. *Non Profit and voluntary sector quarterly,* 45 (1), pp. 28–51. Sage.

Kotler, N. (2001). New ways of experiencing culture: The role of museums and marketing implications. *Museum Management and Curatorship, 19*(4), 417–425.

Kotler N., Kotler P. (1999). Marketing dei musei, Milano: Edizioni di Comunità.

Kuhn, H. (2020). Reducing inequality within and among countries: Realizing SDG 10—A developmental perspective. *Sustainable development goals and human rights, 5*, 137–153.

Magliacani, M. (2008). L'approccio etnografico all'attività dei musei. Aracne.

McCullough, B., Timothy, K., & Melton, E. N. (2022). *The Routledge handbook of sport and sustainable development.*

Nussbaum, M. (2002). Capabilities and human rights. De Greiff, P., Cronin, C, (Eds.), Global justice and transnational politics: Essays on the moral and political challenges of globalization (117–149). Cambridge. MA: MIT Press.

Oestreich, J. E. (2018). SDG 10: Reduce inequality in and among countries. *Social Alternatives, 37*(1), 34–41.

Pelligra, V. (2008). Vulnerabilità e dipendenza. Dal contratto alla responsabilità…e ritorno. Pelligra, V., (ed.). Imprese sociali. Scelte individuali e interessi comuni. Varese: Mondadori, 1–15.

Raymond, C. M., Frantzeskaki, N., Kabisch, N., Berry, P., Breil, M., Nita, M. R., & Calfapietra, C. (2017). A framework for assessing and implementing the co-benefits of nature-based solutions in urban areas. *Environmental Science & Policy, 77*, 15–24.

Regional Braille Stamperia Social Report (2022).

Sandell, R. (1998). Museums as agents of social inclusion. *Museum Management and Curatorship, 17*, 401–418.

Sandell, R. (2000). The strategic significance of workforce diversity in museums. International Journal of Heritage Studies, 6(3), 213–230.

Sandell, R. (2003). Social inclusion, the museum and the dynamics of sectoral change. Museum & Society, 191, 45–62.

Sandell, R, Janes, R.R., (eds.). (2007). Museum Management and Marketing. Routledge: London and New York.

Scapens, R. W. (2004). Doing case study research. *The Real Life Guide to Accounting Research* (Eds)C. Humphrey, B. Lee, Oxford: Elsevier,257–279.

Scapens, R. W. (2011). The case study as research method: A practical handbook. *Qualitative Research in Accounting & Management, 8*(2), 201–204.

Tang, F., Morrow-Howell, N., & Hong, S. (2009). Inclusion of diverse older populations in volunteering. The importance of institutional facilitation. *Non Profit and voluntary sector quarterly, 38*(5), 810–827.

Maria-Gabriella Baldarelli PhD, CPA, is Associate Professor of Accounting, at University of Bologna, Department of Management—Rimini Campus. Full professor availability. Envited professor at Sophia University Institute. SIDREA board member until 2018. She is a member of international scientific networks: the Centre for Social and Environmental Accounting Research (CSEAR) and the European Business Ethics Network (EBEN). Key-note Speaker second International Conference on Economics, Business, Finance and Governance (ICEBFG) by Economics and Business Faculty of University of Bandar Lampung-Bali-Indonesia-Dic. 4–5, 2019. Research interests includes: accountability and gambling enterprises; corporate social responsibility; ethical, social and environmental accounting and accountability, sustainability in tourist enterprises; responsible and accessible tourism for blind people, economy of communion; gender accounting; accounting history, accounting education and Feminist Economics.

Eleonora Cardillo is Associate Professor of Business Economics at the Department of Economics and Business of the University of Catania. She was Visiting Scholar at the CSEAR (Centre for social and environmental accounting research), School of Management of the University of St Andrews (Scotland) for the research project: "Study and analysis of the methodological and operational paths of environmental and social reporting in the evolution process of accounting information systems". Professor of Accounting and Financial Statements and Public accounting iin local administrations. She was Director and Scientific Coordinator of the Master in Accounting and Control in Local Authorities, organized by the Department of Economics and Business of the University of Catania. Her research topics are public accounting systems, performance measurement, socio-environmental reporting, social inclusion in tactile museums, sustainability and accountability.

Chapter 6
Social Inclusion and Technological Innovations in Tactile Museum Accounting and Management

Maria-Gabriella Baldarelli and Eleonora Cardillo

Abstract In the context of museums, technological innovations play an important role in promoting inclusion and strengthening the creation of social value. Museums and cultural institutions are oriented towards offering an accessible cultural product, where culture is shared and accessible to users. Technology is linked to the theme of accessibility and inclusion, as technological innovations represent tools to improve collaboration and sharing. The chapter analyzes the relationship among technological innovations, social inclusion, accounting and management. Starting from the theoretical approach of the inclusive museum model and the role of technological innovation in museum institutions, the case study of the Omero Museum in Ancona is presented, with the aim of evaluating and interpreting the managerial action towards inclusion processes supported by technology.

6.1 Technology to Support accessibility and Inclusion in Museums

Cultural institutions, such as museums, play an essential role in generating social inclusion and sharing processes (Baldarelli, 2004; Fujimoto et al., 2023; McMillen & Alter, 2017; Pegno & Brindza, 2021) and new technologies can contribute in achieving this purpose (Lazzeretti & Sartori, 2016; Navarrete, 2013). Technologies can support inclusion in tactile museums, making art and culture accessible to a wider audience, including those with visual impairments or other specific needs. They have a very important role in developing art sharing and inclusion (Kawashima, 2024; Sandell, 1998). They give the possibility for cultural and museum institutions to act and use digital tools to manage visits, visitor flows, methods of enjoyment and

M.-G. Baldarelli
University of Bologna, Bologna, Italy
e-mail: maria.baldarelli@unibo.it

E. Cardillo (✉)
University of Catania, Catania, Italy
e-mail: cardillo@unict.it

M. Baldarelli et al. (eds.), *Accounting and Accountability for Social Inclusion*, CSR, Sustainability, Ethics & Governance, https://doi.org/10.1007/978-3-032-09271-7_6

socio-environmental monitoring (Darcy, 2005). Literature identified innovative categories to understand the role of digital technologies within the museum (Bakhshi & Throsby, 2012).

The issue of accessibility is strengthened by national and international bodies which underline the importance of promoting accessible tourism (art. 30 of the United Nations Convention on the rights of persons with disabilities ratified in Italy by Law no. 18 of 24/2/09 and the "Manifesto for the promotion of accessible tourism" of the Italian Ministry of Tourism). The theme of accessibility and fruition to culture is part of the broader debate on social inclusion in museums. As highlighted by the UK Department for Digital, Culture, Media and Sport (DCMS), social inclusion activity should "promote the involvement in cultural and leisure activities of those at risk of social disadvantage or marginalization, particularly based on the area they live in; their disability, poverty, age, race or ethnic origin" (Social Exclusion Unit, DCMS 1999). Social inclusion is declined with respect to each territorial context that presents specific needs and conditions (Joseph & Van Buren III, 2022).

Museums move in a specific context and develop policies and initiatives to promote inclusive programs (Museums and Social Inclusion. The GLLAM Report, October 2000). Literature highlights the museum's role as an agent of social inclusion (Belfiore, 2002; Coffee, 2008; Kotler, 2001; Sandell, 2000, 2002; Sandell & Janes, 2007). Inclusion can arise through a combination of a functional and social approach to the creation of inclusive groups (Fredette et al., 2015; Fujimoto et al., 2023). Accessibility, inclusion and sharing are three fundamental elements of the museum. This is evident from the definition of museum suggested by ICOM: "a museum is a not-for-profit, permanent institution in the service of society that researches, collects, preserves, interprets and exhibits tangible and intangible heritage. Open to the public, accessible and inclusive, museums foster diversity and sustainability. They operate and communicate ethically, professionally and with the participation of communities, offering varied experiences for education, enjoyment, reflection and knowledge sharing" (26th ICOM General Conference held in Prague, the ICOM Extraordinary General Assembly, 2022). Information and communication technologies facilitate learning and enjoyment of heterogeneous groups of individuals. Recently, museum and educational spaces integrate different multimedia tools (interactive scenarios, virtual reality, spatial reconstructions, photographic enlargements, projections and holograms) to improve sensory immersion in art and fruition of its historical context (Todino, 2023). The use of these tools makes visitors more autonomous in their enjoyment and favors the creation of diversified and more engaging paths (Belardi & Menchetelli, 2023; Todino, 2023). Numerous devices that interact with each other (audio guides, tablets and smartphones) can integrate Augmented Reality (AR) or Virtual Reality (VR) to enrich the visit and provide different levels of interaction with the aim of supporting inclusivity (Brischetto et al., 2023).

6.2 Inclusion and Technology: Conceptual Frameworks

The use of technology is becoming essential for access to culture and to facilitate enjoyment and participation for people with disabilities. Collaborations between museums and institutions in this area can enhance planning, information exchange, and the implementation of actions to improve access to cultural spaces (Llamazares de Prado & Arias Gago, 2023).

The use of assistive technology, developed for use in museums by people with sensory disabilities or learning difficulties, facilitates the museum experience. In this sense, technology is developed and designed to increase the participation of people with sensory disabilities and promote cultural learning and inclusion (Garcia Carrizosa et al., 2020; Iodice et al., 2023).

Based on the literature on the topic (Bakhshi & Throsby, 2012; Belardi & Menchetelli, 2023; Llamazares de Prado & Arias Gago, 2023; Sandell, 1998, 2000; Todino, 2023), it emerges that technology can foster social inclusion and play a fundamental role in breaking down barriers and promoting inclusion in museums. It can enable people with disabilities to actively participate in cultural life and interact with other visitors, creating a more engaging and rewarding cultural experience.

Sandell (1998) states that, although social exclusion is linked to the concepts of "poverty" and "deprivation", for the cultural sector the term remains ambiguous, in fact "although museums and other cultural organizations face increasing pressure to respond to issues of social exclusion, an analysis of its relevance to them is hindered because the terms, concepts and associated language in relation to arts, heritage and the wider cultural sector, remain undeveloped" (Sandell, 1998, 404). Furthermore, technological innovations can help limit barriers by supporting the culture of social inclusion. For example, the digital transformation process underlying the sharing economy determines the creation of new roles and functions among actors (Massi et al., 2021). This requires greater clarity in defining areas and opportunities for cultural users in using the potential of digital technology (Furness, 2018). Technological innovations are supporting museums and cultural institutions in carrying out their mission (Lazzeretti & Sartori, 2016; Navarrete, 2013). They have the capacity to favor public-private collaboration networks and implement investment projects that innovate the structure and opportunities of the museum (Esposito et al., 2023). The process of applying new technologies is also strongly influenced by the institutional and cultural characteristics of the regulatory context of reference. This generates limitations to the potential that new technologies could offer (Esposito et al., 2023). Some studies (McMillen, 2015; McMillen & Alter, 2017) focus on the importance of using new technologies to make museums more accessible, since "with the increasing use of technology, especially via the web and access via mobile devices, technological, digital and information access barriers have become as important as physical ones" (McMillen, 2015, 95). Bakhshi and Throsby (2012) give a definition of innovation technology in art institutions and consider innovation important for solving various problems relating to cultural institutions. According to these authors, in fact, "although the term 'new technologies'in the cultural field could be used to describe any form of technical advance affecting cultural production from the invention of the printing press onwards, it is used nowadays as shorthand for new information and communication technologies arising from two related late twentieth century sources: the explosion in computational speed and capacity that has transformed day-to-day life in countless ways, and the advent of the Internet" (Bakhshi & Throsby, 2012, 208). Authors highlight problems related both to the decrease in state funds intended to cover needs of users, and to make the culture of these institutions more accessible and widespread. Bakhshi and Throsby (2012) identify four possible categories to understand the role of digital technologies within the museum. The first concerns "*Innovation in audience reach*" and relates to the generation of new audiences, through the use of digital technologies such as live high-definition (HD) broadcasts for theater and opera companies, and providing online access to collections for art galleries and museums. Cultural institutions may also innovate in the depth of their engagement with audiences, for example, by using online knowledge resources to inform and educate their consumers, by interacting with audiences on social networks, or by providing opportunities presented by digital technology for audiences to get involved in artistic creation itself. The second refers to the "*Innovation in artform development*". It represents one of the most significant innovative contributions cultural institutions can make. In this context museum develops the artform in which they move, through the encouragement of new and experimental work. This area includes all actions that have the aim of implementing new technologies in the field of musical performances, theatrical production and the exhibition of paintings and sculptures. The third category is about the "*Innovation in value creation*". Cultural institutions are searching for new ways and areas to measure the economic and cultural value they create for audiences and their wider group of stakeholders, and to translate these into terms that policymakers, funding agencies, donors and private investors can relate to. The fourth area is relative to the "*Innovation in business management and governance*". It concerns the activity of cultural organizations that face challenges in strategic management and in artistic or cultural area in which they operate; dealing with these challenges requires a constant review of the organization's business model and a search for innovative financing strategies in response to a changing funding environment. Based on the literature on the topic (Bakhshi & Throsby, 2012; Sandell, 1998, 2000) some dimensions are highlighted describing how technology can influence inclusion and accessibility (Fig. 6.1). Technological innovations support methods to reach audience, artform development tools, social and economic value creation and new business areas.

Fig. 6.1 -Technology innovation and social inclusion *Source: Authors' elaboration based on* Sandell *(1998) and* Bakhshi and Throsby *(2012) frameworks*

6.3 Technological innovations and Inclusion in Tactile museum management and Accounting: Some Empirical Evidence

6.3.1 Background

The problem of sharing economy and cultural products accessibility to "vulnerable" people is currently very important, in order to spread a new and more inclusive approach. Starting from the theoretical approach of Sandell's model (Sandell, 1998) and Bakhshi and Throsby (2012), empirical analysis tries to evaluate inclusive and sharing processes and new technologies relationships and their achievement in tactile museum accounting and management (Baldarelli & Cardillo, 2022). The integration of digital technologies in museums can enhance inclusion by providing wider access to collections, interactive experiences, and educational programs for diverse audiences. The ability to manage inclusive processes is relevant to promote art sharing for broad social change in tactile museums (Baldarelli & Cardillo, 2022). An empirical study, based on qualitative approach, had been conducted at the Omero Museum in Ancona (Italy) with the aim of evaluating and interpreting the managerial action towards inclusion and sharing economy processes supported by technological innovations. By analyzing the areas proposed by Bakhshi and Throsby (2012), it is possible to highlight how each of them contributes to improving inclusion with respect to specific dimensions of the museum (Sandell, 1998), such as: inclusion, social regeneration, and social change.

The Omero Museum of Ancona (Italy) plays an essential role in terms of accessibility to culture, transferring the historical and artistic value of cultural products mainly to the blind. The study examines the role of digital strategies within tactile museums in order to evaluate how they reflect on accessibility and managerial choices aimed at supporting social inclusion paths by creating a link between accessible culture and historical heritage. The adopted framework expresses the dimensions of inclusion according the three typologies of inclusive museum (Sandell, 1998) such as finalist (objective of the inclusive museum); instrumental (actions for inclusion); motivational (cultural activities to limit exclusion); critical (reduction of problems related to exclusion). They are influenced by the technological innovations produced (Bakhshi & Throsby, 2012), enclosed in the four categories (Innovation in audience reach; Innovation in artform development; Innovation in value creation; Innovation in business management and governance) which have an impact on the dimensions that explain the different forms of inclusive museum. A questionnaire was administered to the Director of the Museum in order to understanding the dimensions of inclusion and technology innovations contributing to managerial systems in the analysis of inclusion measurement processes.

The semi-structured questionnaire was addressed to the museum director and it reports issues on the relationship between technology and inclusion with respect to specific areas: technological innovation projects, inclusive initiatives supported by digital technology, innovation in inclusive processes, impact on enjoyment and accessibility, limits in the use of technology, experiences for disabled and non-disabled visitors, collaborations with other museums in strengthening technology and inclusion. By adopting the conceptual approach outlined above, the case study aims, on the one hand, to acquire data to interpret and evaluate on the topic of technology and inclusion, and, on the other, to offer initial evidence capable of enriching the theoretical framework.

6.3.2 Mission and Governance of the Omero Tactile Museum

The Omero Tactile Museum is managed by the Municipality of Ancona in agreement with the Ministry of Culture as can be deduced from the Act signed on August 3, 2001 and subsequently amended on February 22, 2002. The museum was born "with the aim of promoting the growth and cultural integration of visually impaired people and spreading the knowledge of reality among them, through the collection of materials, objects and reproductions of the different forms of plastic arts and historical-cultural manifestations, the organization of the environment, space and life of people"(Municipality of Ancona and Ministry of Cultural Heritage Agreement, August 3, 2001, p. 1).

As established by the Regulations, the Museum is directed by a Committee of Management, in office for five years, supported by an Advisory Committee. The organizational structure is divided into the following units: 3 municipal employees, 14 operators, 2 collaborators, 1 president / director, 9 civil service and non-profit volunteers. The technical services of the Museum are currently managed by the Temporary Business Association consisting of Opera (Social Cooperative Society) and Coopculture which have provided operators with many years of experience in activities aimed at satisfying the needs with particular reference to people with visual disabilities. The Municipality of Ancona has made available three administrative officials who work in the Omero Museum.

The idea of creating a "special" museum came from two blind people who love art, the current Director and his wife. In 1985 they thought of creating a museum where everything could be touched with the slogan: "Forbidden not to touch" unlike traditional museums where there is a ban on touching works of art. On 29 May 1993 the Municipality of Ancona, with the contribution of the Marche Region and with the support of the Italian Blind and Visually Impaired Union, established the Omero Museum, which was initially located in the classrooms of the "Carlo Antognini" elementary school in Ancona, with 19 plaster copies of classical sculpture and an architectural model. In 1997 the Museum moved with an expanded collection to another school facility. With the Law n. 452/1999, the Italian Parliament recognizes it as the State Museum. The purpose of the Museum is to "promote the growth and cultural integration of visually impaired people and to spread knowledge of reality among them" (Article 2 of Law no. 452/1999). However, the Museum is not only a place reserved for blind people, but represents a cultural space where everyone can share experience as a constructive experience. In 2012, the Museum moved to the Mole Vanvitelliana in Ancona, the current headquarters, occupying a space of about 3000 square meters on different floors where the collections, educational laboratories, offices, conference room, documentation center and others are exhibited. Since September 2017, the Museum has offered over 200 works including plaster and resin copies of classical masterpieces, architectural models and original contemporary sculptures. In 2021 the Museum presents the Design Collection: a new space inside the Mole, which offers a multisensory experience and the opportunity to learn about different styles of Italian design. Between August and October 2022 there had been an internal exhibition: "Touching the Lombards" created by the Italia Langobardorum Association in collaboration with the Omero State Tactile Museum, with the aim of raising awareness of the the extraordinariness and complexity of the UNESCO site "The Lombards in Italy—The places of power (568–774 AD)".

The Museum therefore represents a cultural venue for the visually impaired but performs a multifaceted function as it is open to all those who want to experience the knowledge of art through multisensory aesthetic canons.

The mission of the Omero Tactile Museum is therefore to promote the usability of culture without barriers to allow a better social integration of the visually impaired in the context of a continuous process of innovation. "Through the use of touch to allow even the blind to enjoy art. Promote the aesthetics of tactility and multi-sensoriality for all museum audiences, therefore a removal of all barriers to full accessibility of cultural heritage" (Director of the Museum, 2022).

The Museum offers a flexible path that adapts to every specific need of the visitor starting from a reception area with Bookshop, cloakroom and mini snack/ cafeteria area and then leading to the area where the permanent collections are located, consisting of many works between casts in plaster and resin of classical masterpieces, architectural models and original sculptures of contemporary art. The structure also offers a documentation center for the consultation of texts in black and

Braille, videos, DVDs, audio cassettes, didactic aids and environments intended for special laboratories.

6.3.3 *Inclusion and technology in Omero Tactile Museum*

The museum's action is aimed at increasing the number of users, including non-disabled ones. Digital tools have the role of increasing interaction between the museum and visitors but also increasing the possibility of access to the cultural experience. In this sense this dimension strengthens the inclusive purpose of the museum and the actions for its pursuit.

The Omero Tactile State Museum is implementing innovation technology to approach new *inclusive audiences reach*, developing knowledge resources online and using the web-site in different languages. Educational area offers a series of activities to stimulate creative learning and to activate specific paths for sensory and cognitive disabilities. The absence of barriers is aimed above all at people with disabilities but the structure also becomes a place of visit for families, groups, associations, teachers even if it can however create a contrast in the objectives pursued. For the public there is the curiosity to learn about art in an alternative way, while for disabled people it represents the only way to learn about art and history. The Director of the Museum has always expressed the importance of the teaching methodology linked to the cognitive dimension of art (Interview by Andreozzi S. to the Director of the Museum, 2018). The website created is navigable both from computers and mobile devices such as tablets and smartphones. In order to pursue accessibility, the responsive design technique is used. It represents a notable advantage for blind and partially sighted people, for whom assistance technologies are being developed, such as speech synthesizers, magnifiers, hardware tools such as the Braille bar. These areas are aimed at strengthening the logic of the museum as an agent of inclusion and also constitute elements for increasing the motivation and personal growth of non-selling people. In the context of technological innovations, an important role is played by the In-VisiBLe (Inclusive and Innovative learning tool for Visually Impaired and Blind people), financed by the European Erasmus+ program (project code 2021–1-IT02-KA220-HED-000031139), started in 2022 and coordinated by the University of Bologna, which is impacting different areas of activity and functions with respect to methods of inclusion and accessibility. The project, whose application activities started in 2022, represents an Innovation in audience reach as it is implementing inclusive teaching modules of Architecture History accessible to both able-bodied students and with visual disabilities ones, through a series of avant-garde methods and tools. The main technologies used are 3D architectural models, tactile tables with architectural drawings, artificial intelligence system to recognize and describe architectural images. These technologies will be adopted within traditional university courses. Furthermore, the innovations introduced include the creation of MOOCs (Massive Open Online Courses), accessible to the blind. With this system the teaching modules will be accessible remotely, facilitating participation and access to learning.

New technologies also contribute to innovation in the *development of art forms* which is relevance in tactile museum. This area tends to strengthen the cultural initiatives and operational tools that impact the social regeneration carried out by the Museum. Innovations in art form development are oriented towards the creation of special opportunities for participation in life improvement and personal development initiatives. The museum, in addition to the Design Collection (Discobolus, Michelangelo's Pietà, Canova's Venus, the Parthenon and St. Peter's Basilica and models of contemporary art such as the sculptures of Giorgio de Chirico, Arnaldo Pomodoro, Marino Marini, Giuliano Vangi, Aron Demetz) houses more than 200 works including casts that reproduce the real, in plaster and resin, original sculptures and architectural models that you can see but and above all touch. The expansion of the museum's collection to include the history of Italian design reinforces this purpose. In 2021, in fact, the Museum has been enriched with a new section dedicated to Italian Design. The proposed objects can be listened to and manipulated, in a path that organizes them by theme, allowing the subject to immerse himself in a cultural reality of interest and attraction.

Innovation in artform development favors the social regeneration process, stimulating a broad social change, through motivational and cultural actions to limit exclusion. Museum offers multisensory education in order to encourage the implementation of techniques and methods of digital use. The Museum offers free itineraries where parents and children together can go in search of some particular works or sculptures. Furthermore, accessible and inclusive workshops are organized for schools where they can experience both the experience of visiting the collections and the creative moment in the laboratory with clay, fabrics, Braille tablets and music. As part of Innovation in artform development, activities aimed at studying and understanding art works with innovative digital tools have been strengthened. In 2022, a training course "All ways to read" was created, organized by the LIA Foundation—Accessible Italian Books, intended for blind and visually impaired children attending middle or high schools. It was aimed at librarians, to communication assistants and families of children with visual disabilities who want to explore the topic of accessible digital reading. The presence of experts and trainers specialized in assistive software is important to explain how the tools to support people with visual disabilities work and how the research and consultation of information relating to the accessibility of born accessible e-books is carried out, illustrating the functioning of the catalog and of the LIA sites and stamps, indicated in these texts and in those present in the digital library. Furthermore, the characteristics of accessible digital publication and the formats and protection systems compliant with accessibility requirements are illustrated. These actions strengthen the esteem of blind individuals as they discover the potential of accessible digital publications and thus can explore new technologies and the use of solutions and tools for reading e-books and accessible texts on smartphones and tablets.

The *value creation* created by technological innovations is not easy to define. The museum creates value in different fields and with respect to a special community. Various activities and initiatives developed by Museum are aimed at increasing creative processes. Museum stimulates families and organizes meetings in which families will draw a work through a tactile experience, sharing of ideas and sensations. An important role in the social value creation is played by the approaches of personal involvement, in the physical participation of subjects and in their human interaction with other subjects to share sensations and emotions. In order to remove the social barriers to tactile accessibility to cultural products, the Museum, to spread the culture and values of inclusion, organizes temporary exhibitions. In addition, the Museum participates with some of its own works in exhibitions organized by other institutes and at the same time it hosts exhibitions or exhibitions of third parties. Very interesting is the participation of the Omero Museum at "The Art and Entertainment Itineraries", for cultural tourism for sensory disabled people. This project aims to use innovation technology to systematize and structure existing experiences through the creation of coordinated tourist packages linked to museum itineraries and accessibility services for sensory disabled people (blind and visually impaired, deaf and hearing impaired) combined with the Opera seasons in some municipalities of the Marche region. The social value produced is linked to the possibilities offered by the Museum to blind people to obtain an inclusive education, to offer accessibility to culture and to also guarantee technological innovations, quality of use and training. This action seeks to address the problems of discrimination and obstacles in access to education and cultural enjoyment by limiting the factors that can exclude or aggravate the social status of disadvantaged people.

The introduction of technological and digitalization *innovates business model and accounting system* that expands assets and resources of Museum. Business and accounting involve new ambits and funds, for example those that derive from networking with organizations and institutions, new cultural initiatives and sharing activities. Initiatives and projects are based on a strong partnership and a complex governance ensuring the contribution of different and complementary areas of expertise and collaborations with museums and cultural institutions, organizations, stakeholders and policy makers. Collaborations with other institutions, private or public, expand accounting to include new revenues, licensing agreements and joint projects. With reference to accounting, the introduction of digital platforms for the management of resources and collections, implies the support of software license costs, maintenance and updates that will be detected by the accounting system. Furthermore, the expansion of collections and the growth of "accessible" artistic and cultural products require more complex accounting to ensure that cultural heritage is correctly inventoried. The management of investments in technological innovation has started a process of managerial renewal in the Museum and has improved inclusive processes. This has created a connection between art sharing, accessible culture and historical heritage in the tactile museum. However, the human element remains fundamental in tactile museums, despite technological advances. Technology can offer powerful tools for accessibility and inclusion, but it is the human contribution that guarantees an empathetic and personalized experience. Omero Tactile Museum operators are crucial in guiding visitors through the experience. They can adapt their language and approach to the specific needs of each individual and listen and respond to needs immediately. The Omero Museum represents a significant place to spread and consolidate the culture of diversity and accessibility through cultural, educational, training and promotional initiatives and greater integration and personal growth for all.

6.4 Advantages and limitations of Technological innovations in Museums

The study of Omero Tactile Museum suggested potential and limitations of technology in the context of museums and cultural institution. The potential concerns the strengthening of services and their usability and accessibility. Technological cultural innovations favor the phenomenon of art sharing in museum. Sharing art is an opportunity to enjoy cultural, historical, pictorial and artistic works and products from different forms of the current digital art world. It realizes the sharing of knowledge through information exchange among people, communities or organizations (Charband & Jafari Navimipour, 2016). In general, the sharing economy represents a new economic and cultural model capable of rationalizing the use of resources based on the exchange or sharing of goods and services rather than their purchase. In this context, accessibility becomes an element that goes beyond possession or ownership. Although the concept is not new, digital technologies have strengthened art sharing creating new relationships between artists and those who wish to enjoy artistic works for various reasons (Lazzeretti & Sartori, 2016). The significant impact of digital and technological tools on inclusion is to promote social regeneration to support the visually impaired and blind in accessing education and cultural enjoyment of the "visual" arts, strengthening their motivation and involvement. In order to remove the social barriers to tactile accessibility to cultural products, museums try to limit factors that can exclude disadvantaged people. In this direction, technology, accessibility and cultural inclusion can become effective strategic tools for creating an inclusive society.

However, technology has limitations. In museums, especially in those for special categories, visitors need physical support to interact with tactile art works, to explore them properly or to access specific sections of the museum. For example, in tactile laboratories or interactive activities within museums, the specialized people are essential to teach specific techniques or to answer questions in real time. Main activities are aimed at strengthening the logic of the museum as an agent of inclusion and as an agent of social regeneration since its action increases the motivation and personal growth of blind people. Museum needs to have specialized operators capable of describing, through a multi-sensory approach, the beauty of sculpture through touch and materials.

Technological innovations are playing an essential role in strengthening social and cultural change and inclusion, through creative learning and the enhancement of perceptive and communicative processes.

The analysis conducted highlighted two different effects of technology on different groups and, specifically, users with disabilities and users without disabilities. The museum, although designed to create a tactile experience, welcomes many visitors without disabilities, precisely because the main purpose is the creation of a sharing space without distinctions and limitations. However, one of the limits of technology in museums in general and, especially for users without disabilities, is the risk of excessive dematerialization. Virtual use can reduce the direct experience with the work of art and its historical dimension. For users with disabilities, technology has an increasing effect on sensorial use. In these cases, technology improves use and accessibility and significantly limits potential barriers to access for some users.

However, the introduction of technological and digital tools should be more evaluated in terms of impacts since the recipients are sensitive and disadvantaged subjects.

In the context of social inclusion, human relationships create a sense of welcome and belonging, promoting social inclusion. A human and warm approach makes the museum experience more engaging and less alienating, as some categories of stakeholder may feel intimidated by the use of technology (Charband & Jafari Navimipour, 2016). The museum experience is not only knowledge, but also emotion. Therefore, a combination of technological innovation and personal interaction is needed to make tactile museums inclusive and educational spaces.

The research has implications for museum managers who welcome technological innovations and provides a starting point for reflecting on an effective management of technological innovations in favor of inclusion. Furthermore, the study can be enriched by analyzing other realities and making useful comparisons and further insights into the impact of technology and digitalization in cultural institutions.

6.5 Conclusions

The chapter addresses the role of cultural institutions in generating processes of social inclusion through the use of new technologies. Technological innovation plays a key role in supporting inclusion in tactile museums, making art and culture accessible to different groups such as those with visual impairments or other specific needs. New technological tools adapt digital strategies to manage visits, visitor flows and modes of fruition. Furthermore, the use of assistive technologies is developed and designed to increase the participation of people with sensory disabilities and promote learning and cultural inclusion. The framework adopted adopts two theoretical approaches: the inclusive museum of Sandell (1998) and the role of technological innovations in the museum defined by Bakhshi and Throsby (2012), which identify four possible categories to understand the role of digital technologies within the museum. The empirical investigation was conducted at the Omero Museum in Ancona (Italy) with the aim of carrying out a preliminary assessment of managerial action towards inclusion and sharing economy processes supported by technological innovations. Furthermore, the four areas of the Bakhshi and Throsby (2012) model were analyzed, specifically innovation in reaching the public, innovation in the development of art forms, innovation in value creation and innovation in management and corporate governance. The results underline that the museum's action is aimed at increasing the number of users, including those without disabilities, and that digital tools have the role of increasing the interaction between the museum and visitors and the possibilities of access to the cultural experience. However, the study of the Omero Tactile Museum highlights the potential and limits of technology in the context of museums and cultural institutions. Technological cultural innovations favor the phenomenon of sharing art and knowledge through the exchange of information between people, communities or organizations. However, one of the limits of technology in museums in general and, above all, for users without disabilities, is the risk of excessive dematerialization through a reduction of the direct experience with the work of art. For users with disabilities, technology has a positive effect on the aspect of fruition. Technology improves use and accessibility and reduces potential barriers to access. However, human relationships continue to play an important role in museums, including tactile ones, creating a sense of welcome and belonging. The case of the Museo Tatcile Omero offers insights into the practical application of theoretical approaches to assess with greater awareness the effects of technology on social inclusion in cultural institutions.

References

Bakhshi, H., & Throsby, D. (2012). New technologies in cultural institutions: Theory, evidence and policy implications. *International Journal of Cultural Policy, 18*(2), 205–222.

Baldarelli, M. G. (2004). Definizione degli obiettivi, modalità di governo e sistema informativo nelle piccole aziende museali: un caso di scuola. In B. Sibilio Parri (Ed.), *Creare e valorizzare i distretti museali* (pp. 297–313). Milano.

Baldarelli, M. G., & Cardillo, E. (2022). Managerial paths, social inclusion, and NBS in tactile cultural products: Theory and practice. *Journal of Hospitality and Tourism Research, 46*(3), 544–582.

Belardi, P., & Menchetelli, V. (2023). 4DGypsoteca. Un'architettura multimediale per la didattica del disegno. In A. Luigini & C. Panciroli (Eds.), *Ambienti digitali per l'educazione all'arte e al patrimonio*. FrancoAngeli.

Belfiore, E. (2002). Art as a means of alleviating social exclusion: Does it really work? A critique of instrumental cultural policies and social impact studies in the UK. *International Journal of Cultural Policy, 8*(1), 91–106.

Brischetto, A., Iacono, E., & Becchimanzi, C. (2023). Digital technologies in museums: Critical issues and opportunities for equal access to cultural heritage. *AHFE INTERNATIONAL*, 32–41.

Charband, Y., & Jafari Navimipour, N. (2016). Online knowledge sharing mechanisms: A systematic review of the state of the art literature and recommendations for future research. *Information Systems Frontiers, 18*, 1131–1151.

Coffee, K. (2008). Cultural inclusion, exclusion and the formative roles of muse-ums. *Museum Management and Curatorship, 23*(3), 261–279.

Darcy, S. (2005). *Disability and tourism. A bibliography, School of Leisure, sport and tourism*. University of technology.

Esposito, P., Braga, A., Sancino, A., & Ricci, P. (2023). The strategic governance of the digital accounting environment: Insights from virtual museums. *Meditari Accountancy Research, 31*(2), 366–380.

Fredette, C., Bradshaw, P., & Krause, H. (2015). From diversity to inclusion. A multi-method study of diverse governing groups. *Nonprofit and Voluntary Sector Quarterly, 45*(1), 28–51.

Fujimoto, Y., Ferdous, A., & Wali, F. (2023). Integrative resource model of workplace inclusion for reduced inequality: Conservation of resources perspective. *Journal of Business Ethics, 187*(2), 301–323.

Furness, H. (2018). Art galleries 'must embrace digital technology' as the battle against phones is lost. *The Telegraph.* Retrieved from https://www.telegraph.co.uk/news/2018/03/07/art-galleries-must-embrace-digital-technology-battle-against/.

Garcia Carrizosa, H., Sheehy, K., Rix, J., Seale, J., & Hayhoe, S. (2020). Designing technologies for museums: Accessibility and participation issues. *Journal of enabling technologies, 14*(1), 31–39.

Iodice, G., Carignani, F., Clemente, L., & Bifulco, F. (2023, October). Museum accessibility: a managerial perspective on digital approach. *2023 IEEE International Conference on Metrology for eXtended Reality, Artificial Intelligence and Neural Engineering* (MetroXRAINE) (1144–1149). IEEE.

Joseph, J., & Van Buren, H. J., III. (2022). Entrepreneurship, conflict, and peace: The role of inclusion and value creation. *Business and Society, 61*(6), 1558–1593.

Kawashima, N. (2024). Audience development and social inclusion in Britain. In *A reader on audience development and cultural policy* (pp. 135–152). Routledge.

Kotler, N. (2001). New ways of experiencing culture: The role of museums and marketing implications. *Museum Management and Curatorship, 19*(4), 417–425.

Lazzeretti, L., & Sartori, A. (2016). Digitization of cultural heritage and business model innovation: The case of the Uffizi gallery in Florence. *Capitale Culturale, XIV*, 945–970.

Llamazares de Prado, J. E., & Arias Gago, A. R. (2023). Technology and education as elements in museum cultural inclusion. *Education and Urban Society, 55*(2), 238–258.

Massi, M., Vecco, M., & Lin, Y. (2021). Digital transformation in the cultural and creative industries. Production, consumption and entrepreneurship in the digital and sharing econom. In *Routledge research in the creative and cultural industries.* Taylor & Francis Group.

McMillen, R. (2015). Museum disability access: Social inclusion opportunities through innovative new media practices. *Pacific Journal, 10*, 95–107.

McMillen, R., & Alter, F. (2017). Social media, social inclusion, and museum disability access. *Museums & Social Issues, 12*(2), 115–125.

Navarrete, T. (2013). *Digital cultural heritage. Handbook on the economics of cultural heritage.* Edward Elgar Publishing.

Pegno, M., & Brindza, C. (2021). Redefining curatorial leadership and activating community expertise to build equitable and inclusive art museums. *Curator: The Museum Journal, 64*(2), 343–362.

Sandell, R. (1998). Museums as agents of social inclusion. *Museum Management and Curatorship, 17*, 401–418.

Sandell, R. (2000). The strategic significance of workforce diversity. *Museums in International Journal of Heritage Studies, 6*(3), 213–230.

Sandell, R. (2002). *Museums. Society.* Routledge.

Sandell, R., & Janes, R. R. (Eds.). (2007). *Museum management and marketing.* Routledge.

Todino, M. D. (2023). Accessibility in museums: how to combine accessible spaces, technology, and "shared languages" to ensure the inclusion of all visitors. *Giornale Italiano di Educazione alla Salute, Sport e Didattica Inclusiva-Italian Journal of Health Education, Sports and Inclusive Didactics* 7.

Maria-Gabriella Baldarelli Maria-Gabriella Baldarelli, PhD, CPA, is Associate Professor of Accounting, at University of Bologna, Department of Management- Rimini Campus. Full professor availability. Envited professor at Sophia University Institute. SIDREA board member until 2018. She is a member of international scientific networks: the Centre for Social and Environmental Accounting Research (CSEAR) and the European Business Ethics Network (EBEN). Key-note Speaker 2nd International Conference on Economics, Business, Finance and

Governance (ICEBFG) by Economics and Business Faculty of University of Bandar Lampung-Bali- Indonesia- Dic. 4-5, 2019. Research interests includes: accountability and gambling enterprises; corporate social responsibility; ethical, social and environmental accounting and accountability, sustainability in tourist enterprises; responsible and accessible tourism for blind people, economy of communion; gender accounting; accounting history, accounting education and Feminist Economics.

Eleonora Cardillo Eleonora Cardillo is Associate Professor of Business Economics – at the Department of Economics and Business of the University of Catania. She was Visiting Scholar at the CSEAR (Centre for social and environmental accounting research) School of Management of the University of St Andrews (Scotland) for the research project: "Study and analysis of the methodological and operational paths of environmental and social reporting in the evolution process of accounting information systems". Professor of Accounting and Financial Statements and Public accounting iin local administrations. She was Director and Scientific Coordinator of the Master in Accounting and Control in Local Authorities, organized by the Department of Economics and Business of the University of Catania. Her research topics are public accounting systems, performance measurement, socio-environmental reporting, social inclusion in tactile museums, sustainability and accountability.

Chapter 7
The State of Art About the Implementation of Social and Environmental Sustainability Drivers in Micro and Small Enterprise in an Italian Region

Maria-Gabriella Baldarelli, Federica Balluchi, Paolo Di Toma, Katia Furlotti, Arianna Lazzini, Patrizia Petrolati, and Stefania Vignini

Abstract This chapter shows the most significant results that emerged from empirical explorative research carried out on the territory of the Emilia-Romagna Region (Italy) and with the aim of analysing the sensitivity of micro and small enterprises with respect to sustainability issues, in its social and environmental dimensions. This sensitivity was "measured" by verifying the spreading of social responsibility

The chapter is the result of the project financed by Emilia-Lab Network. We thank you very much to Doct. Macarena Paz Velasco Rosalez for her support to elaborate the data in the first vertion of the report, but all the Graph was made by Authors.

M.-G. Baldarelli (✉) · P. Petrolati · S. Vignini
University of Bologna, Bologna, Italy
e-mail: maria.baldarelli@unibo.it

P. Petrolati
e-mail: patrizia.petrolati@unibo.it

S. Vignini
e-mail: stefania.vignini2@unibo.it

F. Balluchi · K. Furlotti
University of Parma, Parma, Italy
e-mail: federica.balluchi@unipr.it

K. Furlotti
e-mail: katia.furlotti@unipr.it

P. D. Toma · A. Lazzini
University of Modena and Reggio Emilia, Modena and Reggio Emilia, Italy
e-mail: paolo.ditoma@unimore.it

A. Lazzini
e-mail: arianna.lazzini@unimore.it

M. Baldarelli et al. (eds.), *Accounting and Accountability for Social Inclusion*, CSR, Sustainability, Ethics & Governance, https://doi.org/10.1007/978-3-032-09271-7_7

practices in respect of the most relevant stakeholders for these categories of companies: employees, customers and suppliers, community, territory and institutions, environment.

7.1 Introduction

7.1.1 Research Aims

The choice to focus on small-sized enterprises is based on the awareness that the intrinsic characteristics of such realities imply in themselves a strong social orientation that is expressed in a strong relationship with the local community and a consequent attention to specific categories of stakeholders, as well as an important focus on environmental issues (among others: Jenkins, 2006; Moore & Spence, 2006; Spence, 1999). At the same time, however, these (often poorly studied) companies, due to a sort of 'cultural resistance' linked, on the one hand, to a lack of awareness of the benefits of implementing sustainability strategies and, on the other hand, to a passive attitude towards such issues, sometimes do not manage or communicate their social and environmental responsibility activities in a structured approach.

The primary aim of the research was, definitively, to analyse some specificities in the application of the drivers of sustainable development in micro and small enterprises and, in other words, to 'take a picture' of the current situation of the diffusion of both social practices towards employees, the community and other stakeholders (customers, suppliers, territory, institutions), and environmental protection and communication strategies (website and social media). In this sense, the focus was on the relationships that companies have with their stakeholders and, in particular, on the following issues:

- employees: hourly flexibility, professional training, welfare, inclusion and equal opportunities, smart working and teleworking, work climate;
- community, territory, institutions: promotion or sponsorship of events of local or national relevance, support for building works, donations;
- customers and suppliers: monitoring of the origin of inputs/products, continuity of relationships, origin (local or non-local) of customers and suppliers;
- environment: environmental impact assessment indicators, recycling and energy saving actions, other environmental protection measures (e.g. separate waste sorting), circular economy, green certifications.

An in-depth study was then carried out on the practices implemented for their involvement and the social communication tools eventually adopted by them. A special focus was also devoted to the topic of the Sustainable Development Goals (SDGs), trying to understand the level of knowledge of the 2030 Agenda and the implementation of the single goals.

7.1.2 Research Methodology

Data on the issues was collected using the questionnaire tool with closed-ended questions (of the type: yes, no, don't know, not applicable) and with questions answered on a value scale of 1 to 7 (1: "minimal commitment", 7: "very high commitment"). The questionnaire was administered in February and March 2024 through interviews using the CATI (Computer Assisted Telephone Interview) method and the CAWI (Computer Assisted Web Interview) method. The telephone interviews were made possible thanks to the financial support provided by EmiliaLab, the network of Emilia-Romagna universities for scientific, educational and training collaboration in the field of economics and business studies (www.emilialab.it). The completed questionnaires were extracted through the use of a spreadsheet (Excel) in order to process the results and perform descriptive analyses that led to preliminary considerations of an exploratory nature.

The total number of companies that participated in the survey was 806, distributed geographically as follows (Table 7.1 and Table 7.2):

After this brief introduction of a methodological nature the peculiarities of the entrepreneurial fabric of the Emilia-Romagna Region and the motivations for choosing this Region as the object of the study are presented. After the Introduction, the next section is about the awareness of the concept of social sustainability involving employees, community, territory and institutions, customers and suppliers. The Third section is about the wareness of the concept of environmental sustainability and SDGs. The fourth section is analysing Stakeholder engagement and social media communication.

Table 7.1 Sample: distribution of companies per province

Province	Absolute values	Percentage values
Bologna	124	15,4
Ferrara	62	7,7
Forli-Cesena	72	8,9
Modena	120	14,9
Parma	120	14,9
Piacenza	68	8,4
Ravenna	61	7,6
Reggio Emilia	114	14,1
Rimini	65	8,1
Total	806	100

Source https://emiliaromagnainnodata.art-er.it/imprese-e-addetti-in-emilia-romagna-asia-2020

Table 7.2 Sample: Distribution of Enterprises by Province

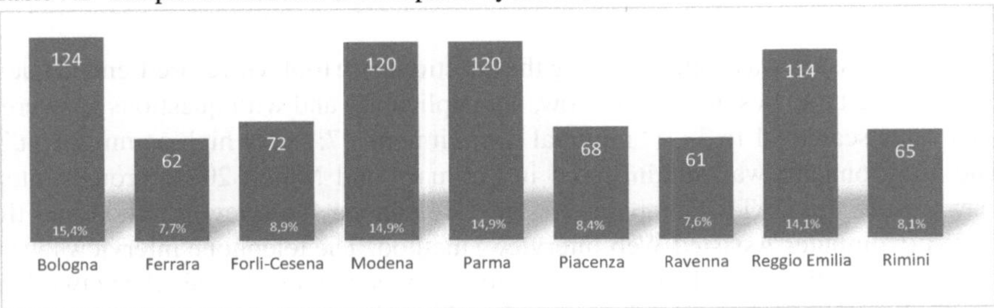

Source Authors' elaboration

7.1.3 Why Emilia Romagna Region?

In light of the above, it is important to briefly dwell now on the economic reasons that led to focusing the investigation carried out on companies in the Emilia Romagna Region, at a time in history in which, notoriously, the entire national economy has been hit by a succession of international crisis situations, first and foremost the Covid-19 pandemic, the Russian-Ukrainian conflict and the resulting energy shock and increase in inflation.

From this perspective, it is important to underline that, although Italy recorded a modest growth in GDP—in volume—of 0.7% in 2024 compared to the previous year, Emilia Romagna achieved growth of 0.9% in the same period, i.e. an increase that, although in line with that of 2023 (0.7%), is still slightly higher than the national figure, supported by the increase in employment, the slight acceleration of consumption and the recovery of exports.

Despite slowing down, therefore, the Region confirms itself as one of the "locomotive" regions of Italy, surpassing Lombardy and Sicily in this, as the first Italian regions for GDP growth rates in the two-year period considered.

At the same time, the labour market in Emilia-Romagna continued to expand during 2024, albeit with a slightly reduced intensity compared to previous years, showing both a substantial stability in the employment rate and a decrease in the unemployment rate, in accordance with equal dynamics observed at the national level (Regione Emilia Romagna, Studi e Analisi, Il mercato del lavoro in Emilia-Romagna nel 2024, 14 marzo 2025. Unioncamere Emilia-Romagna—Regione Emilia-Romagna RAPPORTO 2024 SULL'ECONOMIA REGIONALE).

To this we must add the factor of digitalization, given that that of companies and that of the territory are closely related, in the sense that digital penetration in the territory creates fertile ground for innovation and the sourcing by companies of human resources with cutting-edge skills and, at the same time, an open and reactive entrepreneurial system with respect to the integration of new technologies gives impetus to the territory in which they exist.

In this perspective, Emilia Romagna undoubtedly plays a leading role in Italy, both in terms of investment in areas of application of Artificial Intelligence, and in the use of the e-commerce distribution channel, just to mention the most significant of the various profiles relevant to this purpose.

These data, although evidently influenced by the unfortunately negative economic dynamics of a national and international nature, nevertheless represent the character of vitality that distinguishes the Emilia Romagna Region in the Italian context.

In this perspective, when the investigation discussed in this work was started, the question was asked whether this dynamism of the regional economic fabric could possibly influence the propensity of companies in the Region to implement measures aimed at including social and environmental issues in their actions.

In particular, the hypothesis that was formulated, and which was then tested, is that the general vitality of the regional economic fabric is actually a factor that encourages and facilitates companies to incorporate social and environmental objectives into their strategy.

7.2 Awareness of the Concept of Social Sustainability: Employees, Community, Territory and Institutions, Customers and Suppliers

Within the scope of the research, the first part of the analysis focused on specified types of stakeholders by examining the main critical relationships that exist between companies and these stakeholders. In fact, corporate social responsibility refers to the responsibility that companies assume towards all their stakeholders, which can be individuals or groups that have interests in companies (Balluchi & Furlotti, 2013; Gössling & Vocht, 2007).

Specifically, this section discusses the main findings from the analysis of the responses given considering the following stakeholders: employees, community, territory and institutions, customers and suppliers. The definitions of CSR by the World Business Council for Sustainable Development, in fact, defines CSR as "the ongoing commitment of companies to behave ethically and contribute to economic development, while improving the quality of life of workers and their families, as well as the local community and society at large".

7.2.1 Employees

The category "employees," represents the unified set of people who, by performing their work in the enterprise, participate in the conduct of the company's business. It is evident that the knowledge, skills and competencies of individuals, who contribute to the operation of the company, determine the characteristics and success of the organization itself (Prami et al., 2022). The skills and experiences gained by those who work within the company constitute resources that can generate value for the company, as well as the ability and motivation of employees determine the way the company works and, therefore, influence its organization and performance. The quality of the companies' product and, even more, the efficiency of the service provided, depends mainly on the skills and behaviors of the people who work for their attainment.

The importance, also in the strategic perspective, of employees is also corroborated by the efforts made by companies to manage and stimulate the workforce by initiating personnel management processes (Shahzadi et al., 2014).

From the employee's point of view, professional experience is a fundamental means of satisfying his or her needs (Maslow, 1954), both in terms of economic security and in aspects related to the individual's social position and professional satisfaction and growth. Therefore, although the main link between company and employee is the economic factor, there are other elements that condition the relationship between company and employee, related to personal relationships, career opportunities, job security and home-work reconciliation. These aspects are crucial in ensuring employee satisfaction, which is a key element in safeguarding a positive company-employee relationship (Spector, 1997).

In this sense, the study of the employee stakeholder is relevant, also from a CSR perspective; the literature, in this regard, offers different possible path of development for the studies.

Specifically, several research studies show how employees can be considered key stakeholders (Pedersen, 2011), but remains space for further investigation about them, especially with regard to the CSR literature (Aguinis & Glavas, 2012; Hansen et al., 2011). In fact, in this area of research, some studies (Story & Neves, 2015; Vlachos et al., 2010, 2013) have investigated the issue of CSR from the perspective of employees, but such research can be further developed, also in view of the widely acknowledged relevance of the employee stakeholder, precisely from a CSR perspective. Some work has investigated the implementation of CSR tools and strategies to improve the work climate (Manley, 1991), or to promote the work well-being of employees (Williams & Murphy, 1990), to ensure health and safety in the workplace (O'Dwyer & Madden, 2006), and with reference to the definition and dissemination of values to which everyone, including employees, in the organization should adhere (Molander, 1987; Weaver, 1993).

In the context of this research, for the employee category, the main topics under analysis were: time of work flexibility (Golden et al., 2014; Kauffeld, 2004), professional training (Burhan Ismael, 2021), and occupational welfare, with special reference to work climate (Chang, 2024; Subagja & Safrianto, 2020).

Regarding time flexibility, the questionnaire investigated the possibility for employees to enjoy forms of time flexibility, such as part-time, continuous hours, or other. The following graph (Graph 7.1) illustrates the results that emerged with reference to the Emilia-Romagna region and, below, the breakdown by individual provinces.

The data show that the possibility for employees to use work-life balance tools related in particular to time flexibility is present in most companies. These possibilities appear to be spread evenly in the various provinces of the region, with a slight decrease in the provinces of Piacenza and Parma.

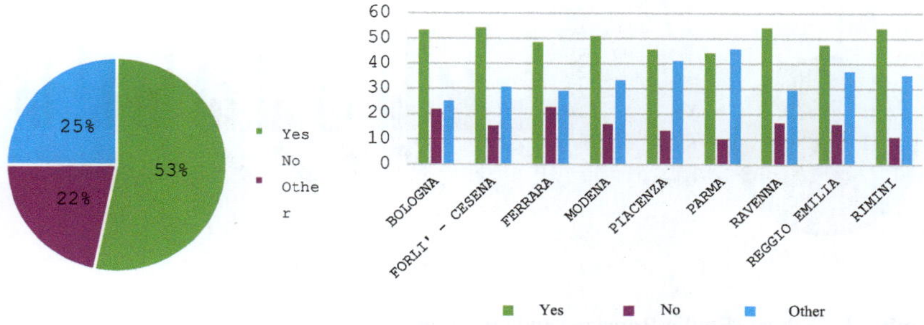

Graph 7.1 Hourly flexibility (Emilia-Romagna and provinces)

A second aspect analyzed, with reference to employees, was the professional training of staff. This issue was investigated, in particular, by surveying the existence of initiatives such as, for example, training courses organized both internally and externally.

Graph 7.2 shows that most of the companies surveyed (52%) declare the possibility of training for employees, again with fairly uniform data in the different provinces and with a slight decrease for the provinces of Parma and Piacenza. In this case, moreover, there are a very small number of companies that explicitly state that they do not provide training, while a significant part (36%) is represented by the item "Other," which includes "don't know" answers and non-answers.

From the point of view of occupational welfare (e.g., initiatives related to parenting support, supplementary health funds, etc.) there is a discrete presence of positive responses and in a similar percentage a lack of responses, highlighting, perhaps, a limited readiness to cover the topic by companies. Again, a minority (17%) of companies expressly state that they do not adopt welfare tools (Graph 7.3).

Lastly, in terms of work climate, the responses show that almost all the companies surveyed evaluate the work environment positively, rating the work climate as satisfactory. Similar results emerge when considering the analysis by province (Graph 7.4).

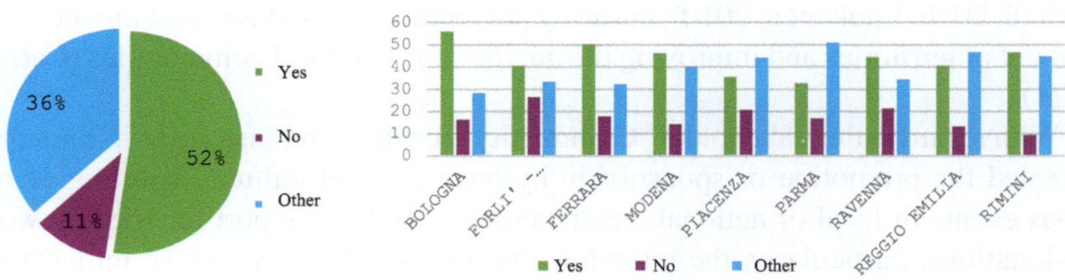

Graph 7.2 Professional training (Emilia-Romagna and provinces)

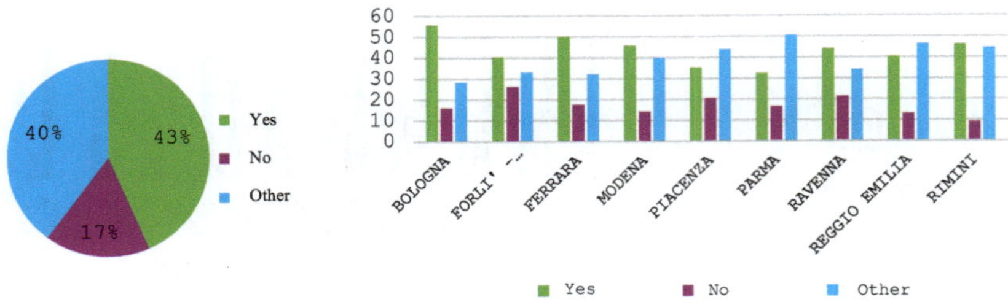

Graph 7.3 Welfare (Emilia-Romagna and provinces)

7.2.2 Community, Territory and Institutions

As mentioned earlier, from the perspective of CSR, companies rethink themselves, moving beyond the purely economic role and reconsider their stakeholders. Accordingly to UE Green Paper (2001):"Corporate social responsibility extends beyond the doors of the company to the local community and involves a wide range of stakeholders in addition to employees and shareholders: business partners and suppliers, customers, public authorities and NGOs representing local communities, as well as the environment". In this sense, the communities of the territories of reference of the company, are fundamental interlocutors to be considered in their own planning processes, making corporate welfare an integral part of public welfare, and generating a sort of extended model of responsible welfare (Cesareo, 2017; Cesareo & Pavesi, 2019) that refers to the entire community. In this perspective, the concept of stakeholder includes not only the local community, but also the broader civil society.

Therefore, companies must extend their accountability beyond simple financial parameters, toward synergistic actions between companies and current and potential stakeholders, including more peripheral ones, such as associations, environmentalists, the third sector, local communities and, with increasing importance, public institutions (Pelanda & Savona, 2005).

In this sense, corporate territorial welfare, represents the most innovative expression of CSR, as a strategic tool to combat even social and geographic marginality (Faludi, 2016; Luukonen, 2010), ensuring polycentric and socially sustainable development of territories and improving the quality of life of local communities (Carrera, 2024).

With regard to the stakeholder "Community, Territory and Institutions," the survey revealed the promotion or sponsorship by businesses of cultural, sporting or religious events of local or national significance, as well as support for specific works or donations. Particularly, the interview investigated the existence of initiatives of implementation (promotion) of such cultural, sports or religious events, as well as participation in events organized by others, for example, through sponsorship (participation). The following graphs illustrate the responses obtained with reference to promotion (Graph 7.5) and participation (Graph 7.6).

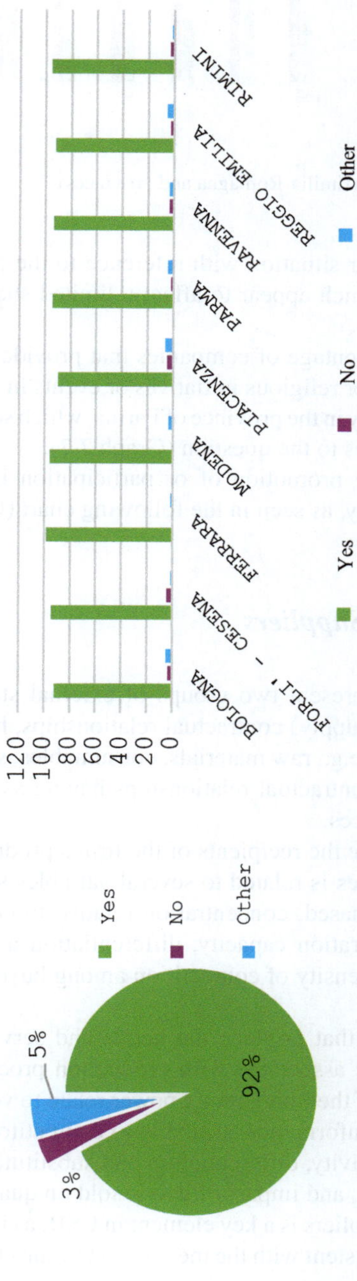

Graph 7.4 Work climate (Emilia-Romagna and provinces)

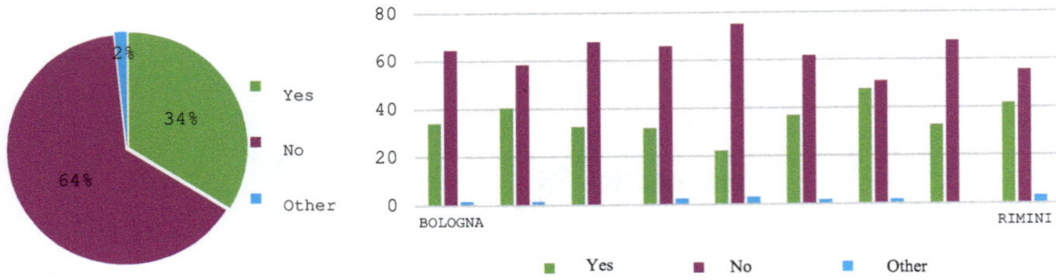

Graph 7.5 Promotion initiatives (Emilia-Romagna and provinces)

The graphs show a similar situation with reference to the promotion and sponsorship of events, both of which appear to affect a limited share of the companies surveyed (34%).

Slightly higher is the percentage of companies that provide donations of money or goods for cultural, sports or religious initiatives or events in the local area, with a particularly positive frequency in the province of Parma, which sees a more significant presence of positive responses to the question (Graph 7.7).

Even more limited is the promotion of or participation in cultural, sports or religious events in the country, as seen in the following chart (Graph 7.8).

7.2.3 Customers and Suppliers

Customers and suppliers represent two groups of external stakeholders linked to the enterprise by purchase (supply) contractual relationships, having as their object inputs of various categories (e.g., raw materials, consumables, semi-finished goods), goods or services or sales contractual relationships having as their object finished products, goods and/or services.

Specifically, customers are the recipients of the firm's products, and their ability to influence the firm's policies is related to several variables such as, for example, the amount of volume purchased, concentration relative to competitors, available information, upstream integration capacity, differentiation and substitutability of purchased goods, and the intensity of competition among buyers (Sütőová & Kóča, 2022).

Suppliers are companies that produce the goods and services acquired by the enterprise to meet the needs associated with production processes. Variables that contribute to the definition of their bargaining power relate to volumes sold, concentration rate of competitors, information available to competitors, downstream integration capacity, price sensitivity, differentiation and substitutability of goods sold, impact of goods sold on cost, and impact of goods sold on quality.

The relationship with suppliers is a key element in CSR, as it is important that the selection of suppliers is consistent with the message one wants to communicate to all

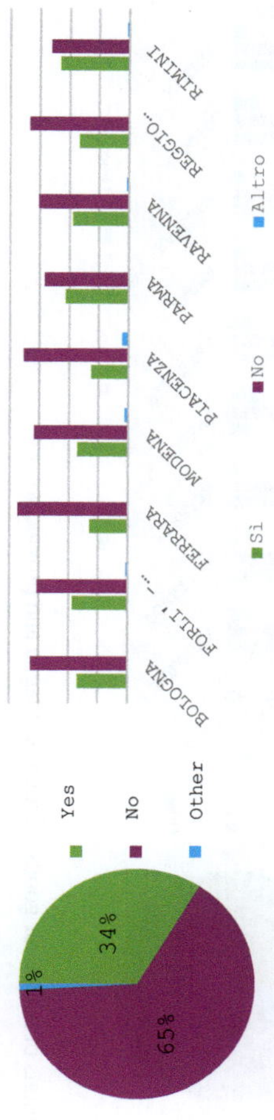

Graph 7.6 Participation to initiatives (Emilia-Romagna and provinces)

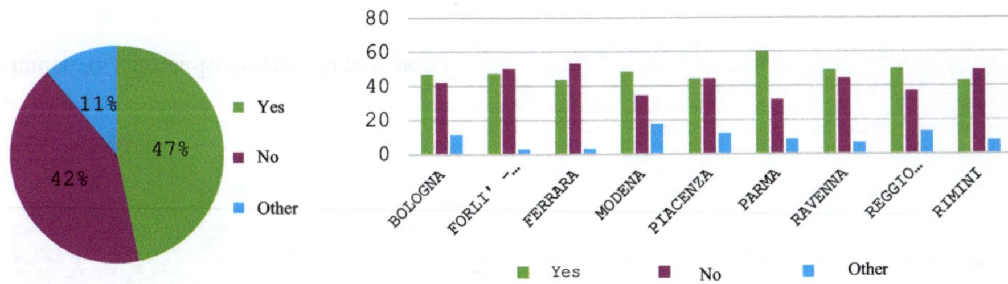

Graph 7.7 Charity—donations of money or goods (Emilia-Romagna and provinces)

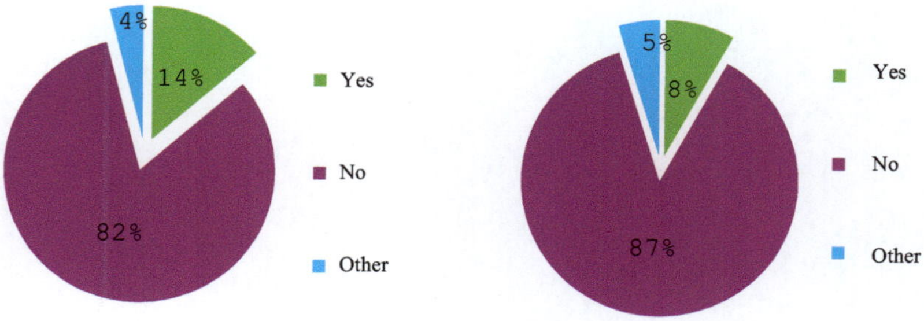

Graph 7.8 Promotion/participation events (Emilia-Romagna)

stakeholders. A "socially responsible" company approaches suppliers who manifest an equally social orientation of their strategies.

In the present research, with reference to customers and suppliers, the interview aimed to analyze the focus on controlling the origin of inputs or products and the constancy of relationships with customers and suppliers. In particular, the results reveal good attention to supply chain sustainability, with a large majority of companies (63%) stating that they adopt tools or implement mechanisms to know the origin of purchased products and ensure supply chain sustainability (Graph 7.9).

7.3 Awareness of the Concept of Environmental Sustainability: Environment and SDGs

7.3.1 Environment and Sustainability

In this section the results of the re-elaborations that concern the part of the questionnaire relating to the environment, sustainability and the 2030 Sustainable Development Goals (SDGs) are evidenced. We begin with a general overview of the main responses at the level of the Emilia-Romagna Region, in particular on the environment and sustainability. Please note that the percentages were calculated with respect to the number of each province.

(Legenda: BO (Bologna), FC (Forlì-Cesena), FE (Ferrara), MO (Modena), PC (Piacenza), PR (Parma), RA (Ravenna), RE (Reggio Emilia), RN (Rimini)).

It emerges (Graph 7.10) that at regional level for micro and small enterprises waste recycling is mainly used but other energy saving and pollution prevention measures are also relevant. In this regard, it can be considered that the measures implemented by the micro and small enterprises under analysis are closely correlated, on the one hand, with company policies aimed at containing operating costs, with a direct impact therefore on net company profitability. Furthermore, with the organizational methods of waste collection implemented at territorial level by the responsible bodies, which

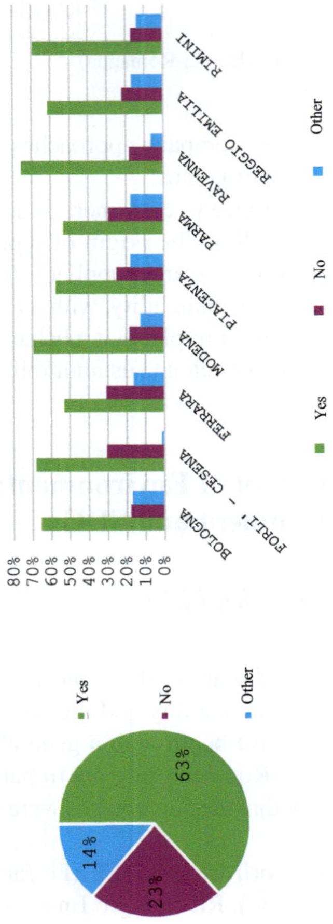

Graph 7.9 Supply chain sustainability (Emilia-Romagna and provinces)

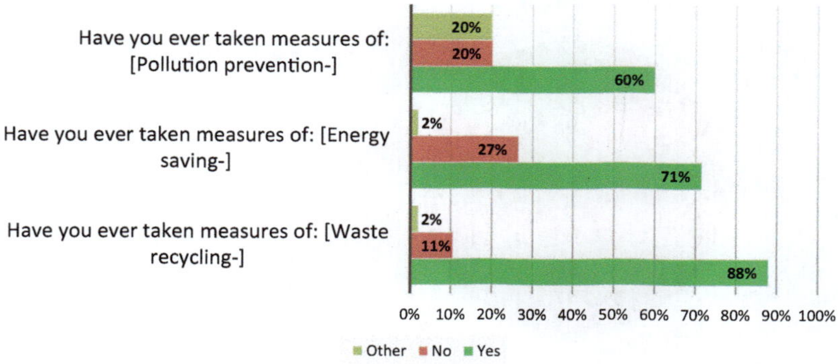

Graph 7.10 Environmental and Sustainability measures adopted by Firms

certainly constitute an incentive and a facilitation to the adoption of environmentally responsible behaviors.

Below the results relating to the proactive attitude of micro and small businesses towards sustainable development are analyzed (Graphs 7.11, 7.12, and 7.13). They represent in detail both the initiatives for promoting sustainability and the commitment to supporting and informing about sustainability topics.

The results that are evidenced (Graphs 7.11, 7.12, 7.13, and 7.14) show that there is little engagement in supporting and promoting environmental and sustainable activities. The first reason of the results derives by the frequent informal involvement in some sustainability activities that are due to the long term practices of micro Firms that sometimes is difficult to report and to account for. So, the results that emerge for the promotion of initiatives and training on sustainable development must be read considering the nature of micro and small-sized enterprises. The second reason is about that individually, each firm has little impact on environmental and sustainability issues, but together they are part of trade associations that promote such projects and in this way shell have more influence on environmental and sustainability topics.

7.3.2 Sustainable Development Goals (SDGs)

The Sustainable Development Goals (from now SDGs) aim to address a wide range of issues related to economic and social development, which include poverty, hunger, the right to health and education, access to water and energy, employment, inclusive and sustainable economic growth, climate change and environmental protection, urbanization, production and consumption patterns, social and gender equality, justice, and peace (UN General Assembly's Open Working Group proposes sustainable development goals, su Sustainabledevelopment.un.org, 19 July 2014. URL accessed 18 October 2016).

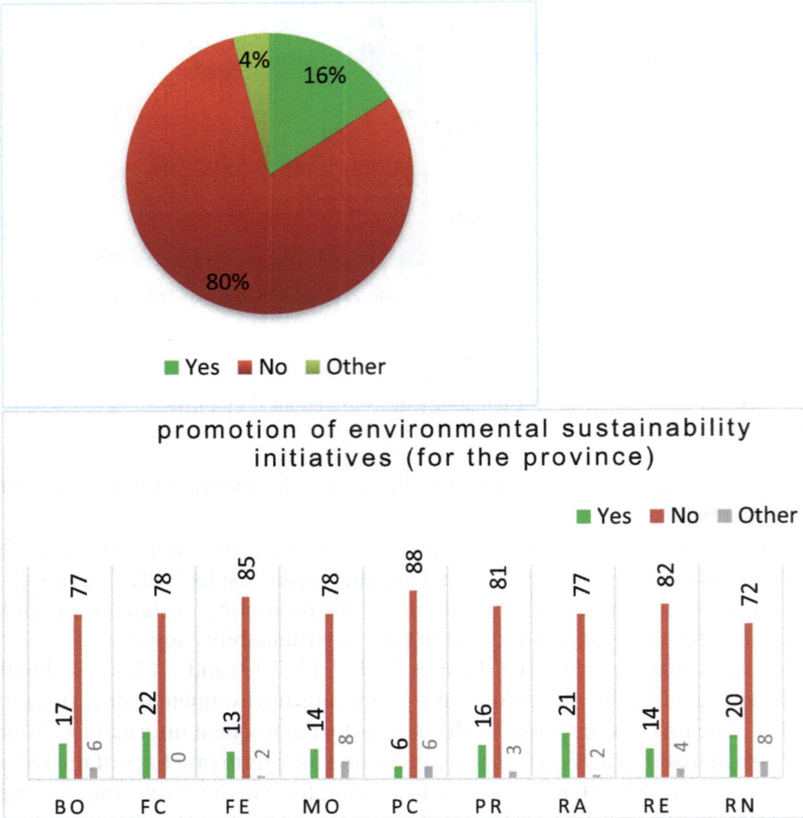

Graph 7.11 Promotion of environmental and sustainability initiatives

Graph 7.12 Promotion and support associations that are involved in environmental protection

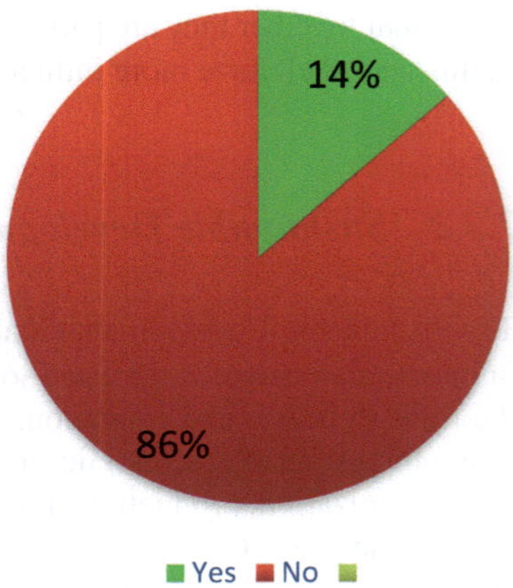

Graph 7.13 Participation in training events on sustainability

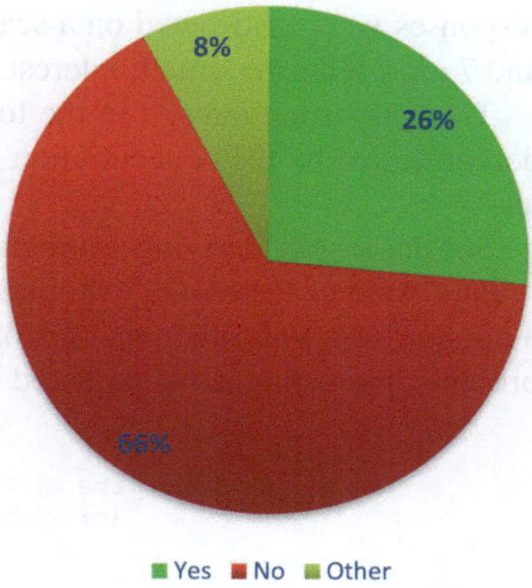

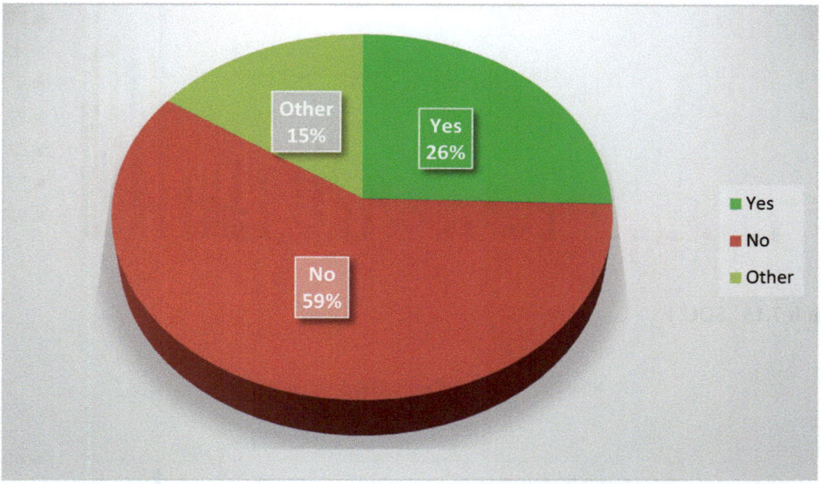

Graph 7.14 The intensity of use of indicators or other tools to assess the environmental impact of Firms activity

The predominant literature on the topic has mostly focused on management (Annan-Diab & Molinari, 2017; Storey et al., 2017), accounting, and accountability (Bebbington & Unerman, 2018; Gray, 2010). Moreover, there is no doubt that pursuing the SDGs (when integrated into business strategies) can help develop innovative solutions to address challenges and alter business models (Boons & Lüdeke-Freund, 2013; Vignini, 2023).

The results are considering some SDGs, in particular numbers 1 (no poverty) (Graph 7.15), 2 (zero hunger) (Graph 7.16), 5 (gender equality) (Graph 7.17), 8 (decent work and economic growth) (Graph 7.18), 10 (reduce inequalities) (Graph 7.19) and 16 (peace justice and strong institutions) (Graph 7.20). The responses were distributed on a scale from 1 to 7, where 1 represents little interest and 7 represents maximum interest.

There is strong interest in the topics and substantially show a consistent trend., demonstrated by the concentration of responses from businesses mainly in zones 6 and 7.

So, the results deriving from survey are comforting and denote a solid interest in the theme of the SDGs. Ultimately, it could certainly be of great utility to make a comparison with other regions of the Italian territory to understand if this zone presents interesting data compared to other areas.

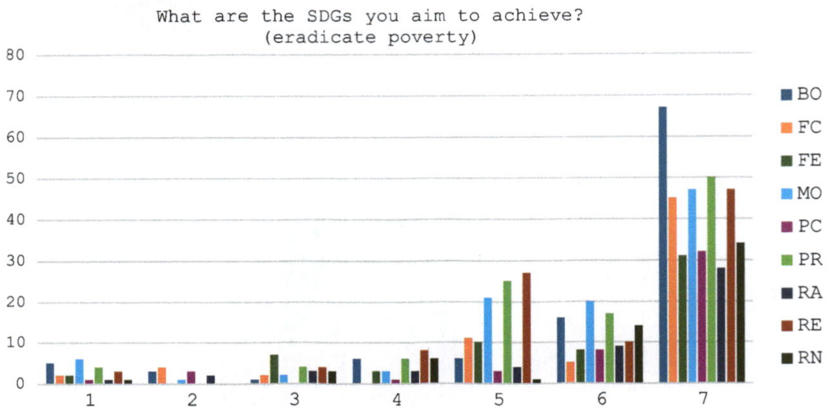

Graph 7.15 SDG 1

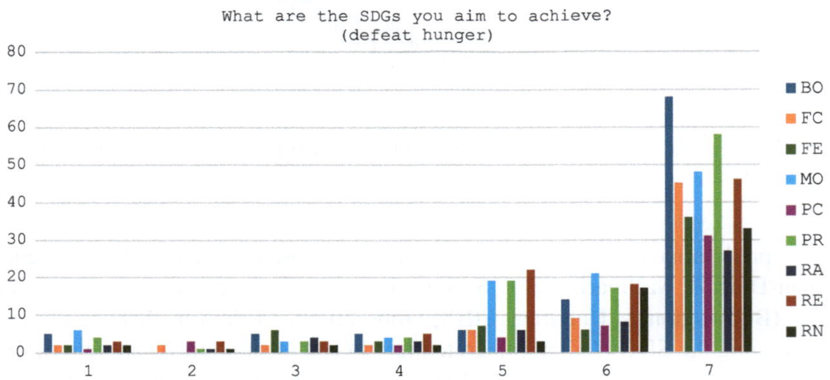

Graph 7.16 SDG 2

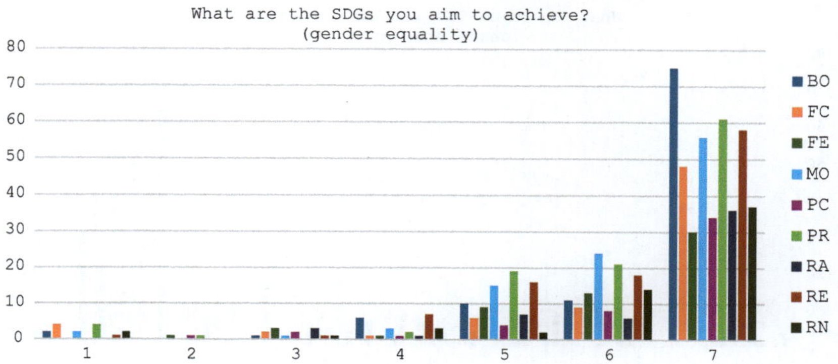

Graph 7.17 SDG 5

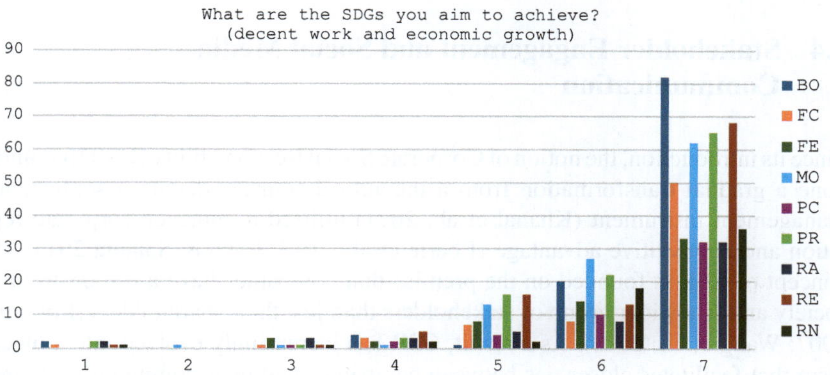

Graph 7.18 SDG 8

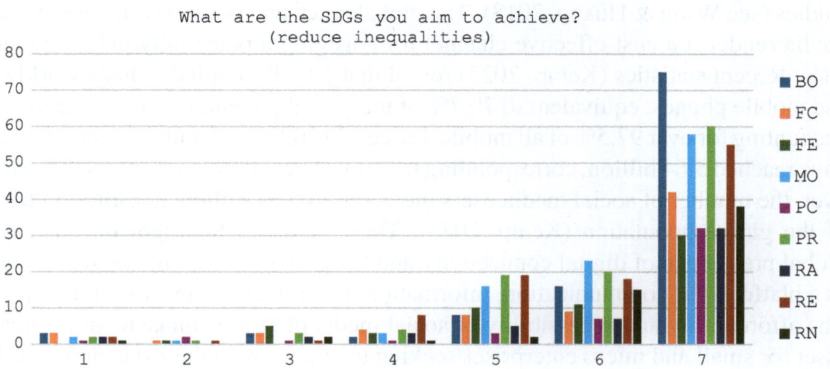

Graph 7.19 SDG 10

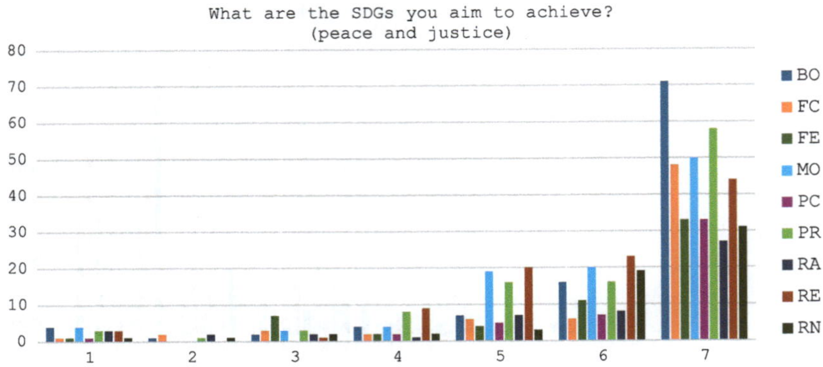

Graph 7.20 SDG 16

7.4 Stakeholder Engagement and Social Media Communication

Since its introduction, the notion of Corporate Social Responsibility (CSR) has undergone a gradual transformation from a theoretical framework into a sophisticated management instrument (Khanal et al., 2021) utilised to enhance corporate reputation and competitive advantage (Eberle et al., 2013; Popa & Salanta 2014). The concept of CSR is founded on the premise that companies have a responsibility to society and to a wider group of stakeholders than just their shareholders (Friedman, 2007; Wang et al., 2016). As a result, CSR has increasingly evolved into a mechanism that facilitates closer ties between companies and their communities, thereby generating substantial positive changes for people, the planet and society.

The potential of social media in this regard has been demonstrated by numerous studies (see Wang & Huang, 2018). The global reach and borderless nature of social media render it a cost-effective channel for engaging a potentially unlimited audience. Recent statistics (Kemp, 2025) reveal that 5.81 billion individuals worldwide use mobile phones, equivalent to 70.7% of the global population, with smartphones accounting for over 97,5% of all mobile devices. In 2025, the number of Internet users have reached 5.64 billion, corresponding to a global penetration rate of 68.7%. Moreover, the number of social media users increased to 5.31 billion, constituting 64.7% of the global population (Kemp, 2025). These statistics highlight the increasing global prevalence of digital connectivity and the growing centrality of social media as a platform for communication, information dissemination, and social interaction. The affordability and accessibility of social media platforms make them a valuable asset for small and micro enterprises seeking to engage with their stakeholders. The effective engagement of stakeholders through social media has been demonstrated to engender reputational advantages, thereby enhancing brand image, customer loyalty, and investor confidence (Islam et al., 2025; Zhou et al., 2024). Furthermore, it has been demonstrated that proactive, stakeholder-centred corporate communication has the capacity to fortify a company's stakeholder relationships and to reduce the impact of public criticism (Camilleri, 2019; Khanal et al., 2021).

In recent years, the concepts of stakeholder engagement and Corporate Social Responsibility have garnered increased attention (Khanal et al., 2021; Kujala et al., 2022; Matarazzo et al., 2025). This is particularly true for small and medium-sized enterprises (SMEs), which are considered the backbone of the European economy. There are some 25 million SMEs in Europe, employing some 100 million people, accounting for more than half of Europe's GDP and play a key role in creating added value in all sectors of the economy (European Commission, 2020).

As SMEs are crucial to Europe's transition to a sustainable and digital economy, there is growing interest in understanding and implementing stakeholder engagement strategies in SMEs. However, despite growing awareness of the issue, the practical implementation of stakeholder dialogue and the use of innovative communication technologies among SMEs in general and micro-enterprises in particular is still underdeveloped.

Nevertheless, the findings indicate a concerning lack of stakeholder engagement among small enterprises. Deriving from the results of the survey (Graph 7.21) emerges a mere 23% of the surveyed companies reported having initiated dialogue with their stakeholders, while a significant 77% admitted to not engaging in such practices. This finding highlights a significant gap in stakeholder management strategies, indicating a widespread lack of culture in micro-enterprises in this area.

A provincial analysis (Graph 7.22) also shows that in no province does the proportion of enterprises engaged in stakeholder dialogue exceed 30%. The highest levels of engagement are reported by Bologna, Parma and Ravenna with 23%, while Ferrara has the lowest with only 17%.

The following table shows the number of companies engaged in stakeholder dialogue by province.

It is possible to identify a number of factors that have contributed to this limited engagement. These include a paucity of dedicated resources, a perceived lack of value in stakeholder dialogue, and organisational difficulties in managing such processes.

A more thorough investigation of the stakeholders involved (Graph 7.23) indicates a discernible tendency to engage with entities that are closely associated with the

Graph 7.21 Companies engaging with stakeholders

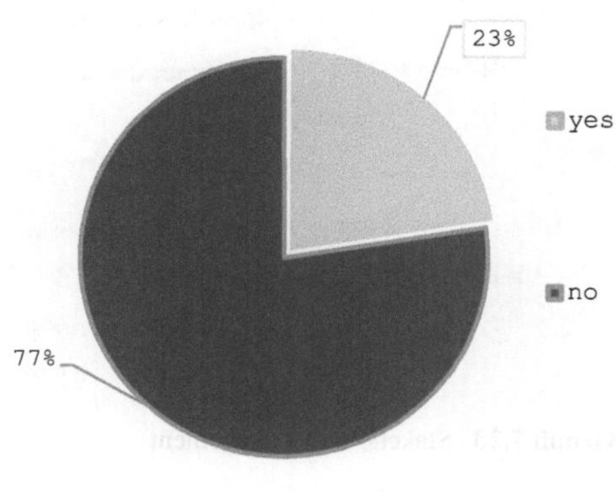

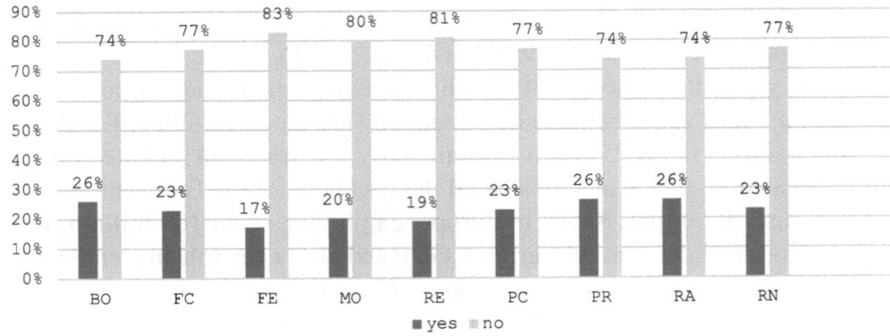

Graph 7.22 Companies engaging with their stakeholders

enterprise's value chain. Specifically, 41% of companies reported engaging primarily with customers, 33% with suppliers, and another 33% with schools. Conversely, engagement with universities (10%), communities (12%), public institutions, and non-profit organisations remains negligible.

This trend suggests that small enterprises prioritise relationships that offer immediate operational benefits, such as market expansion and supply chain optimisation, while neglecting broader social and institutional networks that could foster long-term sustainability and innovation.

This study also explores the adoption of communication technologies among small enterprises. It is evident that a significant proportion of the companies that have participated in the survey have a proprietary website, which suggests a relatively high level of digital presence (Graph 7.24).

However, significant provincial disparities are evident: Reggio Emilia (80%), Modena (77%), and Rimini (77%) show the highest rates of website ownership, while

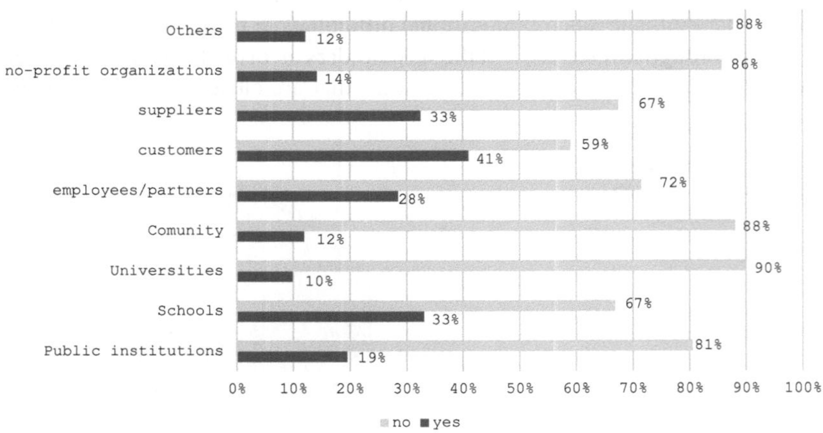

Graph 7.23 Stakeholders engagement

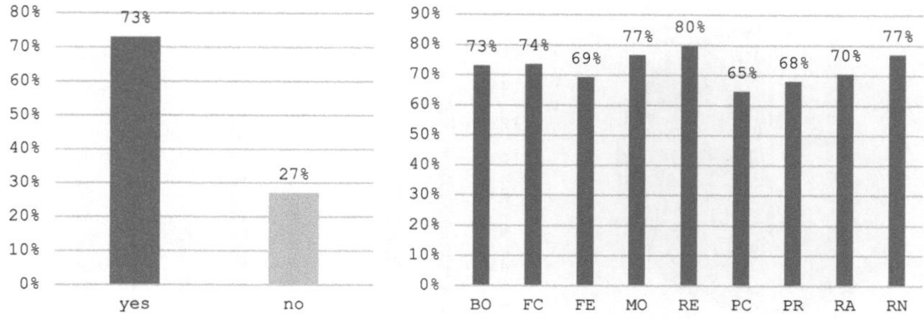

Graph 7.24 Companies with a website (regional and provincial level)

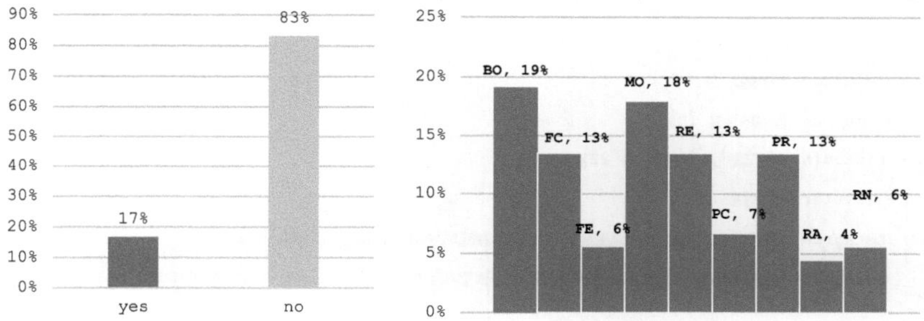

Graph 7.25 Companies with a page dedicated to sustainability

Piacenza (65%), Ferrara (69%), and Parma (68%) show lower rates. A noteworthy finding is that among companies lacking a website, a mere 19% are contemplating website development in the near future. This observation underscores a pervasive underestimation of the strategic significance of a digital presence. With regard to the communication of sustainability practices, a mere 17% of companies with a website have a dedicated page for sustainability (Graph 7.25).

Bologna leads in this aspect (19%), followed by Modena (18%). This limited emphasis on sustainability communication suggests that, despite increasing societal expectations, small enterprises still view sustainability as a peripheral concern rather than a strategic priority.

Social media platforms have emerged as critical tools for stakeholder engagement. According to the study, 62% of small enterprises use social media (Graph 7.26).

Modena has the highest adoption rate, followed by Bologna, Reggio Emilia and Parma. With regard to platform preferences (Graph 7.27), Facebook has emerged as the predominant channel, with 85% of enterprises utilising it. This is followed by Instagram (67%), LinkedIn (22%), YouTube (10%), and Twitter (8%). The findings of this study indicate that SMEs are prioritising platforms that offer broad reach and ease of customer engagement over more niche or professional networks.

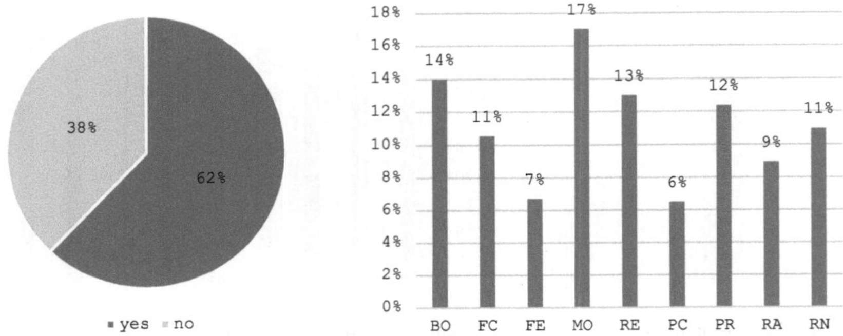

Graph 7.26 Social media adoption (regional and provincial level)

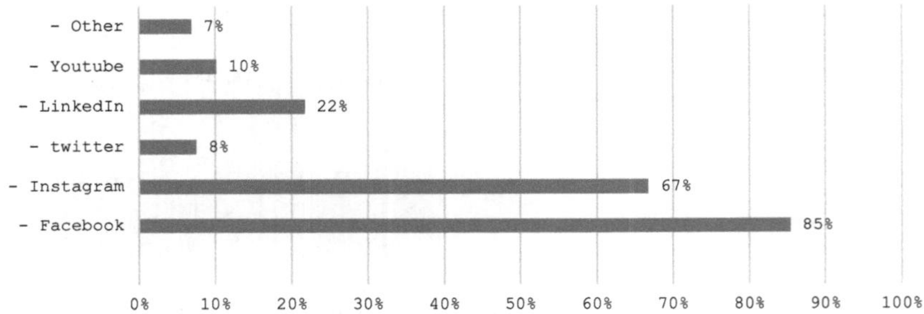

Graphure 7.27 Social media adopted

The primary purposes for using social media (Graph 7.28) are marketing (25%) and customer engagement (25%), emphasising the tactical use of these tools for business promotion rather than for strategic sustainability communication. A mere 11% of companies employ social media as a tool to communicate their social and environmental initiatives, thereby indicating a significant missed opportunity to enhance transparency and corporate reputation.

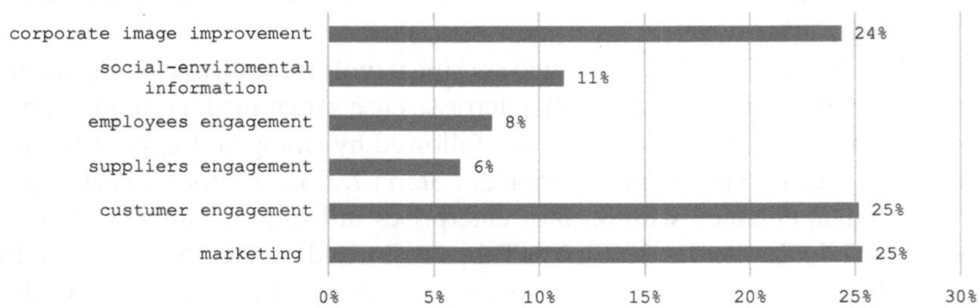

Graph 7.28 Purpose of social media use

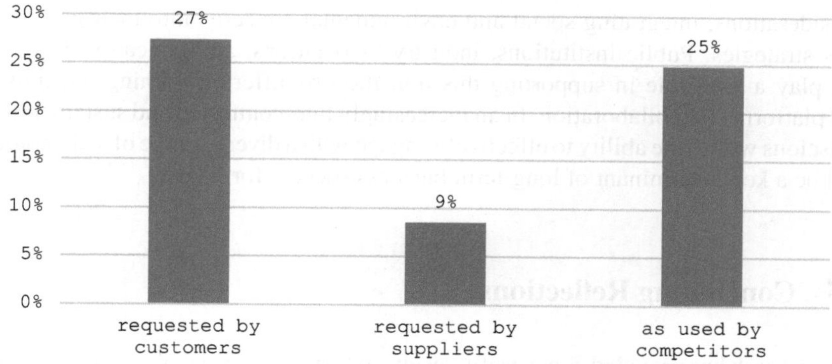

Graph 7.29 Reasons for using social media

Moreover, the reasons for social media usage (Graph 7.29) reveal that 27% of companies are driven by customer demand, while 25% cite competitive pressure as the main reason. Very few (9%) are motivated by supplier requirements, suggesting that market forces, rather than proactive strategic planning, largely dictate social media adoption.

The findings present a multifaceted picture of stakeholder engagement and communication practices among small enterprises in Emilia-Romagna. On the one hand, the relatively high adoption rates of websites and social media platforms reflect a growing awareness of the importance of digital communication. incidental deployment of these tools, primarily for marketing purposes, and the limited focus on sustainability communication, indicate a significant gap in strategic thinking.

The low levels of stakeholder engagement are particularly troubling, as effective stakeholder dialogue is increasingly recognized as a cornerstone of corporate social responsibility and sustainable business practices. SMEs' preference for engaging primarily with customers and suppliers, while understandable from a short-term operational perspective, limits their ability to build resilient, socially embedded business models.

Furthermore, the minimal interaction with universities and research institutions points to an underutilization of potential innovation drivers. Strengthening ties with the academic world could help SMEs access new knowledge, enhance their technological capabilities, and better respond to societal challenges.

The provincial disparities in digital adoption and sustainability communication also warrant attention. Targeted policy interventions and support programs could help bridge these gaps, fostering a more homogeneous regional development.

Data highlights critical areas for improvement in the stakeholder engagement and communication practices of small enterprises in Emilia-Romagna. While digital tools such as websites and social media offer significant opportunities for enhancing stakeholder relations and promoting social sustainability, their current use remains predominantly tactical and market-driven. To fully realize the potential of stakeholder engagement, SMEs need to move beyond mere compliance and marketing considerations, integrating social and environmental concerns into their core business strategies. Public institutions, industry associations, and educational entities can play a vital role in supporting this transition by offering training, incentives, and platforms for collaboration. In an increasingly interconnected and sustainability-conscious world, the ability to effectively engage with a diverse range of stakeholders will be a key determinant of long-term business success for SMEs.

7.5 Concluding Reflections

The research has provided some useful results to formulate initial observations on the sensitivity of micro-small businesses in the Emilia Romagna region to sustainability, which often escape broader databases. In particular, the aspects relating to awareness of the concept of social sustainability in relation to the main corporate stakeholders (employees, community, territory and institutions, customers and suppliers) were investigated with a particular focus on environmental sustainability aspects. The research also examined the level of knowledge on the subject of Sustainable Development Goals (SDGs) and verified the presence of stakeholder involvement initiatives and the use of social communication tools.

The results outline a picture of fair attention to all the aspects analysed even if sometimes different trends can be observed in the different provinces of the Region.

In some cases, elements emerge that are contradictory in some respects, partly probably also linked to an incomplete and incorrect understanding of the questions being investigated by the companies interviewed. These aspects can certainly be better examined through future in-depth studies, also in relation to specific best practices.

On the other hand, these risks are implicit in the choice to focus on micro and small-sized companies that, due to their culture and available resources, often do not have mature experience in the field of social responsibility and sustainability, but that have always had in their management methods those "drivers" of sustainable development, both social and environmental. This misalignment between awareness and CSR tools and daily operations is also one of the reasons that motivated this research.

Despite the limitations highlighted, we believe that these initial results can be useful for reflections by trade associations and public institutions, in order to promote initiatives and policies that can support companies in defining systematic strategies of social responsibility and socio-environmental communication.

References

Aguinis, H., & Glavas, A. (2012). What we know and don't know about corporate social responsibility: A review and research agenda. *Journal of Management, 38*(4), 932–968.

Annan-Diab, F., & Molinari, C. (2017). Interdisciplinary: Practical approach to advancing education for sustainability and for the Sustainable Development Goals. *The International Journal of Management Education, 15*(1), 73–83.

Balluchi, F., & Furlotti, K. (2013). *CSR disclosure by Italian companies. An empirical analysis.* LAP Lambert Academic Publishing.

Bebbington, J., & Unerman, J. (2018). Achieving the United Nations Sustainable Development Goals an enabling role for accounting research. *Accounting, Auditing & Accountability Journal, 31*(1), 2–24.

Boons, F., & Lüdeke-Freund, F. (2013). Business models for sustainable innovation: State-of-the-art and steps towards a research agenda. *Journal of Cleaner Production, 45*, 9–19.

Burhan, I. N., Jabbar, O. B., Gardi, B., Abdalla, H. P., Sorguli, S., Mahmood, A. H., & Anwar, G. (2021). The role of training and development on organizational effectiveness. *International Journal of Engineering, Business and Management, 5*(3), 15–24.

Camilleri, M. A. (2019). The SMEs' technology acceptance of digital media for stakeholder engagement. *Journal of Small Business and Enterprise Development, 26*(4), 504–521.

Carrera, L. (2024). Public and corporate socio-territorial policies. CSR as strategy for a new and enlarged social sustainability. *Journal of Emerging Perspectives, 1*, 23–32. https://doi.org/10.36253/jep-16897

Cesareo, V. (Ed.). (2017). *Welfare responsabile.* Vita e pensiero.

Cesareo, V., & Pavesi, N. (Eds.). (2019). *Il welfare responsabile alla prova: una proposta per la società italiana.* Vita e pensiero.

Chang, R. (2024). The impact of employees' health and well-being on job performance. *Journal of Education, Humanities and Social Sciences, 29*(1), 372–378.

Commission of the European Communities, Green Paper Promoting a European Framework for Corporate Social Responsibility, Brussels. (2001).

Eberle, D., Berens, G., & Li, T. (2013). The impact of interactive corporate social responsibility communication on corporate reputation. *Journal of Business Ethics, 118*, 731–746.

European Commission. (2020, March). Communication from the commission to the European parliament, the council, the European economic and social committee and the committee of the regions.

Faludi, A. (2016). EU territorial cohesion, a contradiction in terms. *Planning Theory & Practice, 17*(2), 302–313.

Friedman, M. (2007). The social responsibility of business is to increase its profits. In *Corporate ethics and corporate governance* (pp. 173–178). Springer.

Golden, L., Henly, J., & Lambert, S. (2014). Work schedule flexibility: A contributor to employee happiness? *Journal of Social Research and Policy.*

Gössling, T., & Vocht, C. (2007). Social role conceptions and CSR policy success. *Journal of Business Ethics, 74*(4), 363–372.

Gray, R. (2010). Is accounting for sustainability actually accounting for sustainability ... and how would we know? An exploration of the narratives of organizations and the planet. *Accounting Organizations and Society, 35*(1), 47–62.

Hansen, S. D., Dunford, B. B., Boss, A. D., Boss, R. W., & Angermeier, I. (2011). Corporate social responsibility and the benefits of employee trust: A cross-disciplinary perspective. *Journal of Business Ethics, 102*(1), 29–45.

Islam, T., Arunachalum, M., Wellalage, N., & Benjamin, S. (2025). Corporate environmental performance leading financial performance: Impacts of social media sentiment and corporate reputation. *Business Strategy and the Environment, 34*(4), 4274–4290.

Jenkins, H. (2006). Small business champions for corporate social responsibility. *Journal of Business Ethics, 67*(3), 241–256.

Kauffeld, S., Jonas, E., & Frey, D. (2004). Effects of a flexible work-time design on employee- and company-related aims. *European Journal of Work and Organizational Psychology, 13*(1), 79–100.

Kemp, S. (2025). Digital 2025 April global statshot report, https://datareportal.com/reports/digital-2025-april-global-statshot

Khanal, A., Akhtaruzzaman, M., & Kularatne, I. (2021). The influence of social media on stakeholder engagement and the corporate social responsibility of small businesses. *Corporate Social Responsibility and Environmental Management, 28*(6), 1921–1929.

Kujala, J., Sachs, S., Leinonen, H., Heikkinen, A., & Laude, D. (2022). Stakeholder engagement: Past, present, and future. *Business & Society, 61*(5), 1136–1196.

Luukkonen, T. (2010). *The effectiveness of the Finnish pre-seed and seed policy schemes to promote innovative high-growth entrepreneurial ventures (1221)* (ETLA-Discussion Papers).

Manley, W. (1991). *Executives handbook of model business conduct codes*. Prentice-Hall.

Maslow, A. H. (1954). The instinctoid nature of basic needs. *Journal of personality*.

Matarazzo, M., Oduro, S., & Gennaro, A. (2025). Stakeholder engagement for sustainable value co-creation: Evidence from made in Italy SMEs. *Business Ethics, the Environment & Responsibility, 34*(2), 347–361.

Molander, E. A. (1987). A paradigm for design, promulgation and enforcement of ethical codes. *Journal of Business Ethics, 6*, 619–631.

Moore, G., & Spence, L. (2006). Editorial: Responsibility and small business. *Journal of Business Ethics, 67*(3), 219–226.

O'Dwyer, B., & Madden, G. (2006). Ethical codes of conduct in Irish companies: A survey of code content and enforcement procedures. *Journal of Business Ethics, 63*(3), 217–236.

Pedersen, E. R. G. (2011). All animals are equal, but …: Management perceptions of stakeholder relationships and societal responsibilities in multinational corporations. *Business Ethics: A European Review, 20*(2), 177–191.

Pelanda, C., & Savona, P. (2005). *Sovranità & fiducia*. Sperling & Kupfer.

Popa, M., & Salanţă, I. (2014). Corporate social responsibility versus corporate social irresponsibility. *Management & Marketing, 9*(2).

Prami, A. I. N. D., Guntar, E. L., & Setiawan, I. P. D. (2022). Pengaruh Kepuasan Kerja Dan Loyalitas Terhadap Kinerja Karyawan Pada PT Cendana Indopearls Buleleng Bali. *Majalah Ilmiah Widyacakra, 5*(2), 47–61.

Shahzadi, I., Javed, A., Pirzada, S. S., Nasreen, S., & Khanam, F. (2014). Impact of employee motivation on employee performance. *European Journal of Business and Management, 6*(23), 159–166.

Spector, P. E. (1997). *Job satisfaction: Application, assessment, causes, and consequences*. Sage publications.

Spence, L. (1999). Does size Matter? The state of the art in small business ethics. *Business Ethics: A European Review, 8*(9), 163–172.

Storey, M., Killian, S., & O'Regan, P. (2017). Responsible management education: Mapping the field in the context of the SDGs. *The International Journal of Management Education, 15*(1), 93–103.

Story, J., & Neves, P. (2015). When Corporate Social Responsibility (CSR) increases performance: Exploring the role of intrinsic and extrinsic CSR attribution. *Business Ethics: A European Review, 24*(2), 111–124.

Subagja, I. K., & Safrianto, A. S. (2020). Pengaruh Kepuasaan Kerja Dan Loyalitas Kerja Terhadap Kinerja Karyawan Pt Bank Sahabat Sampoerna Jakarta. *Jurnal Manajemen Bisnis Krisnadwipayana, 8*(2), 118–128. https://doi.org/10.35137/jmbk.v8i2.428

Sütőová, A., & Kóča, F. (2022). Corporate social responsibility standards: Is it possible to meet diverse customer requirements? *Management Systems in Production Engineering, 30*(1), 54–61. https://doi.org/10.2478/mspe-2022-0007

Vignini, S. (2023). Sustainable Development Goals: How do companies react? *Australasian Accounting, Business and Finance Journal, 17*(3), 124–139.

Vlachos, P. A., Panagopoulos, N. G., & Rapp, A. A. (2013). Feeling good by doing good: Employee CSR-induced attributions, job satisfaction, and the role of charismatic leadership. *Journal of Business Ethics, 118*, 577–588.

Vlachos, P. A., Theotokis, A., Pramatari, K., & Vrechopoulos, A. (2010). Consumer-retailer emotional attachment: Some antecedents and the moderating role of attachment anxiety. *European Journal of Marketing, 44*(9/10), 1478–1499.

Wang, H., Tong, L., Takeuchi, R., & George, G. (2016). Corporate social responsibility: An overview and new research directions—Thematic issue on corporate social responsibility. *Academy of Management Journal, 59*(2), 534–544.

Wang, R., & Huang, Y. (2018). Communicating Corporate Social Responsibility (CSR) on social media: How do message source and types of CSR messages influence stakeholders' perceptions? *Corporate Communications: An International Journal, 23*(3), 326–341.

Weaver, G. R. (1993). Corporate codes of ethics: Purpose, process and content issues. *Business & Society, 32*(1), 44–58.

Williams, O. F., & Murphy, P. E. (1990). The ethics of virtue: A moral theory for marketing. *Journal of Macromarketing, 10*(1), 19–29.

Zhou, J., Ye, S., Liu, X., & Tang, Y. (2024). The role of social media in CSR performance: An integrated institutional and resource dependence perspective. *Journal of Business Research, 184*, 114880.

Maria-Gabriella Baldarelli , PhD, CPA, is Associate Professor of Accounting, at University of Bologna, Department of Management- Rimini Campus. Full professor availability. Envited professor at Sophia University Institute. SIDREA board member until 2018. She is a member of international scientific networks: the Centre for Social and Environmental Accounting Research (CSEAR) and the European Business Ethics Network (EBEN). Key-note Speaker 2nd International Conference on Economics, Business, Finance and Governance (ICEBFG) by Economics and Business Faculty of University of Bandar Lampung- Bali- Indonesia- Dic. 4-5, 2019. Research interests includes: accountability and gambling enterprises; corporate social responsibility; ethical, social and environmental accounting and accountability, sustainability in tourist enterprises; responsible and accessible tourism for blind people, economy of communion; gender accounting; accounting history, accounting education and Feminist Economics.

Federica Balluchi PhD Full Professor of Business Economics, She is a member of several national and international academic associations, and is a reviewer for Italian and international journals. He is a member of the Scientific Committee of the National Association GBS (Bilanci e Sostenibilità Group). Her studies focus on: voluntary disclosure, sustainability, management control and history of accounting. The results of his research have been presented at national and international conferences and published in monographs and national and international journals.

Paolo Di Toma PhD CPA is Full Professor of Business Economics—University of Modena and Reggio Emilia—Department of Communication and Economics. His main research interests are: Corporate governance, entrepreneurial strategies and innovation of business models; Composition, functioning and evaluation of Boards of Directors and corporate governance systems; Family Business and entrepreneurial families; Industrial plans, strategy execution and performance control.

Katia Furlotti PhD is full Professor of Business Economics, University of Parma Vice Dean of the Department of Economics and Management, University of Parma, since January 2017. Member of: European Accounting Association (EAA); European Business Ethics Network (EBEN); Centre for Social and Environmental Research—CSEAR; Accademia Italiana di Economia Aziendale—AIDEA (Italian Academy of Business Administration); Società Italiana di Storia della Ragioneria—SISR (Italian Academy of Accounting History); Società Italiana dei Docenti di Ragioneria e Economia Aziendale -SIDREA (Italian Academy of Accounting and Business Economics Teacher). Author of publications regarding: Corporate Social Responsibility, Social Report and Corporate Governance, accounting history.

Arianna Lazzini PhD is Associate Professor of Business Economics at the Faculty of Communication Sciences and Economics, University of Modena and Reggio Emilia. She is member of the Scientific-Editorial Committee of the series Strategy, Management and Control—Giappichelli; Member of the Scientific-Editorial Committee of the series Information Systems, Management and Control—Franco Angeli. She is Referee for national and international journals/series.Since 2020 Member of the study group Guidelines for Management Control—Management control in small and medium-sized enterprises; Since 2017–2018 External adjunct member of the research group "New perspectives on governance, audit, risk and performance management".

Patrizia Petrolati is a Confirmed Associate Professor at the Department of Management—DISA of Alma Mater Studiorum—University of Bologna. She teaches "Financial Accounting" and "Business Combination" at its Bologna Campus. She has long been involved in the evolution of corporate information systems in the context of international accounting harmonization within the European Union and in the methodologies for the interpretation of the economic and financial positions for the management of for-profit and cooperative companies through the analysis of financial statements by the means of ratios and financial flows. On these topics, she has produced several essays and participated in various conferences, also at an international level.

Stefania Vignini PhD, is an Assistant Professor of Accounting, at the University of Bologna, Department of Management, Bologna, Italy. Associate professorial availability. Principal research interests include: accountability; ethical, social and environmental accounting; gender accounting; accounting history, accounting systems, managerial control in non profit organizations; International Accounting Standards; Corporate Social Responsibility; Financial Statement Analysis.

Chapter 8
The Social and Inclusive Accounting Perspective of Economy of Communion: Firm Research Cases

Maria-Gabriella Baldarelli and Eleonora Cardillo

Abstract This chapter has the objective to answer to the research question: "What are the results deriving form the implementation of the specificities in EoC Firms starting from Stakeholder theory?" The research design is based on literature relative to the social and inclusive accounting perspective following Economy of Communion (EoC). The theoretical framework, that is implemented in this work, derives from the Stakeholder Theories and EoC in dialogue (Baldarelli & Rusconi, 2024). The empyrical analysis is based on two research cases, that are taking part of different sectors.

8.1 Introduction

This chapter has the objective to answer to the research question: "What are the results deriving form the implementation of the specificities in EoC Firms starting from Stakeholder theory?". The research design is based on literature relative to the results of theoretical dialogue between the Stakeholder Theories and EoC (Baldarelli & Rusconi, 2024).

It also refers to the systemic view of Rusconi (2019), that proposes a sort of "merger" between the Italian Systemic Economia Aziendale and Stakeholder Theory, enlarging the analysis of responsibility from the manager to each and every stakeholder. Thus is highlighting certain aspects of responsibility and communitarian elements that may derive from the dialogue with EoC.

The empirical analysis is based on two research cases taking part of diverse sectors, because is important to study the implementation of EoC specificities on service and on production Industries, that are based on Stakeholders Teories in different contexts.

M.-G. Baldarelli (✉)
University of Bologna, Bologna, Italy
e-mail: maria.baldarelli@unibo.it

E. Cardillo
University of Catania, Catania, Italy
e-mail: cardillo@unict.it

M. Baldarelli et al. (eds.), *Accounting and Accountability for Social Inclusion*, CSR, Sustainability, Ethics & Governance, https://doi.org/10.1007/978-3-032-09271-7_8

The general characteristics of EoC are described in the first section, with specific emphasis on what is relevant for the aim of this paper. In the second section methodology of survey of research cases are analyzed. In the third section the Ornella Insurance Agency case is presented and in the fourth section Cialotti Fishing case is describe. Discussion and conclusion are presented in Sect. 8.5, considering that EoC requires a profound change of mentality within the firm, towards the logic of gratuitousness, reciprocity and communion.

Therefore, a dialogue and reciprocal influence between the two perspectives examined can help either Stakeholders Theories to enlarge their perspective, in order to influence practical management behaviour towards personal communitarian and not only economic values, or EoC to apply the stakeholder theory of synergic cooperation between ethics and business to concrete govern in the best way, so as to investigate the advantages and dis-advantages of the best applications of EoC specifities.

Furthermore, some suggestions an be drawn for possible advancements in Firm literature.

After the Introduction, in the next section the EoC specificities literature are described.

8.2 EoC Specificities in Relationships with Stakeholders' Theories: Conceptual Framework

This section has the objective to focus on the debate suggested by Elms et al. (2010) which invite to deepen some research paths, in particular: "normative aspects of stakeholder theory … ethics in strategy as practice." (Elms et al., 2010, 412). So: "Furthermore, the pursuit of this convergent research agenda has potential to produce its own practical considerations. Not only have scholars that "shaped the fields of corporate strategy and organizational behavior… Joined the call to encourage and guide firms in taking on a larger role in society" (Margolis & Walsh, 2003, 270) " (Elms et al., 2010, 412).

Additionally, also from a religious perspective, the need to deepen the analysis of the dynamics linked to the tensions between conflicting interests, that could prevent development processes from being effective, is emphasized: "… in development work is the struggle to articulate shared interests. Stated in the broadest terms, it is difficult to imagine and articulate how the interests of people with social and legal control over material resources might fully align with the interests of those, who lack the material resources needed for social and economic development " (Moràn & Uelmen, 2020, 37).

In this sense: "The EoC requires an important and radical change in the business management. It promotes a commitment of owners (shareholders) to operate their businesses both for profit and for the benefit of society. They operate in normal market conditions with all its requirements, restrictions, and competition. However, the EoC businesses are the places where the culture of giving is executed in practice, where both profits and needs are shared in an atmosphere of mutual support and trust. Interpersonal relationships are based on mutual trust and create an organizational atmosphere in the company, in which each employee can find suitable conditions in the extent of performing his / her tasks and in building fraternal relations with collaborators (Biener, 2002; Gallagher & Buckeye, 2014)." (Grochmal, 2016, 5).

Another important reflection is interesting to introduce the EoC." In particular, in the trinitarian vision of inter-personal and social relationships, which is at the basis of the economy of communion, some people glimpse a new key of interpretation which could also enrich the understanding of economic interactions and therefore contribute towards going beyond the individualistic foundation that prevails today in the science of economics" (Lubich, 2020, 15, or.ed., 1991).

Gallagher (2020) gives an interesting interpretation of the matter. Indeed, the author bases his thoughts on a book by Brueggemann (2001). In these writings, Brueggemann deems the "prophetic imagination" as deriving from interior aspects that mature a vision of reality and culture which are more directed towards the common good and quality of life than the dominant culture of the moment which is instead mainly oriented towards the culture of individualism and individual advantage which generate "wastage". Brueggemann considers the Prophetic Imagination to come from a profound intrinsic thought that, may potentially be able to overturn, partially, the dominant culture in favor of the common good.

To clarify the different perspectives the macro and micro dimensions are synthesized (Tables 8.1 and 8.2 [ed or: 2 and 4 by Baldarelli & Rusconi, 2024]).

In order to try to make a synthesis for the implementation in real firms, the EoC specificities are underlined starting from: work communion, sharing the production process and the result of profits; reciprocity; selfishness and gratuity.

Table 8.1 EoC Macro and Micro dimensions—synthesis

	EoC
Macro	- Focus on poors and human dignity; attention to solve poor's problems, gratuity Baldarelli et al. (2015), Crivelli (2020), Frémeaux and Michelson (2017), Grochmal (2016), Gustafson and Harvey (2020) - the dynamics that put the person at the center, that transform society (to promote universal fraternity) that are involving EoC and consider in general the position of EoC between shareholders theory and stakeholders one moving toward a a "third way" between Marxism and Capitalism Baldarelli et al. (2015), Esteso-Blasco et al. (2021), Gallagher (2014, 2020), Harvery (2019), Linard (2003), McNerney (2020), Zamagni (2014)
Micro	Helical dynamic using the word of life Pillars: Dialogue, trust and reciprocity(based on gratuity) Argiolas (2017), Baldarelli and Del Baldo (2013, 2017), Bruni et al. (2008), Bruni and Héjj (2011), Gui and Sugden (2005), Pelligra (2010, 2011); Instruments, Rainbowscore Golin and Parolin (2003), Van Marrewijk (2003)

Source Baldarelli and Rusconi (2024, 255–256)

Table 8.2 Stakeholders theory and EoC– common dimension synthesis

	Common areas
Macro	Not separation thesys, work in communion, sharing production process and profit
Micro	link between ethics and business, reciprocity, selfishness, gratuity

Source Baldarelli and Rusconi (2024, 256)

Regarding this, certain aspects of the relevant literature concerning EoC, amongst which we find Harvey (2019, 2020) and Gallagher (2014), Baldarelli and Rusconi (2024).

The first area concerns the EoC project is work communion, sharing the production process and the result of profits, that are very important but there are some specific elements which are presented.

Indeed, theoretical thoughts by the EoC practice are generated, which derive out of the aim of concretely contributing to universal fraternity and trying to bring about efficacious improvements to the issue of poverty (Del Baldo & Baldarelli, 2019; Linard, 2003; Lubich, 2001).

With regard to this aspect, we may affirm that EoC is much more important as an "antidote" against strategic-reductivist interpretations of Stakeholders (Rusconi, 2019). Furthermore, EoC is pushing to a regeneration and active participation of the poors inside of the stakeholder map.

The stakeholder map is oriented to satisfying the same aims, whereas in EoC the relation dynamic leads to precisely identifying one's own needs by way of relations with the other: person and/or Firm. It is the relationship with the "other" which better clarifies one's own identity and one's own aims and objectives. Moreover, in EoC, besides the market negotiation, that is nevertheless important, enterprises act through dialogue and reciprocity, as later we will see.

In Economia Aziendale (Business Economics) the company is considered a system that is forever in unstable and dynamic balance (Amaduzzi, 1956); this implies, and is tied, to the concept of creative entrepreneurship talked about by Freeman et al. (2010). In the concept of creative entrepreneurship a continual innovation allows better facing the natural instability of company systems. EoC helps to enhance the person and relative relationships as much as possible and may contribute towards having the silent stakeholders come to the fore. Thus is allowing a more open and more collaborative vision even among Stakeholders.

The second area concerns reciprocity, which in EoC includes also the environment, taken in its broadest sense, wherein the company finds itself operating and which is a fundamental aspect for the management of the company, both the surrounding area and the ethical and value background from where it comes. In stakeholders' theories, even in the summary undertaken and thought of by Rusconi (2019), the problem that is posed is a partially different one, in that gratuity which also depends on the "ethical base" is not so important (Bruni & Sena, 2013).

In EoC, ethics is not external, but it creates an internal synergy with the mission, governance and accountability processes. Indeed, stakeholder theory may provide us with a possible direction in order to solve conflicts between company and environment. The solution consider the process of involvement of the same stakeholders, through also using an ethical approach to these conflicts.

Furthermore, the ethics and business balance is considered to be fundamental in EoC (Bruni & Uelmen, 2006). In the "stellar" Stakeholders perspective (Baldarelli et al., 2005), these aspects consider that which refers to the company, in EoC the focus is on: "che tutti siano uno" (*that all are one*) (Lubich, 2001) therefore, it comes from a common anthropological and ethical base. So, a "helical" path towards a greater fraternity can be seen (Gallagher, 2020), coupled with a growth in quality of dynamic and creative relations, which flows out more into the "taking care" than into the stake of the various stakeholders.

Therefore, the EoC proposes the activation of "bridges of fraternity", which as far as gratuity and selfishness are concerned are very important. Gratuity is important also in order to better understand EoC culture, which places it at the base of the process, while the Stakeholders perspective refers only to the ethical base.

Finally, EoC bases its activities and processes of gratuity on voluntary choices. Therefore, the "stake" alone is not sufficient (Harvey, 2019), which may be considered as a "right" or as an "interest" but it is integrated by the concept of "gift" (Gallagher, 2014).

This aspect accepts into the analysis even elements, which concern the common good, and particularly that of the human person, and, therefore, aspects which consider the value not just from an economics point of view.

Should we consider Stakeholders Theories as being not tied to the purely economic value, but also to the values as part of the stake (Rusconi, 2019), but EoC requires a broadening of the concept, which is at the bottom of the ethics vision of Stakeholders and on the basis of the EoC culture of giving (Grochmal, 2016).

In this sense, Gallagher (2020) considers the concept that every person may be involved within the EoC, in order to aim for the maximum "disinterested and free" involvement. In such a way, as to enlarge the concept of Stakeholders with a culture coming from EoC, rooting it in particular ethical principles that would involve also the 'silent' Stakeholder.

If 'stake' is a personal interest, it has nothing to do with 'gift', if, however, it is considered on a group level, it may be rescuable. The gift, upon which EoC is based, may widen the concept of stake and base it upon particularly "sound" ethical values, tied to the Social Doctrine of the Catholic Church on the Common Good (Argandona, 2011).

The meaning of stake in the EoC project is "translated" with the concept of "gift". The viewpoint is not of he who acts, and he who receives. The point of view is of the set of the two people: the giver and the receiver, within the logic of each being a gift for the other and, therefore, generating profound and sincere relations. Futhermore, that which characterises the activities of EoC is generating deep relations, which open up to a new dimension, which does not limit itself to collaboration in reciprocal interest but which includes the gift of unconditional love (Coda, 2010).

The dynamics generated in EoC, is that we are all brothers, so welcoming the other is a very important aspect, and being a "gift" for the other highlights a quality of relations even if they refer to the economic field.

The stakeholder map is oriented towards satisfying the same objectives. While in EoC, the relational dynamic leads to a more precise identification of one's own needs through the relationship with the other: whether person and/or company. It is the relationship is able to actively respond to the various forms of poverty: material, communitarian and ethical (Gustafson, 2020), helping to know and protect the distant stakeholders, the weakest and quietest, including the "discarded ones".

In religious terms, stakeholder theory takes possession of the "golden rule", which is present in every religion: "do onto others as you would have them do onto you". Therefore, it draws from a root of a religious nature, from which it derives, but it opens up to the consideration of every economic enterprise and circumstance, that have an approach diffferent from that religious one, but with which occasion to collaborate for objectives, for improvements in the quality of life may be found. Thoughts widen and broaden to understand areas of collaboration in the marketplace, whether understood as "invisible hand", according to Adam Smith, but also as a system of social relationships (Bruni & Zamagni, 2016).

The apparent alignment to the ideas of the "sister" enterprise or competitor enterprise may falsely make us think of an apparent fragility of the relationship where one of the two parties gives in to the other, because it is more amenable and compliant and more propense to operate. The economic theory, and company theory as well, have underlined the aspects of the quality of business relationships for a long time (Baldarelli, 2010; Gui & Sugden, 2005), and how defeat or situations of profound dfficulty lead to intensifying creativity and sharpening the methods of continuing to run the business with solutions that are often innovative and never thought of in the past.

The characteristics of these businesses make the development of networks which get wider and wider progressively: from a company to industrial EoC poles, to the network of incubators, which have developed to support and sustain start-ups, that have the characteristics of such businesses, to the definition of openness to actively taking part in initiatives like that one named: Economy of Francesco.

The EoC enterprises have inscribed the tension to feed relational networks of peculiar quality in their purpose and values (Baldarelli & Ceraulo, 2024). That generative activity derives out of a community that has made fraternity in its life style, they feel a living and essential part of society. "They are main actors, connected in a network with all the other vital forces of civil coexistence, change and development, promoting the common good – and it is within this dynamic that, as it is clear to everyone, the conditions needed for producing sustainable worth are created" (Davos—Manifesto, 2020).

After the specific aspects of EoC have been defined, in the following section we will present the empirical application to the research cases analysed.

8.3 Methodology of Empirical Research

The selection of firms as research cases considered the following criteria. The first is to taking part of The Economy of Communion Association (AIPEC) that has the objective to spread EoC culture and to pursue the Common good:" 4. The Association, in this regard, undertakes to: a) to preserve and enhance the reputation of the business class and of everyone in the civil society, contribute with their work and their professionalism to the common good" (AIPEC Ethics Code, p. 2; https://www.aipec.it). The second reason is the diversity of the sector and the third is the geographical location. The session intervews with the Firms was about one hour each one and they were specifically recorded and stored.

The choice to analyse the research case (Naumes & Naumes, 2006) Ornella Seca Insurance Agency is due to the specific activity that the Firm is implementing and the need to better understand the implementation of EoC specifities in service sector, in order to relate to Stakeholders and to answer to the research question.

The choice to analyse the research case (Naumes & Naumes, 2006) Cialotti and C. a family-owned firm of 42 years of fishing entrepreneurship, that is part of the "Fishermen house cooperative of Cesenatico" (Italy) is due to the need to better understand the implementation of EoC specifities in fishing sector, in order to answer the research question.

The second reason is that Cialotti firm is looking forward a more sustainable way to practice fishing. The company case is confirming to have a very sustainable activity in carrying out fishing activities in the Adriatic Sea (Cesenatico-FO), not using bottom trawl fishing systems. Moreover the company is activating fishing activities for blue fish and ecological methods of processing it.

In order to ensure rigor and reliability to the research case (Naumes & Naumes, 2006), the research protocol is presented below (Yin, 2018) (Table 8.3).

Methodology is involving some steps. The first step is about the preliminary on line meetings with the owners and members of the firms (Naumes & Naumes, 2006). The second step is about the definition and dialogue about quantitative and qualitative indicators. The tool is the questionnaire to submit to owners and staff of the firms (Golin & Parolin, 2003).

The third step consisted in the submission of questionnaires to company members, using Google docs and the elaboration of the results. Finally, the discussion with the owners of the two Firms was provided about the collected and elaborated results.

The timing involved two calendar years (2021–2022) and the phases of the research are summarized (Table 8.4).

After the methodology description in the next sub-section Ornella Seca research case is analysed.

Table 8.3 Ornella Seca Insurance Agency and Cialotti Roberto and C. Unlimited Family busisess: cases study research protocol

Introduction	Objectives: studying the specificities of EoC in two research cases
	Research question: "What are the results deriving from the implementation of the specificities in EoC Firms starting from Stakeholder theory?"
	Literature: EoC specificities deriving from the dialogue with Stakeholders' Theories
information gathering procedure	Semi-structured interviews from February to July 2021 lasting 1 h each one. Online meetings by Zoom, that had been recorded. Document analysis: Income statement 2019 and 2020, value added analysis. Videos stored on internet and local newspaper articles
Protocol questions	Enterprise description (history, mission, governance, strategy, accountability) and company performance to study: reciprocity; selfishness; gratuity; work in communion, sharing the production process and the result of the profits
Report framework	Quantitative and qualitative. Starting from April 2021 to September 2022, the income statements of the company were obtained to start the re-elaboration of added value produced and distributed according to the model prepared by the Study Group for the Social Report (http://www.gruppobilanciosociale.org/) which is particularly useful for reading the results of the company in a perspective of distribution of the wealth it produces, rather than in that of the production of profit. These re-elaborations required the preparation of matrices using the Excel Program and the preparation of the financial statement data and the initial summary graphs

Source Author's elaboration

Table 8.4 Research steps activities description

Timing	Firms involved	Referent	Instruments
(I) 2 months up to 1/03/ 2021	(1)Ornella Seca-Insurance agency (2)Cialotti & C	(1)Ornella Seca (2) Maurizio Cialotti	Two Online meetings (1 h.) Semi-structured interviews with questionnaire to know the firms Golin and Parolin (2003)
(II) 4 months / 30 June 2021	(1)Ornella Seca-Insurance agency (2)Cialotti & C	(1)Ornella Seca (2) Maurizio Cialotti	Two Online meetings (1h each one) Definition and dialogue about quantitative and qualitative indicators and measurements using questionnaire to submit to owners and staff of the firms Golin and Parolin (2003) and comparison with pre-existing models
(III) 4 months/Dec 2021 4 months / April 2022	(1)Ornella Seca-Insurance agency (2)Cialotti & C	(1)Ornella Seca (2) Maurizio Cialotti and other firms staff	-administration of questionnaires to firms members and discussion with the owners on the collected results -Financial statements analisys by Value Added ratios

Source Author' s elaboration

8.4 Work in Communion, Sharing the Production Process and the Result of Profits in: Ornella Seca Insurance Agency

In 1996, Mrs. Ornella Seca began working as an employee at the Fondiaria-Sai Agency in Lanciano in the life insurance sector. In 2001 you were entrusted with the role of general agent with a fixed-term contract until 2003. Contract was renewed later.

In 2004, at the request of the SAI Company, the Lanciano agency was joined by that of Vasto (in the South of Italy) creating a general partnership in which Seca held eighty per cent of the capital.

The mission of the Firm is to satisfy customers with a high quality and competent insurance service by putting the quality of the relationship first to achieve universal fraternity and working in communion (Baldarelli & Rusconi, 2024).

About the governance, the agency's staff is made up of 9 people in total, of which 7 employees and 2 collaborators are distributed in different territories of the South of Italy.

Ethics within insurance agencies is certainly a topic that is still not very widespread, Ornella was the first insurance agency in Italy that decided to apply the principles of the EoC, it is a project in which she strongly believes as she considers ethics a central element of the economy without which the market would become a place of speculation only. In the context of the EoC, insurance companies can play an important role by promoting an insurance model inspired by solidarity and social responsibility. This could include the creation of insurance programs that take into account the needs of local communities, with rates and policies that reflect values such as social justice and sustainability.

Furthermore, companies that adopt the EoC often try to involve their employees and the local community in business decisions, thus helping to build a sense of community and solidarity. This participatory approach can also be extended to the design and management of insurance programs. What differentiates Ornella's insurance agency from other agencies is precisely the ethics that accompany its actions, starting from the relationship with employees up to that with customers. The service offered by insurance agencies includes adequate training of staff that can generate trust in their customers and create lasting relationships over time, in this regard it is important to offer personalized solutions that are adequate to their needs. Over time, Ornella has focused on creating a work team made up of people who are always up to date on insurance and pension issues, ready to provide specialist advice and recommend personalized strategies with respect to the needs of each customer. The orientation towards continuous improvement is an ever-present theme within the agency, especially with regard to the administrative and commercial sectors, which, in order to keep up with market changes and meet customer needs, require continuous updates.

The entrepreneur cares a lot about the relationship with her collaborators, so much so that every month she plans a meeting with them in which they discuss and try to resolve any problems, sometimes finding extraordinary solutions.

The purpose of these meetings is also to achieve balance between the three human dimensions which, according to Ornella, are: the relational, spiritual and material dimensions. In this way there is the implementation of reciprocity in the logic of gift (Gallagher, 2014).

From 2007, and in the following years, the insurance world suffered a strong collapse which led to a very critical economic situation for insurance agencies, in particular Ornella's company was also affected. During a meeting Ornella explained the situation to her employees who, after countless discussions and clashes, proposed a solution: all the employees offered to reduce their working hours as much as was necessary to avoid firing the other two people.

The Firm is creating shared value (Graph 8.1).

The Value Added is distributed with 46% to employees to underline the importance that the firm is giving to work in communion and sharing production process and profit (Graph 8.1).

To complete the analysis the main results of the survey are showed below (Graphs 8.2, 8.3, 8.4, 8.5, 8.6, and 8.7).

As evidenced (Graphs 8.2 and 8.3), the firm is considered a place to improve both professional competences and human growth. Furthermore, It is underlining that

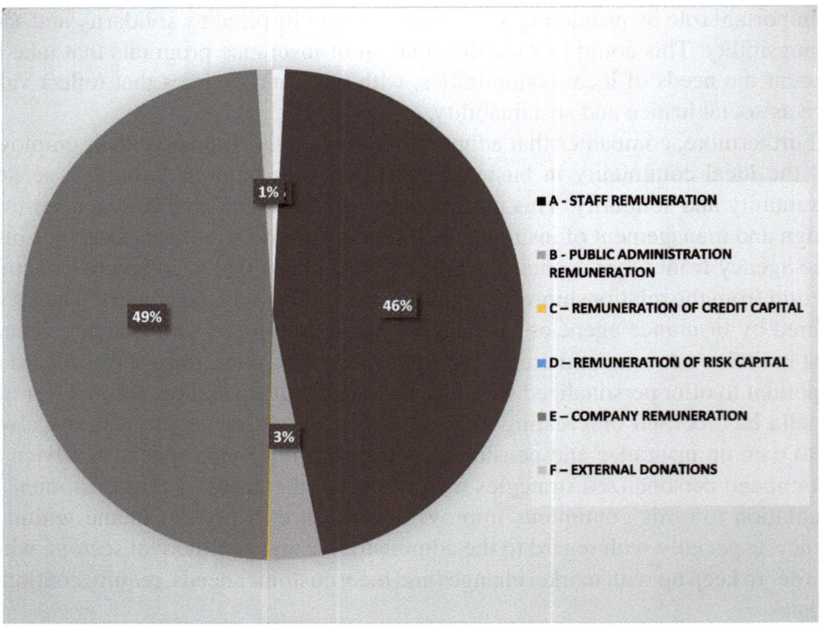

Graph 8.1 Value added distribution 2020- Ornella Seca

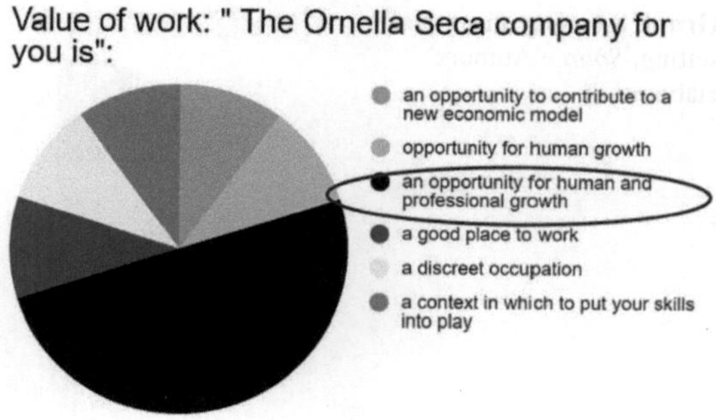

Graph 8.2 Value of work. *Source* Authors' elaboration

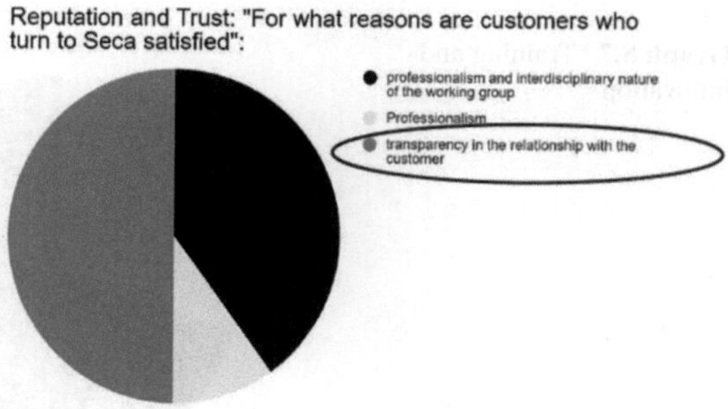

Graph 8.3 Reputation and trust

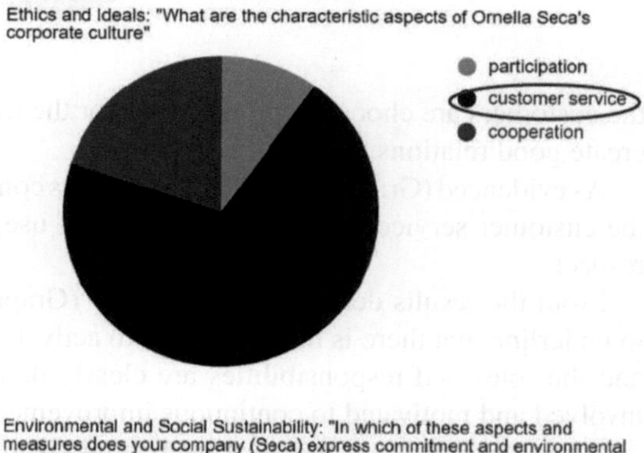

Graph 8.4 Ethics and Ideals. *Source* Authors' elaboration

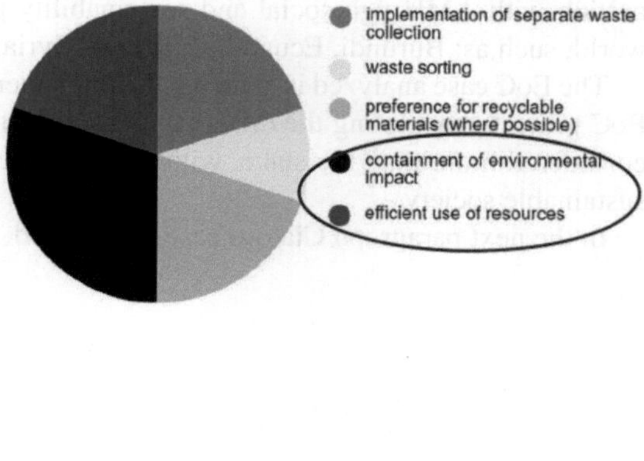

Graph 8.5 Environment and social sustainability

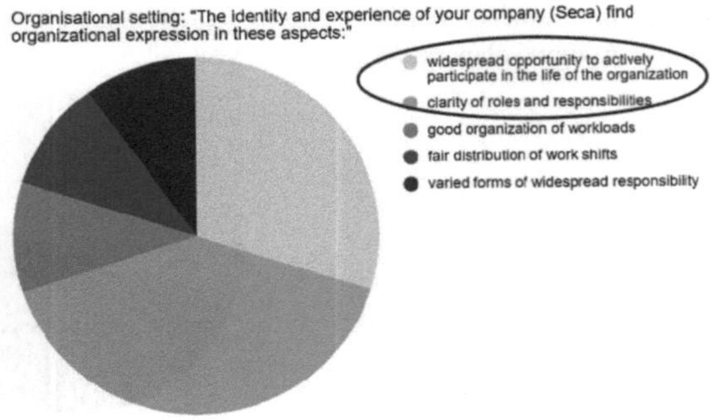

Graph 8.6 Organisational setting. *Source* Authors' elaboration

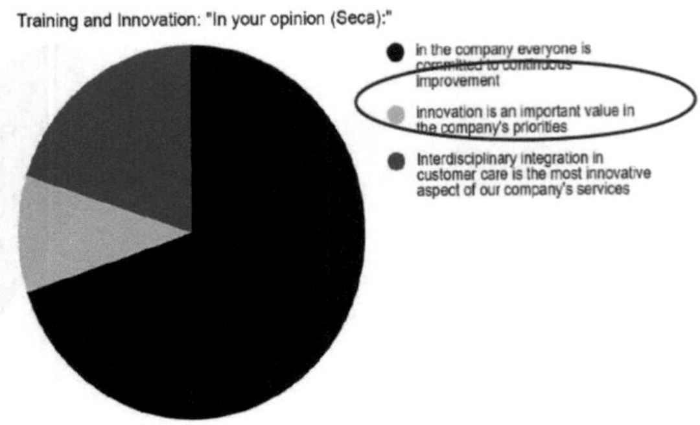

Graph 8.7 Training and innovation

the customers are choosing Ornella Seca for the transparency and the availability to create good relations.

As evidenced (Graphs 8.4 and 8.5) the firm is considering at the core of Its activities the customer service and there is an efficient use of resources with environmental respect.

From the results deriving by the survey (Graphs 8.6, 8.7 and 8.8) It is possible to underline that there is the possibility to actively participate to the life of the Firm and the roles and responsibilities are clearly defined. Furthermore, all people are involved and motivated to continuous improvements.

After the analysis of the most interesting results of the questionnaire, the collaboration with AMU ngo social and sustainability projects are financed all over the world, such as: Burundi, Ecuador, Cuba and Syria.

The EoC case analyzed is showing the implementation of the main specificities of EoC project considering the different difficult situation in which always people are considered more than the stake, with active participation and inclusion for a more sustainable society.

In the next paragraph Cialotti case is analyzed.

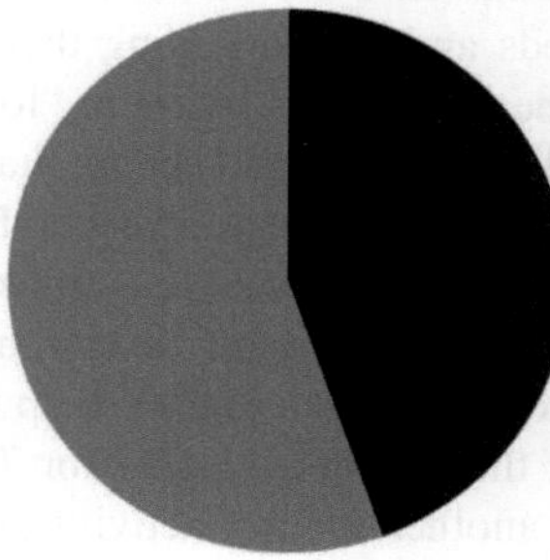

Graph 8.8 Internal commucation. *Source* Authors' elaboration

8.5 Work in Communion, Sharing the Production Process and the Result of Profits in: Cialotti Fishing Case

From the analysis of the research case, work in communion is the first feature that arises.

In fact, during the description of the dialogue among Stakeholders and EoC,the idea of the meaning of "stake" emerged and one of the most important assention are that EoC can contribute to anlarge the concept inserting the ethical basis and the concept of "gratuity" and gift. Reading the case following this idea It is possible to find both of them in different steps of the activities.

8.5.1 Work in Communion-First Step (More "Stake" than "Gift"?)

The firm had an important passage when the old owner of one boat wanted to stop his work. He wished that the boad had been managed by Cialotti and his present collegue that has completely different culture then the italian one. In the past Cialotti sustained bad experiences to be partner in managing both fishing and boat, so He didn' t accept immediately. In this first step at this stage the "stake" and selfish is prevailing. One year after, He asked to his collegue what to do about the offer of the boat management. His collegue accepted and Cialotti said: "we are put into play" (Int. 26th March 2021) and He decided to try again. In this passage there is the prevailing of "gift" that changed strategically the finshing activities involving not only one boat but contemporarly two boats.

After this choice, their work started to have different depth, i.e. from a predictable action to a way of working that takes into account the richness of the diversity of cultures. Some examples of the relationships among cultures had been about the way to manage money, work time and the strategic perspectives of the firm.

What had been written previously can be read as the implementation of the dynamic of communion. Especially living with the concept that the "other" is

Cialotti's "brother" (in this case the owner of the second boat). The first phase is "uderstanding" the needs and not forgetting them during the time is passing; the second phase is to "experiment" this living in "love" of brother(s) (about the daily fishing activities with the collegues and seeing that the different culture is requiring sacrifice, but become an enrichment to everybody). The third phase is communicating (asking to the collaborator what He is thinking about the management of the second boat). Finally the "gift of oneself" to start again, to risk but, at the same time, to have trust that the providence would have help them.

The management of the two boats lasted for 7 years and after that the collegue wanted to try to have another fishing activity and they shared profit. Today, his collegue has one of the largest boats in Cesenatico and Cialotti says:" I am very proud to have contributed to his success introducing him to fishing activities and donating all my experience". The last statement is again the implementation of "giving oneself" and enlarging the Stakeholders.

8.5.2 Work in Communion-Second Step (Human Dignity, Community)

The second step is about fishing activity paired with two boats with totally 9 workers and so there are the relationships to manage with the other partner (Cialotti wife) and with the other fishing boat. "The seeds of relationships sown every day make also your own economy and that of others go well". But inside of the cooperative, time by time, they lost the opportunity to discuss about personal problems but is more becoming an accounting service centre only, but people accept easily to collaborate for solidarity initiatives. In this second step even if there are conflicts, what matters is maintaining relationships that are base on ethical base of the consideration of each one as "brother" respecting dignity and working to create the community (Gustafson & Harvey, 2020). Moreover He said: "indeed the creation of deep inter-personal relationships and friendship collaboration, both during work activities and during daily life, have had a very positive impact on the economic result".

In this way they olso accept easily to take part to solidarity initiatives.

8.5.3 Work in Communion -Third Step (Altruism and Sharing the Production Process and the Result of Profits)

At the third step and in order to understand relational dynamics the stakeholders map members are presented: the sea, workers, public administration, firm ownerships, customers, Ecopesce, Fishermen house cooperative of Cesenatico -Italy; Association

"Tra il cielo e il mare" (between sky and sea) Cesenatico -Italy, AIPEC and AMU ngo.

To be part of EoC the Owner of the Firm experimented solidarity and the benefit to became part of a national and international EoC network. So, had been easier then understood in the daily activity the term: "Providence" by carrying out the activity of fisherman without excessive rational calculations but trusting in the sea (Graphs 8.9, 8.10, and 8.11).

There had been an increasing both of Value of production and value added.

About the distribution of the value added there is an increasing especially during Pandemic From the graphs highlighted, a significant percentage of the company's wealth distribution to staff emerges. This recalls and confirms the logic underlying EoC companies, that consider the person at the center of the firm. Furthermore, these companies consider, in some cases, the consolidation of the company to be very relevant.

Furthermore, the creation of deep relationships during fishing activities gives the opportunity to open people to solidarity for individual (He said; "widows and

Graph 8.9 Value of production. *Source* Authors' elaboration

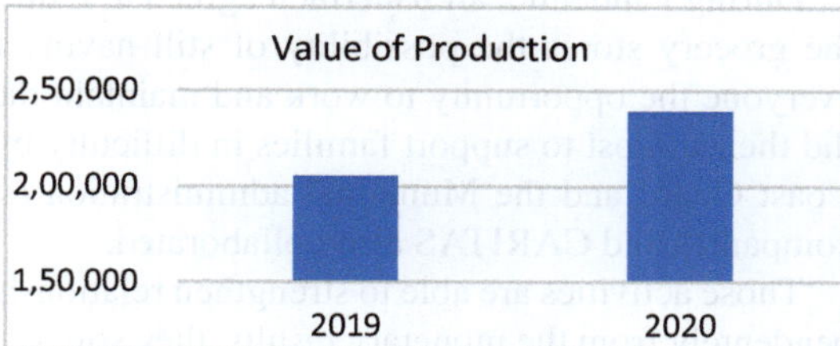

Graph 8.10 Net value added production

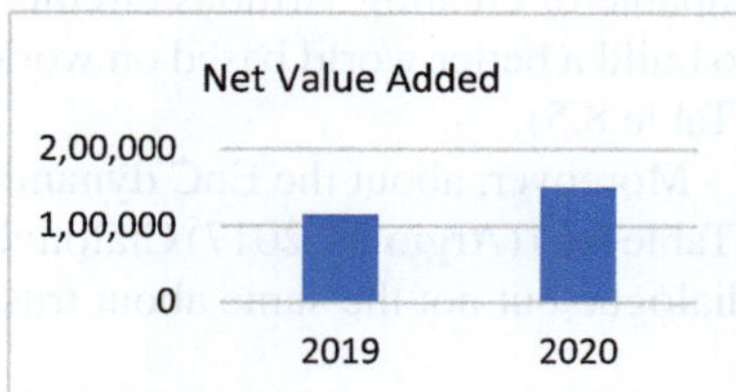

Graph 8.11 Distribution of the value added. *Source* Authors' elaboration

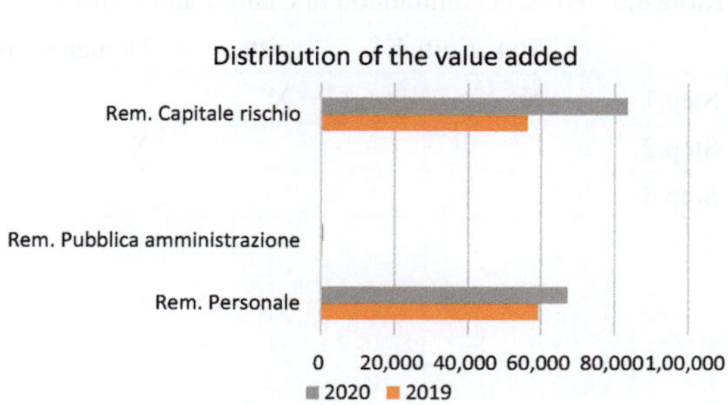

pensioners have the right to receive fish for free" (Int. 30/04)) and family needs (for example: spontaneous fundraisers for a colleague, who has urgent need for paid treatment that he cannot sustain).

Inside of EoC and AIPEC had been possible to share experiences to deep motivate the overcoming of selfish to embrace altruism (Esteso-Blasco et al., 2021) to drive the creation of solidarity networks more and more at large and this is very important dialogue with Stakeholders (Argandona, 2011; Rusconi, 2019).

Among the initiatives that Cialotti's firm promoted, some of them are described, such as the organization of charity dinners, from 200 to 1000 people, for solidarity initiatives: on 2002-in favor of the people of Kenya to build a school; on 2004 to send aid for the reconstruction after the Tsunamy in Thailand; on 2009 f to contribute to CARITAS to sustain families' needs at Cesenatico territory; on 2012 to finance cultural initiative of Gen-Fest; on 2012 to raise funds for the earthquake in central-northern Italy an the testimony of Cialotti: "*I feel I have to thank each and everyone, because, once again, the thought that I take away is the confirmation that only to love wins, especially if it requires sacrifice* "; on 2015 for Aleppo-Syria. Those solidarity activities consider the silent stakeholders.

During Pandemic, all fishermen agreed to reduce working hours, in order to give the grocery stores the possibility of still having the supply of fish and of giving everyone the opportunity to work and maintain their respective families. They also did their utmost to support families in difficulty by providing free fish to which the Coast Guard and the Municipal administration (social services), private transport companies and CARITAS also collaborated.

Those activities are able to strengthen relationships, to create fraternity and, independentely from the monetary results, they sow seeds for the common good (Argandona, 1998) involving different cultures, believing and not believing people, and capable of creating virtuous circuits that other territories imitate and so very useful to build a better world based on work in communion (Baldarelli & Del Baldo, 2017) (Table 8.5).

Moreover, about the EoC dynamic and the pillars: dialogue, trust and reciprocity (Table 8.6) (Argiolas, 2017) Cialotti Firm self evaluation is considering the best about dialogue but not the same about trust and reciprocity.

Table 8.5 Work in communion in Cialotti and C. firm

	Stake/selfish	gift	Human dignity/ community	altruism
Step 1	X	X		
Step 2			X	
Step 3				X

Table 8.6 Cialotti EoC pillars implementation

EoC pillars	From 1 to 10
Dialogue	10
Trust	5
Reciprocity	(Only some times) 9

8.6 Discussion and Conclusion

The chapter has the objective to answer to the research question: "What are the results deriving form the implementation of the specificities in EoC Firms starting from Stakeholder theory?".

In order to answer to the research question, literature about the EoC specificities based on dialogue with Stakeholders'Theories was presented. Among the micro and macro features, the Economy of Communion project originates from the beginning with a peculiar characteristic, which is that of "building bridges" and developing a way of being a company that cooperates in courageous reciprocity (Bruni & Uelmen, 2006) and in gratuitousness and that trying to "discover" the most depressing and difficult aspects of the economy to transform them into a gift.

The tension towards the achievement of the most distant and ambitious goal of universal brotherhood, that considers the EdC companies always oriented to "taking care" of the "waste" of the economy and to operate in the condition in which the company operates by examining the common good which is also the good of the individuals who work in it. This creates situations of different approaches and diversity of processes, that however have a single common thread, which is that of "equal" collaboration despite the different roles. This by activating processes and tools that are based on traditional ones but whose use becomes particular in the relational and social dynamics that are grafted into such circuits.

The two cases contribute to answer to the research question and in their analisys the results showed that is possible, but It is very difficult, to implement EoC specificities on the base of Stakeholders' theories.

Furthermore, one can also consider the orientation to go "beyond" the vector of objectives in the search for "terms", that can describe in the immanent what "immanent", by its very nature, is not, while the vector of objectives is framed within a very precise conceptual map.

The objectives of the companies of the EoC could be better expressed by the image of a range of various colors and meanings that, distinguishing themselves by culture, management and religion. EoC firms tend however, to find and try to give "hope" and resolve problematic situations of varying severity, as the first step of that objective that unifies them all to pursue the final objective that is the universal fraternity.

The two research cases underlined the implementation in their governance and the measurement of the pillars and aspect of communion for more inclusive society.

The limitations of the work are about the absence of critical discussion on the difficulties in conciling the reasons of Business with the reasons of ethics and Spirituality. That, because sometimes the prevalence of the economy of Business is able to create discrepancy with Ethics in EoC firms too. In other cases the prevalence of ethics and Spirituality is able to arise some difficulties about to fulfil the economic sustainability. But these temes are topics for further reflections and researches.

References

Amaduzzi, A. (1956). *Il sistema dell'impresa nelle condizioni prospettiche del suo equilibrio*. Signorelli.

Argandona, A. (2011). *Stakeholder Theory and Value Creation*. Iese Business School University of Navarra.

Argiolas, G. (2017). *Social management. Principles, governance and practice, CSR, sustainability, ethics & governance*. Springer.

Baldarelli, M. G., & Rusconi, G. (2024). Stakeholder theory(-ies) and economy of communion: Common features and specificities. *International Journal of Business Governance and Ethics*. https://doi.org/10.1504/IJBGE.2024.10064604.

Baldarelli, M. G., & Ceraulo, S. (2024). Collective value co-creation and accountability in purpose-driven place-based companies: Theory and practice. In M. Del Baldo, M. G. Baldarelli & E. Righini (Eds.), In *Place based approaches to sustainability volume II. Palgrave studies in sustainable business in association with future earth* (pp. 177–199). Palgrave Macmillan. https://doi.org/10.1007/978-3-031-41610-1_8

Baldarelli, M. G., Santi, M., & Signori, S. (2005). Chiacchierando con E. Freeman. Non Profit, 1, 225–238.

Baldarelli, M. G. (2010). An Italian note on social responsibility, catholic social teaching and the economy of communion. *Social and Environmental Accountability Journal*, April (ed or. 2006). Published on line 22 Nov. 2010, 7–12. https://doi.org/10.1080/0969160X.2006.9651748

Baldarelli, M. G., & Del Baldo, M. (2013). The question of pendulum between entrepreneurship and managerialism: New challenges in theory and in practice. *Ideas and Ideals (Idei i Idealy), 4*(18) T. 2, 63–74. ISSN: 2075-0862.

Baldarelli, M. G., & Del Baldo, M. (2017). From weak to strong CSR: The contribution of new categories in the account(ing) ability of EoC industrial parks, Springer International Publishing Switzerland 2017. In S. Vertigans, & S. O. Idowu (Eds.), *Corporate social responsibility, CSR, sustainability, ethics & governance*. https://doi.org/10.1007/978-3-319-35083-7_3

Baldarelli, M. G., Del Baldo, M., Ferrone, C. (2015). The relationships between CSR, good governance and accountability in the economy of communion (EoC) enterprises. In S. O. Idowu, C. S. Frederiksen, A. Y. Mermod, & M. E. J. Nielsen (Eds.), *Corporate social responsibility and governance: Practice and theory* (pp. 3–38). Springer.

Biener, H. (2002). *Economy of communion*. Paper presented at the world conference on religion and peace. Peace Education Standing Commission (PESC). Report 2001/2002. Retrieved May 12, 2012, from http://www.evrel.ewf.uni-erlangen.de/pesc/R2001-EoC.html

Brueggemann, W. (2001). *The prophetic imagination* (2nd ed.). Fortress press

Bruni, L., Gilli, M., & Pelligra, V. (2008). Reciprocity: Theories and facts (introduction to the special issue). *International Review of Economics, 55*(1–2), 1–12.

Bruni, L., & Héjj, T. (2011). The economy of communion. In L. Bouckaert, L. & Zsolnai (Eds.), *Handbook of spirituality and business*. Palgrave Macmillan. https://doi.org/10.1057/9780230321458_45

Bruni, L., & Sena, B. (Ed.). (2013). *The charismatic principle in Social life*. Routledege, N.Y.

Bruni, L., & Uelmen, A. J. (2006). Religious values and corporate decision making: The economy of communion project. *Journal of Corporate & Financial Law, 11*, 645–680.
Bruni, L., & Zamagni, S. (2016). *Civil economy. Another idea of market*. Agenda.
Coda, V. (2010). *Entrepreneurial values and strategic management. Essays in management theory*. Palgrave Macmillan.
Davos Manifesto. (2020). *The universal purpose of a company in the fourth industrial revolution*.
Del Baldo, M., & Baldarelli, M. G (2019). Serving the poor: The case of the EoC enterprise 'Mercurio Net. In L. Luk Bouckaert & S. C. Van Den Heuvel (Eds.), *Servant leadership, social entrepreneurship and the will to serve* (pp. 255–285) Spiritual Foundations and Business Applications. Palgrave Macmillan. https://doi.org/10.1007/978-3-030-29936-1_13
Elms, H., Brammer, S., Harris, J. D., & Phillips, R. A. (2010, July). New directions in strategic management and business ethics. *Business Ethics Quarterly, 20*(3). https://doi.org/10.5840/beq201020328
Esteso-Blasco, M. A, Marqués M. G., & Sapena J. (2021). Leadership in economy of communion companies. *Contribution to the Common Good through Innovation, Humanistic Management Journal, 6*(1), 77–101. https://doi.org/10.1007/s41463-020-00095-6
Frémeaux, S., & Michelson, G. (2017). The common good of the firm and humanistic management: Conscious capitalism and economy of communion. *Journal of Business Ethics, 145*, 701–709. https://doi.org/10.1007/s10551-016-3118-6
Freeman, R. E., Harrison, J. S., Wicks, A. C., Parmar, B. L., & De Colle, S. (2010). *Stakeholder theory: The state of the art*. Cambridge University Press.
Gallagher, J., & Buckeye, J. G. (2014). *Structures of grace: The business practices of the economy of communion*. New City Press.
Gallagher, J. (2014). Communion and profits: Thinking with the economy of communion about the purpose of business. *Revista Portuguesa de Filosofia, 70*(1), 9–27.
Gallagher, J. (2020). the economy of communion as an exercise of prophetic imagination. In A. Gustafson & C. Harvey (Eds.), *Business, faith, and the economy of communion, journal of religion & society-supplement series 22* (pp. 50–60).
Golin, E., & Parolin, G. (2003). *Per un'impresa a pi_u dimensioni. Strategie e bilancio secondo il metodo Rainbowscore*. Citta' Nuova.
Grochmal, S. (2016). Spirituality of unity in management—Economy of communion. *Cogent Business & Management, 3*(11), 1–18. https://doi.org/10.1080/23311975.2016.1140618
Gui, B., & Sugden, R. (2005). *Economics and social interactions: Accounting for interpersonal relations*. Cambridge University Press.
Gustafson, A. (2020). Practicing entrepreneurship as an agent of communion. *Journal of Jesuit Business Education*, 1–30. September 2 SKU: BUS-006970.
Harvey, C. (2019). *A person-centered theory of the firm: Learning from the economy of communion*. Presentation for International Vincentian Business Ethics Conference, Dublin Ireland 2019.
Harvey, C. (2020). Business, faith, and the economy of communion. *Journal of Religion & Society-Supplement Series, 22*(2020), 50–60.
Linard, K. T. (2003). Economy of communion: Systemic factors in the rise of a new entrepreneurship systems. *Research and Behavioral Science, 20*, 63–175, Published online in Wiley InterScience, https://doi.org/10.1002/sres.539
Lubich, C. H. (2001). *Economia di comunione. Storia e profezia*. Città Nuova.
Lubich, Ch. (2020). For an economy based on communion. *Journal of Religion & Society-Supplement Series, 22*, 12–15.
Margolis J. D., & Walsh, J. R. (2003). *Misery loves companies: Rethinking social initiativebs business*. University of Michigan@2003 by Johnson Graduate School, Cornell University. https://doi.org/0001-8392/03/4802-0268/$3.00
McNerney, J. (2020). The business of business. Recapturing a personalist perspective. *Journal of Religion & Society-Supplement Series 22*, 107–121
Moràn, J., & Uelmen, A. (2020). Pope Francis and the economy of communion. *Journal of Religion & Society-Supplement Series, 22*, 27–48.

Naumes, W., & Naumes, M. J. (2006). *The art and craft of case writing* (2nd ed.). M.E. Sharp.

Pelligra, V. (2010). Trust responsiveness. On the dynamics of fiduciary interactions. *The Journal of Socio-Economics, 39*, 653–660.

Pelligra, V. (2011). Intentions, trust and frames: Note on sociality and theory of games. *Review of Social Economy, 69*, 163–188.

Rusconi, G. (2019). Ethical firm system and stakeholder management theories: A possible convergence. *European Management Review, 16*(1), 147–166.

Van Marrewijk, M. (2003). Concepts and definitions of CSR and corporate sustainability: Between agency and communion. *Journal of Business Ethics, 44*, 95–105. https://doi.org/10.1023/A:1023331212247

Yin, R. K. (2018). *Case study research and applications: Design and methods*. Sage Publications.

Zamagni, S. (2014). The economy of communion project as a challenge to standard economic theory. *Revista Portuguesa de Filosofia, 70*(1), 44–60.

Maria-Gabriella Baldarelli , PhD, CPA, is Associate Professor of Accounting, at University of Bologna, Department of Management- Rimini Campus. Full professor availability. Envited professor at Sophia University Institute. SIDREA board member until 2018. She is a member of international scientific networks: the Centre for Social and Environmental Accounting Research (CSEAR) and the European Business Ethics Network (EBEN). Key-note Speaker 2nd International Conference on Economics, Business, Finance and Governance (ICEBFG) by Economics and Business Faculty of University of Bandar Lampung- Bali- Indonesia- Dic. 4-5, 2019. Research interests includes: accountability and gambling enterprises; corporate social responsibility; ethical, social and environmental accounting and accountability, sustainability in tourist enterprises; responsible and accessible tourism for blind people, economy of communion; gender accounting; accounting history, accounting education and Feminist Economics.

Eleonora Cardillo is Associate Professor of Business Economics—at the Department of Economics and Business of the University of Catania. She was Visiting Scholar at the CSEAR (Centre for social and environmental accounting research) School of Management of the University of St Andrews (Scotland) for the research project: "Study and analysis of the methodological and operational paths of environmental and social reporting in the evolution process of accounting information systems". Professor of Accounting and Financial Statements and Public accounting iin local administrations. She was Director and Scientific Coordinator of the Master in Accounting and Control in Local Authorities, organized by the Department of Economics and Business of the University of Catania. Her research topics are public accounting systems, performance measurement, socio-environmental reporting, social inclusion in tactile museums, sustainability and accountability.

Part III
Accounting and Accountability for Social Inclusion: Interdisciplinary Dialogues

Chapter 9
Multidimensional Model for Social Tagging of Environmental Investment Costs (STEIC)

Ninel Nesheva Kiosseva

Abstract Environmental (green) investments that promote environmental sustainability are often seen as the dominant tool for achieving sustainability goals. Environmental and social sustainability are linked. However, the lack of integration of social criteria in the evaluation process of these green investments limits the understanding of their impact by society. The idea of Social Tagging of Green Investments (STEIC) may appear as a promising method to overcome this shortcoming. This approach combines the environmental and social aspects of sustainability, creating a holistic framework for social evaluation of green investments. In this way, social tagging has the potential to increase transparency, accountability, trust of investors and the public, as well as be useful for the assessment of the activities of enterprises in the direction of sustainability. The present article proposes a multidimensional model of social tagging (STEIC) based on a structural equation model (SEM) that integrates observable and latent variables of social and environmental impact. It includes analysis through regression methods that assess the correlation between environmental performance and social impact, as well as the concept of social return on investment (SROI). This methodology allows for a more accurate assessment of the overall impact of environmental investments and their economic dimension.

9.1 Introduction

Green investments have long been viewed primarily through the prism of their environmental impact—reducing carbon emissions, improving energy efficiency and minimizing resource use. However, the academic literature increasingly emphasizes the importance of social aspects as an integral part of sustainability. Social tagging aims to bring these two aspects together, creating a model for transparently evaluating the social results of green investment spending.

N. N. Kiosseva (✉)
University of National and World Economy (UNWE), Sofia, Bulgaria
e-mail: ninel.kiosseva@unwe.bg

M. Baldarelli et al. (eds.), *Accounting and Accountability for Social Inclusion*, CSR, Sustainability, Ethics & Governance, https://doi.org/10.1007/978-3-032-09271-7_9

By environmental (green) investments we understand here all investment costs of enterprises (environmental investment costs of enterprises (EICE))—the costs necessary to reduce a selected set of environmental requirements for enterprises from IFRS S 1 and IFRS S 2 and ESRS.

The social effect to be tagged to the environmental investment costs also means social performance criteria from the specified standards.

This model is designed to integrate social considerations into green investment spending, similar to the budget's green marking system.

There are a number of serious practical reasons for developing this question (Lost in the green transition? Measurement and stylized facts 2024). In Commission Delegated Regulation (EU) 2023/2772 for supplementing Directive 2013/34/EU of the European Parliament and of the Council of 26 June 2013 (European Commission, 2013) through sustainability reporting standards, Art. 52 (a) of the Commission Delegated Regulation requires "*The action plan for the decarbonisation of production, may have a material negative impact on the enterprise's own workforce and lead to material risks due to severance benefits.*" This document also raises the concern that in its sustainability reports, as required by ESRS S1 AR 24 e), "*[...] an Enterprise should disclose how it interacts with individuals in its workforce and with workers' representatives regarding impacts on its own work force that may arise from the reduction of carbon emissions and the transition to greener and climate-neutral activities, in particular restructuring, job loss or creation, training and upskilling/reskilling, gender and social justice, and health and safety.*" (European Commission, 2023a, p. 1).

Whether these concerns, which are written into law, are justified, we aim to investigate in this research, through the created tagging methodology.

And one more important reason: In Art. 35 of Regulation (EU) 2020/852 of the European Parliament and of the Council of 18 June 2020 on the Establishment of a Framework to Facilitate Sustainable Investment, and Amending Regulation (EU) 2019/2088 clearly states that they **will not be recognized environmental activities, if basic social rights and principles are not respected**: "*Recalling the joint commitment of the European Parliament, the Council and the Commission to pursuing the principles enshrined in the European Pillar of Social Rights in support of sustainable and inclusive growth, and recognizing the relevance of international minimum human and labor rights and standards, compliance with minimum safeguards should be a condition for economic activities to qualify as environmentally sustainable. For that reason, economic activities should only qualify as environmentally sustainable where they are carried out in alignment with the OECD Guidelines for Multinational Enterprises and UN Guiding Principles on Business and Human Rights, including the declaration on Fundamental Principles and Rights at Work of the International Labor Organization (ILO), the eight fundamental conventions of the ILO and the International Bill of Human Rights. The fundamental conventions of the ILO define human and labor rights that undertakings should respect*" ((Regulation EU), 2020/852, 2020).

The main objectives of the study consist of developing a methodological approach and framework for social labeling of green investment costs, Evaluation of the relationship between environmental investment costs and social impact through SEM and regression analysis, calculation and application of SROI for assessing the social return on green investments (EICE).

The research questions in the article are: Does every environmental investment have a social projection and, if so, to what extent? How can social criteria be integrated into green investment evaluation (EICE) to assess their overall impact on sustainability? This question encapsulates the paper's focus on developing a social tagging model that integrates both environmental and social aspects to comprehensively assess the impact of green investments (EICE) on the social component of sustainability.

The research hypothesis to be investigated is: "Green investments (EICE) not only benefit the environment but also contribute positively to social dimensions or they do not contribute to social issues." The hypothesis is designed to be tested using modeling of structural equations (SEM), regression analysis and SROI calculations, in accordance with the methodologies described in the article.

Following this approach, the paper brings together theory, tools and methodology aimed at practical applications to propose a model that evaluates by labeling the social effectiveness of green investments (EICE).

9.2 Literature Review

This question is not directly present in the scientific literature, it is an author's idea inspired by the possibilities to integrate environmental and social aspects, using the Balanced System of Indicators and the marking of green budget expenditures.

A number of articles explore the possibilities of integrating environmental and social indicators using the BSC created by Kaplan and Norton (Kaplan & Norton, 2005) to evaluate the performance of organizations. Such studies have been published (Dias-Sardinha et al., 2007; Duman et al., 2018; Eifert & Julmi, 2019, 2022; Jassem et al., 2020; Kaplan & Ramanna, 2022; Khalid et al., 2019; Schaltegger & Wagner, 2010).

Green budgeting at the government level, which is the starting point for the Green Budgeting article, mainly focuses on categorizing and tracking government spending related to environmental goals. It is an administrative tool used in the budgeting process to ensure that funds are directed towards environmental protection and sustainability. This is a simpler, more administrative approach that involves labeling budget expenditures according to environmental criteria. It focuses primarily on environmental outcomes, although in some implementations it may include social dimensions (Blazey & Telong, 2022; Darvas & Wolff, 2022; OECD, 2021; Guariso et al., 2023; Pindiriri & Kwaramba, 2024). Guariso et al. even use artificial intelligence for tagging. But it inspires with its approach to the goal of improving transparency and accountability in the allocation of resources to achieve sustainable goals(European Commission, 2023b).

9.3 Methodology

The Social Tagging of Environmental Investment Costs (STEIC) model differs from the Balanced Scorecard (BSC) model developed by Kaplan and Norton. The BSC framework is a strategic planning and management system used to align business activities with an organization's vision and strategy.

The STEIC methodological framework relies on structural equation modeling (SEM) that combines latent and observed variables (Kline, 2023), regression analysis (Chatterjee & Hadi, 2006) and SROI (SROI Value Map—Social Value International, n.d.).

A structural equation modeling (SEM) approach is here tasked with assessing the social impact of green investments (EICE). SEM is a method used to test and evaluate causal relationships using a combination of data and qualitative causal assumptions. It is particularly useful for modeling complex relationships and evaluating model fit using goodness-of-fit indicators.

BSC is a strategic management and performance measurement system (Kaplan & Ramanna, 2022). Both approaches have their unique objectives and methodologies and can be used to assess organizational performance and sustainability.

The choice between structural equation modeling (SEM) and balanced scorecard (BSC) depends on the specific research objectives, data availability, and the nature of the relationships being investigated. Both models have their strengths and weaknesses. It is precisely because of these characteristics that we use the SEM model here.

The use of SEM allows analysis of the complex relationships between these variables, assessing both direct and indirect effects. This methodology is widely used for multivariate analyzes in the social and economic sciences (Kline, 2023).

Regression analysis and SROI are used to achieve another goal—theoretical justification of the possibility to assess the social contribution of green investment costs, looking for a causal relationship between investment costs and social indicators required by the European Social Sustainability Standards ESRS S1 and ESRS S2.

Model Limitations: The model currently relies on hypothetical data, which limits its real-world applicability. Real data is essential to validate the model assumptions and ensure its reliability. At the moment it is not possible to develop sectoral models, this is a future task. Different interpretations of social criteria in different regions and sectors can lead to inconsistencies in labelling. Future research should prioritize collecting data from actual green investment projects to increase the credibility of the model.

Table 9.1 Investment amounts in € for each initiative

Initiative	Total Costs (€)
Energy Efficiency Program	500,000
Training Programs	200,000
Waste Management	300,000

While SEM and regression analysis are appropriate for investigating causal relationships, the inclusion of qualitative data can provide a more comprehensive understanding of social impacts. Future research could explore mixed methods approaches to enrich the analysis.

Data on Green Investments (EICE) are illustrative and not based on actual case studies. We accept sample data because of our desire to provide an exemplary theoretical and conceptual model that can be easily used and supplemented according to the needs of enterprises, since this methodology has not yet been implemented.

Table 9.1 presents the investment amounts in € for each initiative as used in the analysis.

9.4 Multidimensional Model for Social Tagging of Environmental Investment Costs

9.4.1 Structural Equation Model (SEM) for Estimating the Social Contribution of Green Investments (EICE)

SEM is a fundamental method for building the social labeling model, which allows the assessment of the relationships between social and environmental indicators through a combination of latent and observable variables.

Here, we have identified latent variables from the set of IFRS S1, IFRS S2 and ESRS that we consider to be representative. In our selection, we adhere to the advice of Kaplan and Ramanna (2021) who suggest that social reports initially focus on issues on which there is a public consensus of importance and what constitutes "good or bad social outcomes, such as employee health and safety, eliminating the use of child and slave labor in supply chains."

Social impact

Environmental efficiency

Observed variables were defined in the same way. The data for the observed variables are based on the indicators provided in the material:

Environmental indicators: carbon emissions, energy efficiency, water usage, waste generation.

Social indicators: Labor practices, Supply chain ethics, Commitment to local communities, Protection of human rights.

The model includes:

Structural relationships between latent variables.
Coefficients for evaluating the impact of environmental indicators on social impact.
Evaluation criteria include:
Appropriate statistical indices.
Reliability and validity of latent variables.
Open source software The R Project for Statistical Computing was used as a tool for the analysis. (R: The R Project for Statistical Computing, n.d.). The operation of the software and its calculation methodology are given in the article by Fox (2006). Results of the SEM analysis are given in Table 9.2.

Analysis of SEM results:

The social impact of environmental investments (EICE) is strongly positively related to work practices ($\beta = 0.67, p < 0.01$), indicating a significant contribution to the sustainability of work ethics in general.
Environmental performance is negatively related to carbon emissions ($\beta = -0.72$, $p < 0.01$), highlighting the complexity of balancing emissions reduction efforts with efficiency improvements.
Environmental performance is positively related to waste management ($\beta = 0.53$, $p < 0.01$), indicating a significant impact of waste management practices on environmental performance.
The results highlight the key role of supply chain labor practices and ethics in improving social impact. Environmental efficiency is directly related to waste management, making it a priority area for interventions.
P-value < 0.05: All relationships are statistically significant.
This means that there is a strong evidence base for a relationship between the latent and observed variables.

Coefficient (beta β):

Positive values (0.67,0.45,0.530.67, 0.45, 0.530.67,0.45,0.53) indicate a positive relationship — when the latent variable increases, the observed variable also increases.
Negative value (−0.72) indicates an inverse relationship — when "Environmental efficiency" increases, "Carbon emissions, Water usage" decrease (Fig. 9.1).

9.5 Regression analysis

Regression analysis complements SEM by providing more precise quantitative estimates of the relationships between observed variables.

Table 9.2 Results of the SEM analysis

Latent variable	Observed variable	Coefficient (β)	P-value	Significance	Meaning
Social impact	Labor practices	0.67	< 0.01	Positive Highly significant **Strong Social Impact**	A one-unit increase in Labor Practices leads to a 0.67 unit increase in Social Impact
Social impact	Community engagement	0.45	< 0.05	Positive Significant **Moderate Social Impact**	A one-unit increase in Community Engagement leads to a 0.45 unit increase in Social Impact
Environmental efficiency	Carbon emissions	– 0.72	< 0.01	Negative Highly significant **Strong Social Impact**	Given the context of environmental benefits, The negative coefficient of – 0.72 indicates that as ecological efficiency improves, carbon emissions decrease, which is a positive outcome for the environment
Environmental efficiency	Waste management	0.53	< 0.01	Positive Highly significant **Strong Social Impact** t	A one-unit increase in Ecological Efficiency leads to a 0.53 unit increase in Waste Management

Strong positive relationship, highly significant ($p < 0.01$)
Moderate positive relationship, highly significant ($p < 0.01$)
Weak positive relationship, significant ($p < 0.05$)
Strong negative relationship, highly significant ($p < 0.01$)
Weak relationship, not significant ($p > = 0.05$)

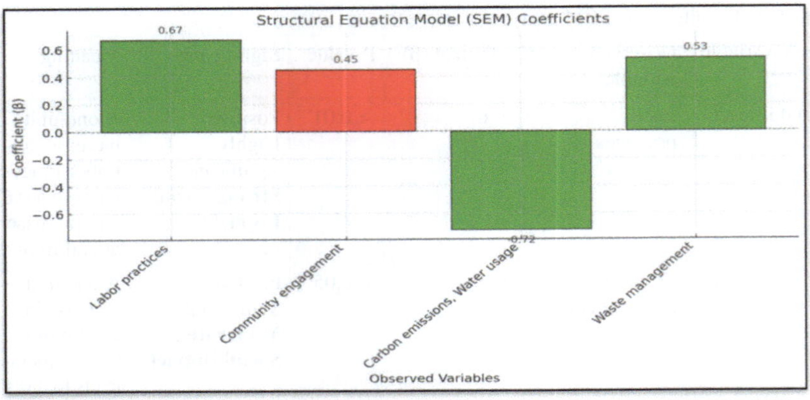

Fig. 9.1 Results of the SEM analysis

Procedure:

1. The data is also arbitrarily and hypothetically taken.

   Reduction of carbon emissions as an independent variable.
   Participation of local communities as a dependent variable.

2. Model:

The regression model is defined as:

$$Y = \beta_0 + \beta_1 X +$$

In our case:
Social Impact (Y) $= \beta_0 + \beta_1$ *Environmental Efficiency(X)* $+ \varepsilon$.
where:
Y: The dependent variable (in this case, "**social impact**").
X: The independent variable, predictor or explanatory variable (in this case, "**environmental efficiency**").
β_0: The intercept (the value of Y when $X = 0$).
β_1: The coefficient that measures the influence of X on Y, showing the change in Y for a one-unit increase in X.
ε: Error representing deviations of observed values from the predicted values (the difference between the observed and predicted values of Y).
Python software was used as a tool.

3. Interpretation of results:

A positive coefficient of β1 indicates a positive relationship between environmental performance and social impact.
The significance of the results is evaluated by p-values ($p < 0.05$) (Table 9.3).

Table 9.3 Results of the regression analysis

Independent variable	Dependent variable	Coefficient (β)	P-value	Significance	Meaning
Energy efficiency	Community involvement	0.34	< 0.05	Significant Moderate Social Return on Environmental Investment **Moderate Social Impact**	A one-unit increase in Energy Efficiency leads to a 0.34 unit increase in Community Participation
Waste management	Labor practices	0.56	< 0.01	Highly significant High Social Return on Environmental Investment **Strong Social Impact**	A one-unit increase in Waste Management leads to a 0.56 unit increase in Labor Practices
Emission reduction	Protection of human rights	0.21	0.12	Not significant Lower Social Return on Environmental Investment **Low Social Impact**	A one-unit increase in Carbon Emission Reduction leads to a 0.21 unit increase in Human Rights Protection, but this is not statistically significant

Lower social return on environmental investment—p-values ≥ 0.05. The relationship between environmental performance and social impact is not statistically significant.

Moderate social return on environmental investment- Regression coefficients with p-values < 0.05 but not highly significant (e.g., p-values close to 0.05). There is a statistically significant but moderate relationship between environmental performance and social impact.

High social return on environmental investment. Regression coefficients with highly significant p-values (e.g., $p < 0.01$). There is a strong and statistically significant relationship between environmental performance and social impact.

Analysis and interpretation of regression analysis results

Increased energy efficiency leads to greater community participation ($\beta = 0.34$), which highlights the social potential of these investments.

Waste management has a significant positive impact on work practices ($\beta = 0.56$), which shows the interrelationship between environmental and social aspects.

The significant relationship between EICE as energy efficiency and social outcomes as community engagement was confirmed.

9.6 Social Return on Investment (SROI)

SROI is an important tool for economic evaluation of social impact. This method translates social benefits into economic (monetary) values. (They may not be converted into monetary values.) Open access software was used for this purpose. (SROI Value Map—Social Value International, n.d.). SROI provides investors with quantitative data on the social impact of projects. Its results help to increase the credibility and accountability of green investments.

For sought results from the EICEs made, according to the data given in Table 9.1, we have assumed a hypothetical:

Improved healthcare in local communities.
Increased employment and qualification.
Social outcomes are monetized, and they are:
Health care: economic value of reduced medical care costs.
Employment: calculating the economic contribution of jobs created.

The total green investment, as shown at the beginning, is 100,000 Euro. Number of people affected amount of change per person and duration of effect (1 year) and results:

Improved air quality: 50,000 people benefit from cleaner air.
Reduced water pollution: 30,000 people benefit from cleaner water.
Protected biodiversity: 10,000 decares benefit from an improved ecosystem.
For the purposes of deriving SROI, we need to identify stakeholders. We assume that these are citizens as well as ecosystems, (according to the requirements of ESRS E4 Biodiversity and ecosystems. The result of green investments will lead to the presence of the following.
Citizens who benefit from cleaner air.
Citizens benefiting from cleaner water.
Ecosystems that benefit from improved biodiversity.
Results should be sought in—Improved air quality, Reduced water pollution, Protected biodiversity.

Impact measurement:

Improved air quality: We assume that each person benefits by €50. annually from cleaner air.
Reduced water pollution: We estimate that each person benefits €40 per year from cleaner water.
Protected biodiversity: We estimate that each hectare of land benefits €100 per year from an improved ecosystem.

SROI is calculated using the following formula:

$$SROI = \frac{Totaleconomicvalueofsocialbenefits}{Totalgreeninvestmentcosts}$$

Improved air quality: 50,000 people x €50 = €2,500,000
Reduced water pollution: 30,000 people x €40 = €1,200,000
Protected biodiversity: 10,000 decares x €100. = €1,000,000
Calculating Total SROI:
Total social value: €2,500,000 + €1,200,000 + €1,000,000 = €4,700,000
Total environmental investment €100,000.
SROI = €4,700,000 / €100,000 = 47

According to the calculations, the social return on the total environmental investment (SROI) is 47. This means that for every 1 BGN invested in the environmental project, a social value of 47 € is generated.

An example set of values to demonstrate the sectoral impact of green investments with key adopted indicators are the following:

1. Social results:

   Increased employment among local communities.
   Improved access to training and qualifications.
   Reduction of negative environmental impacts on health.

2. Quantitative Meters:

   Number of people affected by the investment (e.g. participants in training programs or workers in green projects).
   Average amount of change per person (for example, increased income or decreased health care costs).

3. Duration:

   For all projects, the duration of the effect is assumed to be 1 year (as indicated in the Table 9.4).

The high value of SROI for waste management (2.0) highlights the significant social and economic contribution of this initiative. Training programs also have a high SROI (1.75), indicating the importance of investment in human capital.

9.6.1 The Combination of Methods

SEM, regression analysis, and SROI work together to provide a multivariate assessment. SEM analyzes the complex relationships between latent and observed variables. Regression analysis provides a detailed quantitative relationship between environmental performance and social impact. SROI provides economic context to these relationships (Table 9.5).

SEM: The results highlight the key role of labor practices and supply chain ethics in improving social impact. Environmental efficiency is directly related to waste management, making it a priority area for interventions.

Table 9.4 Calculations for SROI

Item	Number of persons affected	Quantitative change man (€)	Total value of benefits (€)	Total expenses (€)	SROI	Interpretation	Meaning
Program for Energy Efficiency	500	1,400	700,000	500,000	1.4	Moderate social return **Moderate Social Impact**	For every € invested, there is a 1.4 € return in social benefits
Training programs	200	1,750	350,000	200,000	1.75	High social return **Strong Social Impact**	For every € invested, there is a 1.75 € return in social benefits
Waste management	300	2,000	600,000	300,000	2.0	High social return **Strong Social Impact**	For every € invested, there is a 1.75 € return in social benefits

Legend for Significance: Highly significant ($p < 0.01$), Significant ($p < 0.05$), Not significant ($p >= 0.05$)

Table 9.5 Summary of the results of the methods used

Methodology	General Conclusions
SEM	Strong dependence between social and environmental indicators
Regression analyses	Positive relationship between energy efficiency and social benefits
SROI	High social return for initiatives with an ecological focus

Regression analysis: The significant relationship between EICE as energy efficiency and social outcomes as community engagement was confirmed.

SROI: Data show that initiatives such as waste management (SROI = 2.0) and training programs (SROI = 1.75) generate high social returns, making them preferred for future investment.

9.6.2 *Tagging Designations*

EICEs that demonstrate a significant social impact can be labeled with positive labels **"Strong Social Impact"**. These labels can be used to highlight investments that contribute positively to both environmental sustainability and social well-being.

EICEs that show low and minimal social impact may be labeled with negative labels such as **"Low Social Impact"**.

These labels can be used to identify EICEs that may require improvement in both environmental and social dimensions.

EICEs that show a moderate social impact can be labeled with balanced labels such as "**Moderate Social Impact**".

These labels can be used to indicate investments that are making progress but still have space for improvement.

9.7 Discussions

The present analysis is based on random sampling and assumes that social outcomes are stable over time. It is recommended that future research expand the scope of the analysis by:

Inclusion of more industries and regions.

Long-term evaluation of the effectiveness of social tagging.

Development of more advanced models for quantitative assessment of combined social and environmental impacts.

With the integration of social branding, investments can not only support environmental sustainability, but also create significant social benefits, becoming a driving force for equitable sustainable development.

This study highlights the importance of integrating both environmental and social dimensions when assessing the sustainability of investments. Future research can continue to refine and validate this model, particularly in different cultural and economic contexts, to improve its applicability and reliability.

Future research could explore the scalability and adaptability of this approach across industries and regions, further refining its application in different contexts.

9.8 Conclusions

The multidimensional theoretical model highlights the multifaceted positive impact of environmental investments on social activities, promoting fair labor practices, enhancing community engagement, improving public health, creating employment opportunities and promoting social cohesion. By integrating social and environmental criteria into EICE labeling, stakeholders can better understand and improve the social outcomes of environmental investments, leading to more sustainable and equitable development. Investments in reducing carbon emissions have a multifaceted impact on social factors, as the article's analysis and related data show. This paper demonstrates the importance of an integrated approach in assessing the social impact of green investments through social branding. By applying structural equation modeling (SEM), regression analysis and social return on investment (SROI) calculations, a framework was created that combines environmental and social criteria and marks indices and significances of the impact of environmental investments on the social obligations of enterprises.

For companies, adopting social labeling can lead to improved social outcomes, aligning their environmental investments with broader sustainability goals. This enables them to identify and prioritize initiatives that offer both environmental benefits and social returns, thereby optimizing their contribution to sustainability.

In conclusion, it can be said that social labeling could be a tool to achieve social impact through environmentally friendly investments. By integrating social and environmental metrics, it provides a comprehensive assessment framework that guides companies towards more sustainable and socially responsible investment strategies.

References

Blazey, A., & Telong, M. (2022). Green budgeting: A way forward. *OECD Journal on Budgeting, 22/2*, https://doi.org/10.1787/dc7ac5a7-en

Chatterjee, S., & Hadi, A. S. (2006). *Regression analysis by example*. John Wiley & Sons.

Darvas, Z., & Wolff, G. B. (2022). A green fiscal pact for the EU: Increasing climate investments while consolidating budgets. *Climate Policy, 23*(4), 409–417. https://doi.org/10.1080/14693062.2022.2147893

Dias-Sardinha, I., Reijnders, L., & Antunes, P. (2007). Developing sustainability balanced scorecards for environmental services: A study of three large Portuguese companies. *Environmental Quality Management, 16*(4), 13–34. https://doi.org/10.1002/tqem.20139

Duman, G. M., Taskaynatan, M., Kongar, E., & Rosentrater, K. A. (2018). Integrating environmental and social sustainability into performance evaluation: A balanced scorecard-based grey-DANP approach for the food industry. *Frontiers in Nutrition, 5*. https://doi.org/10.3389/fnut.2018.00065

Eifert, A., & Julmi, C. (2022). Challenges and how to overcome them in the formulation and implementation process of a Sustainability Balanced Scorecard (SBSC). *Sustainability, 14*(22), 14816. https://doi.org/10.3390/su142214816

European Commission. (2013). Directive 2013/34/Eu of the European Parliament and of The Council of 26 June 2013 on the annual financial statements, consolidated financial statements and related reports of certain types of undertakings, amending Directive 2006/43/EC of the European Parliament and of the Council and repealing Council Directives 78/660/EEC and 83/349/EEC. (2013). *Official Journal of the European Union, European Commission*. https://eur-lex.europa.eu/legal-content/EN/TXT/PDF/?uri=CELEX:32013L0034

European Commission. (2023a). Commission delegated regulation (EU) 2023/2772 of 31 July 2023 supplementing directive 2013/34/EU of the European Parliament and of the council as regards sustainability reporting standards (Text with EEA relevance), *Official Journal of the European Union EN Series L*. Retrieved November 29, 2024, from https://eur-lex.Europa.eu/legal-content/EN/TXT/HTML/?uri=OJ:L_202302772

European Commission. (2023b, November 24). *Green budgeting in the EU, Economy and Finance*. https://economy-finance.ec.Europa.eu/economic-and-fiscal-governance/green-budgeting-eu_en

Fox, J. (2006). Teacher's corner: Structural equation modeling with the sem package in R. *Structural Equation Modeling a Multidisciplinary Journal, 13*(3), 465–486. https://doi.org/10.1207/s15328007sem1303_7

Guariso, D., Guerrero, O. A., & Castañeda, G. (2023). Automatic SDG budget tagging: Building public financial management capacity through natural language processing. *Data & Policy, 5*. https://doi.org/10.1017/dap.2023.28

Jassem, S., Zakaria, Z., & Azmi, A. C. (2020). Sustainability balanced scorecard architecture and environmental investment decision-making. *Foundations of Management, 12*(1), 193–210. https://doi.org/10.2478/fman-2020-0015

Kaplan, R. S., & Norton, D. P. (2005). The balanced scorecard: measures that drive performance. *Harvard Business Review, 70*, 71–79. https://images.template.net/wp-content/uploads/2016/04/11122659/balanced-scorecard-key-performance-indicators.pdf

Kaplan, R. S., & Ramanna, K. (2021). How to fix ESG reporting. *SSRN Electronic Journal*. https://doi.org/10.2139/ssrn.3900146

Kaplan, R. S., & Ramanna, K. (2022). *Reimagining the balanced scorecard for the ESG era (BSG Working Paper Series, Working Paper 22-005)*, 1–12. https://papers.ssrn.com/sol3/papers.cfm?abstract_id=3900146

Khalid, S., Beattie, C., Sands, J., & Hampson, V. (2019). Incorporating the environmental dimension into the balanced scorecard. *Meditari Accountancy Research, 27*(4), 652–674. https://doi.org/10.1108/medar-06-2018-0360

Kline, R. B. (2023). *Principles and practice of structural equation modeling*. Guilford Publications.

Lost in the green transition? Measurement and stylized facts. (2024). In *OECD Economics Department Working Papers*. https://doi.org/10.1787/dce1d5fe-en

OECD. (2021). *Green budget tagging*. https://doi.org/10.1787/fe7bfcc4-en

Pindiriri, C., & Kwaramba, M. (2024). Climate finance in developing countries: Green budget tagging and resource mobilization. *Climate Policy, 24*(7), 894–908. https://doi.org/10.1080/14693062.2024.2302325

R: The R Project for Statistical Computing. (n.d.). https://www.r-project.org/

Regulation (EU) 2020/852 of the European Parliament and of the Council of 18 June 2020 on the Establishment of a Framework to Facilitate Sustainable Investment and Amending Regulation (EU) 2019/2088 (Text with EEA relevance): L 198/13. (2020, June 22). *Official Journal of the European Union*. https://eur-lex.Europa.eu/legal-content/EN/TXT/HTML/?uri=CELEX:32020R0852

Schaltegger, S., & Wagner, M. (2010). Sustainable entrepreneurship and sustainability innovation: Categories and interactions. *Business Strategy and the Environment, 20*(4), 222–237. https://doi.org/10.1002/bse.682

SROI Value Map—Social Value International. (n.d.). Social value international. https://www.socialvalueint.org/sroi-value-map

Ninel Nesheva-Kiosseva Ninel Nesheva-Kiosseva holds a master's degree in History from Sofia University "St. Kliment Ohridski" and a master's degree in Accounting and Auditing from the University of National and World Economy, Sofia, Bulgaria. She holds a state-certified PhD and the academic rank of Associate Professor of Economics. She is an Associate Professor at the University of National and World Economy, Sofia, Institute of Economics and Politics. Her professional experience includes working as an independent auditor and consultant for small and medium-sized enterprises (SMEs). Dr. Nesheva-Kiosseva's international academic engagements have included visiting professorships at institutions such as the University of Bologna, the University of Aveiro, the University of Molise, and the University of Urbino, among others. Her research interests encompass a broad range of interdisciplinary topics, including institutional economics, economic theory and history, sustainable water and energy pricing, environmental and social performance in water supply companies, and ESG (Environmental, Social, and Governance) accounting and reporting. Her scholarly work demonstrates a dedicated effort to advancing knowledge at the intersection of economic systems and sustainability.

Chapter 10
Accounting and Economic Inclusion: Transparency, Innovation, and Social Impact in Marginalized Communities

Vedrana Stermasi

Abstract This chapter examines how accounting procedures can enhance the distribution of resources to underserved communities that have historically been shut out of the financial system, thereby promoting economic inclusion. Achieving sustainable development requires transparent and efficient resource management, especially in the context of global issues like unemployment, social exclusion, and poverty. It further explores how accounting can serve as a mechanism for tracking financial support and improving transparency in initiatives that aim to support communities facing systematic exclusion and inequality. Examples will be drawn from initiatives such as microcredit programs, small business development, and employment training in disadvantaged areas. The chapter emphasizes the importance of clear performance reporting and institutional responsibility for the outcomes of such initiatives. Accounting helps identify how resources are used, which strategies yield the most impact, and how they affect the lives of marginalized populations. This approach enables organizations to demonstrate responsibility toward stakeholders while pursuing the goals of poverty reduction and long-term social development. Accounting plays an important role in promoting both economic inclusion and social justice, not only as a financial management tool but also as a way to support fairer decision-making. By improving transparency and data accessibility, accounting can empower communities to better understand and influence how resources are used. The chapter argues that long-term growth and sustainability in marginalized communities depend on transparent and accountable resource management practices.

10.1 Introduction

Confronting global challenges such as unemployment, poverty, and social exclusion requires an integrated approach to address global issues that combine financial, social, and economic strategies (Idowu, 2014). Among these difficulties, disadvantaged

V. Stermasi (✉)
University of Dubrovnik, Dubrovnik, Croatia
e-mail: vstermasi@net.efzg.hr

M. Baldarelli et al. (eds.), *Accounting and Accountability for Social Inclusion*, CSR, Sustainability, Ethics & Governance, https://doi.org/10.1007/978-3-032-09271-7_10

groups, include individuals with limited access to healthcare, income, or formal banking services. These challenges include restricted access to financial resources, education, and job prospects. Therefore, their economic marginalization impedes sustainable development and adds to the escalation of structural inequality such as women in rural areas, migrants, etc. The most important issue in this situation is how to allocate resources to these communities and how to guarantee their efficient use—both non-financial (digital infrastructure, healthcare, education) and financial.

Accounting is not only a financial management tool, but also a powerful instrument for advancing economic inclusion. The ability to accurately record, track, and transparently report financial flows can increase accountability and ensure that resources are directed most effectively. Visibility refers to the recognition and acknowledgment of marginalized communities within the institutional financial system, while transparency is the open and understandable disclosure of how resources are allocated and what results they generate. Combining these two aspects can lead to more effective resource allocation and increased accountability toward those most at risk of exclusion. In such a manner, accounting will not only contribute to financial sustainability but also to creating a framework for the economic empowerment of marginalized communities, as seen in microfinance programs where financial tracking and transparent reporting are key to building trust and ensuring fair loan distribution. This chapter focuses on how accounting can support social progress through increased inclusion and transparency.

Recent events like digital transformation, pandemic, and climate change have significantly changed how people live and work. These changes have also made economic inclusion more urgent, especially for those without access to digital tools. Marginalized communities, often lacking access to education, basic infrastructure, and finance—are disproportionately affected. To address these obstacles, transparent financial reporting, stakeholder engagement, and equitable resource allocation are necessary. Finding methods for efficiently managing resources, like digital technologies, education, money, and infrastructure, that can support community growth and provide equitable access to economic opportunities is essential in such a setting. Access to microcredit, education, and even instruments for civic involvement can be provided by innovative financial technology like mobile banking and Internet platforms. By doing so, people from marginalized communities will get a chance for personal development, which will lead to their economic progress.

A major challenge lies in the lack of visibility, these communities are often absent from decision-making processes and official data. To ensure adequate allocation of resources and to monitor performance, there must be clear data on how funds are used, what goals are set, and which results are achieved. This chapter explores how financial reporting, performance tracking, and transparency can support economic inclusion for marginalized communities. It will also explore best practices to improve the current financial management system and promote fairer distribution.

The fact that underprivileged communities frequently represent unrealized potential for economic growth makes the topic crucial. Reducing poverty and promoting wider social and economic development are both possible by guaranteeing their inclusion in economic flows, such as access to employment, credit, investment, and public services. Proper implementation of accounting procedures can offer a framework for improved resource allocation, well-informed decision making and tracking of results. The chapter explores the role of accounting in promoting sustainable development and reducing inequality through the use of theoretical perspectives and practical case studies. It also considers how openness in reporting and institutional responsibility can foster trust among stakeholders. This chapter aims to show how transparent reporting, investment performance analysis and financial flow tracking can advance economic inclusion for marginalized communities. Furthermore, it explores systemic practices that promote efficient resource allocation and outlines potential reforms to enhance institutional management structures.

10.2 Literature Review and Conceptual Framework

This chapter builds on three interrelated areas: financial inclusion theory, sustainable development goals (SDGs), and critical accounting literature. Accounting is not treated solely as a technical or reporting function but as a social and institutional practice that can influence visibility, resource distribution, and inclusion (Burns & Jollands, 2020; Carnegie & Napier, 2012). The framework draws on practical tools such as Social Return on Investments (SROI), GRI guidelines, and development in digital finance to examine how transparency and accountability can lead to fairer outcomes. At the same time, it highlights that digital access alone does not guarantee genuine change. Issues like poor infrastructure, restrictive regulation, and limited financial literacy continue to block progress. By connecting academic research with examples from practice, the chapter offers a perspective on accounting that is both grounded in reality and focused on social outcomes.

10.2.1 Economic Inclusion and Sustainable Development

Economic inclusion refers to broader access to economic opportunities, while financial inclusion specifically focuses on access to financial services. It involves the removal of barriers that prevent individuals from fully engaging in economic activities. In this text, the focus is on financial inclusion as a key component of economic inclusion. Financial inclusion caused greater interest in the economic and finance literature which is defined as the access and use of financial services given its relevance as an important driver of economic growth. It is now seen as not only a tool for improving access to credit, but also as a key element of individual empowerment, local development, and gender equality. However, despite significant progress made in promoting financial inclusion globally, the lack of financial inclusion remains a major challenge (Taylor et al., 2024). Financial inclusion can drive economic development and reduce poverty by improving access to credit for both production and consumption, generating employment, developing human capital, and increasing income, assets, and household expenditure. Additionally, it mitigates exploitation by informal financial systems, fostering economic stability (Van & Nguyen, 2019). Financial inclusion, through microfinance, which provides services to communities that do not have access to traditional financial institutions, is a key factor that contributes to achieving and improving people's quality of life. One of the best examples of microcredit is the Grameen Bank (rural bank), which Muhammad Yunus founded in the late 1970s. As Yunus recounted, "*I wanted to see if I could make myself useful to people living in a remote village, even if just for a day*" (Yunus, 1999). The goal of the Grameen Bank is to reduce poverty by providing microcredit, or loans with small denominations. Yunus created the idea of microcredit when he started giving extremely poor Bangladeshis living in remote rural villages small loans, usually between $5 and $100. This approach proved to be extremely successful and became a model for similar initiatives around the world (Yunus, 1999). Although microfinance has made a strong impact in some regions, particularly in rural communities, many people still struggle to access traditional financial services. Applying for a loan usually requires paperwork, good credit, and access to a bank, things that are not available to everyone, especially in poorer or remote areas. In the past decade, different forms of finance have started appearing more frequently. Mobile apps, online lending, and platforms like Alipay or WeChat Pay let people send and receive money without needing a bank account. In China, millions now use their phones to do just that (Yao et al., 2018). These options do not just improve convenience, they allow people who have been left out for years to finally take part in a formal financial system. They also contribute to larger goals, like tackling poverty (SDG 1), improving work opportunities (SDG 8), and building infrastructure (SDG 9). Traditional finance still plays a role, but these tools are now letting people do things that were not possible for them before. Microfinance not only has a direct impact on the individual, but it will be able to contributes to broader economic development. True development requires individual socioeconomic progress, not just improvements at the macro level. Increased income, healthcare, better education, and other various aspects provide a better position for the individual and offer greater opportunities for prosperity and contribution to society. However, access alone is not sufficient. Without a system in place to monitor, report, and assess the use of financial support, resources risk being misallocated or underused. Reducing poverty in all of its dimensions is a challenge because it has a significant impact on people's opportunities and living standards. Fighting poverty is only one aspect of sustainable livelihoods, they also guarantee steady access to social infrastructure, health care, education, etc. To achieve sustainable livelihoods and raise people's standard of living, development should be inclusive and equitable (Niaz, 2022). Having access to financial services helps people deal with unforeseen costs and make investments in education or their businesses thereby promoting poverty reduction and economic resilience. Apart from these direct benefits financial inclusion is a key foundation for achieving Sustainable Development Goals (SDG). There are 17 sustainable development goals, and financial inclusion deals with three of them, such as no poverty (1), gender equality (5), and last but not least, reducing inequalities (10). These efforts collectively promote inclusive and fair economic growth (Klapper et al., 2016). However, achieving these goals is not without challenges. For example, the country that has remained steadfastly on the path of development despite internal political unrest and natural disasters is Bangladesh. Bangladesh's per capita income has increased by more than 130%. By that, the country has made steady progress in reducing poverty by more than half (Mazumred & Lu, 2015). While Bangladesh represents how financial inclusion can help fight poverty, the World Bank emphasizes that 1.7 billion adults globally still lack formal access to financial services (World Bank, 2017). By restricting access to financial resources and keeping marginalized communities from fully participating in economic activities, financial exclusion may prevent sustainable development, perpetuating inequality and poverty while negatively affecting environmental and social well-being (Yap et al., 2023). While this analysis focuses on financial inclusion's role in poverty, gender equality, and reducing inequalities, recent studies or other research also underscore its critical contribution to the other two SDGs such as ending hunger and promoting economic growth. Financial inclusion and sustainable development were once considered as two separate agendas, now, they are deeply intertwined. Initially, the focus of financial inclusion was exclusively tied to a specific number of sustainable development goals, such as reducing inequality, promoting gender equality, and reducing poverty. Financial inclusion includes now some additional SDGs, including zero hunger, good health and well-being, fostering economic growth, and supporting industry, innovation, and infrastructure (Ozili, 2022).

Since financial inclusion is no longer linked to just a few sustainable development goals, but also encompasses other goals, financial inclusion acts as a foundation for making progress in multiple areas of sustainable development. For instance, the role of financial inclusion and its ability to stimulate economic growth through the expansion of bank branches in rural areas, improved access to credit, and the mobilization of savings (Burgess & Pande, 2005). By removing credit restrictions on the impoverished and boosting their productive assets and productivity, financial deepening helps to reduce poverty (Inoue & Hamori, 2011).

Even though financial inclusion proves to be an important tool for achieving sustainable development goals and fostering economic growth, there are for sure some obstacles. Rural areas present unique challenges that restrict the implementation of financial inclusion initiatives. According to a European Parliament report, rural areas make up 83% of the total European territory, where around 137 million people live (30% of the European population). Rural areas face challenges such as limited access to services and infrastructure, limited transportation options, and a lack of high-speed broadband internet, drainage, water services, healthcare, childcare, training, and quality education (European Parliament, 2022).

Due to limited employment and educational opportunities, as well as unequal access to public services, women in rural areas face several social and economic obstacles (Bokan et al., 2024). A successful example of financial inclusion is the SEWA (Self-Employed Women's Association Bank in India. SEWA is a membership organization, its objective is to empower poor women working in the informal sector so they can achieve secure employment and self-reliance. Large numbers of members have increased their incomes through both the collective pressure that organizing allows them to exert and the creation of alternative employment opportunities.

They have gained access to markets through information campaigns, assistance with product improvement, and SEWA-run marketing services; they have gained access to services that are essential to a secure livelihood; and they have gained access to banking facilities that allow them both to save and borrow in small amounts and on reasonable terms and so gradually build up assets. (World Bank, 2007). The gender gap in employment rates is still greater in rural areas, even though the overall employment rate for women in the EU has improved. Compared to both men and women in urban and rural areas, women in rural areas have fewer job options (Copa-Cogeca, 2020). Rural women also frequently lack cultural, social, and economic capital, which further restricts their options. Increasing mobility and education could lead to positive changes for rural women, highlighting the significance of formal education and training as the first step toward empowerment (Šikić-Mićanović, 2012).

10.2.2 The Role of Accounting in Enhancing Transparency and Accountability

In addition to financial inclusion itself, accounting plays a crucial role in ensuring that available resources are used transparently and equitably. Accounting literature has evolved to emphasize its social dimension, where accountability and transparency are key to building stakeholder trust and improving outcomes in disadvantaged communities. This shift reflects the growing view that accounting should act in the public interest, especially by addressing the needs of vulnerable populations (Burns & Jollands, 2020). One of the most important factors in achieving economic inclusion-especially for communities often left behind—is maintaining open and accountable financial practices. According to Carnegie and Napier (2012), accounting should not be seen solely as a technical task, but as a social and institutional practice that shapes how resources are managed and decisions are made. Similarly, Lionzo (2012) emphasizes how accounting frameworks, even when technical in nature, carry embedded assumptions that influence how economic priorities are shaped and enacted. Without proper oversight, money meant to help local projects can get lost in the system or used inefficiently, making it harder to close economic gaps. Having strong investor backing can make a big difference. When large investors support a social project, they do more than just provide funding; they help make sure that financial decisions are handled responsibly and transparently. One of the most prominent examples of impact investing is the Acumen Fund. Acumen is an impact investment fund that focuses on low-income communities in developing nations. In the clean energy, agriculture, and healthcare industries, Acumen has a proven track record of finding and implementing equity investment opportunities that have an impact on the environment and livelihoods (Acumen n.d.). As Rodriguez Lopez et al. (2023) argue, transparency is not about the volume of available data, but the clarity with which financial realities are communicated to stakeholders. Building on this idea, Wong and Yap (2019) explain that when social projects gain the trust of institutional investors, they are more likely to secure funding, improve management, and enhance overall financial accountability. In this context, the focus should be on how clearly an organization can communicate its actual financial situation, rather than simply presenting large amounts of information. Effective and sustainable international aid between two countries or international organizations, within and across the humanitarian, development, and peacekeeping nexus, requires transparency and accountability. Moreover, this efficiency should be planned, taking into account the most vulnerable groups in society. Financial transparency is, therefore, not just a technical issue but also to ensure that aid reaches where it is most needed (Callies et al., 2021). Low accounting transparency, may raise investor concern about information asymmetry and increase perceived risk. Companies with lower levels of accounting transparency often respond to investor concerns by adopting more conservative accounting practices, aiming to reduce perceived information risks (Gyu et al., 2017). Since accounting transparency can lower risks and boost investor confidence, the question of what instruments are available to evaluate the sustainable long-term effects of financial decisions emerges. According to Dumay et al. (2010), the United Nations Sustainable Development Goals (SDGs) and the Global Reporting Initiatives have recently offered standardized metrics and frameworks for businesses thereby increasing financial transparency and accountability in reporting. Principles for Responsible Investments adopters currently manage assets worth nearly 60 trillion US dollars, about half of all global institutional assets. This shows the growing commitment of financial markets to social, environmental, and governance factors. On the other hand, mainstream investors' large-scale adoption of sustainable investment practices is still moving slowly (Friede et al., 2015).

The Social Return on Investment (SROI) framework offers a way to evaluate the broader social, environmental, and economic impact of projects and organizations. It aims to minimize inequality and environmental harm while improving overall well-being. SROI can focus on a specific aspect of an organization or evaluate its total impact. The analysis may be conducted internally or in collaboration with external researchers, depending on scope and capacity (Nicholls et al., 2012). For instance, Manetti et al. (2015) illustrate how SROI can be applied to assess the social return of investments in volunteer management, training, and local engagement strategies. Growing interest in such impact measurement tools is also reflected in regulatory developments. The Corporate Sustainability Reporting Directive (CSRD) mandates that businesses operating in the EU as well as certain non-EU entities, disclose detailed information on their social, environmental, and governance performance (European Commission, 2023). Frameworks such as GRI and the Corporate Sustainability Reporting Directive (CSRD) assist organizations aligning financial disclosure with sustainable development goals, especially those related to transparency, equity, and sustainability. This alignment represents a major step toward increased accountability in business financial practices (European Commission, 2023; Dumay et al., 2010). The use of advanced data analytics in sustainability reporting helps improve the reliability, clarity, and credibility of published information (Wanner & Janiesch, 2019). This further highlights the essential role that modern technologies play in strengthening accountability and transparency within accounting processes.

Taken together, these developments show that accounting is no longer just a technical tool for tracking numbers. As such, it has become a central discipline that supports responsible, evidence-based, and transparent decision-making in today's global context. This aligns with critical accounting perspectives that emphasize the importance of addressing social themes such as migration and inclusion, as discussed by Rubino and Veltri (2017).

10.2.3 Technology and Innovations in Accounting for Inclusive Growth

Today we are witnessing rapid development and innovation in the world of technology. Big data analytics, artificial intelligence (AI), and blockchain are digital technologies used in public sector accounting. These technologies are especially relevant in the public sector, where transparent and accountable financial reporting is essential for managing public funds and building trust among citizens. They also modernize accounting by streamlining financial reporting, improving verifiability, and aligning it with data-driven governance models. (Gunasilan n.d.). As Yawe and Prabhu (2015) highlight, financial innovation is a key influence on financial inclusion, and some significant policy issues are brought up by its connection to income and opportunity disparities. Because innovative tools, like mobile banking or microcredit, give low-income individuals access to services they were previously excluded from, financial innovation helps reduce income gaps and improve equal access to economic opportunities. This aligns with Galović's (2016) view of innovation ecosystems, where skills, finance, institutions, and digital infrastructure all interact to enable inclusive progress. Their realization depends on various factors, or rather, on their environment. Such an environment consists of a complex innovation system, an interconnected network of institutions, research infrastructure, policies, workforce skills, and financial entities (Galović, 2016). A vast array of financial operations carried out via digital platforms, such as digital payment systems, online banking, and mobile banking applications are collectively referred to as digital banking. Because of these advancements, banking services are no longer limited by location or time, enabling clients to manage accounts, conduct transactions, and access financial data whenever and wherever they choose (Nnaomah et al., 2024). Social inclusion and financial inclusion remain linked in the digital age. This situation reflects the broader digital divide, where lack of access to the internet, devices, or digital skills prevents certain groups from participating in modern financial systems. Due to geographical limitations or a lack of traditional banking infrastructure, mobile banking has had a notable impact on financial inclusion. It is important to ensure that marginalized communities are not excluded and unbanked from financial opportunities hence most personal financial transactions are switching from cash currency to digital transactions (Cnaan et al., 2021). Due to geographical limitations or either lack of traditional banking infrastructure, mobile banking has a notable impact on financial inclusion by providing banking services to people who previously did not have access (Nnaomah et al., 2024). To reduce financial exclusion, new information and communication technologies (ICTs) are essential. Online banking and ATM are examples of a few financial service technologies that lower bank operating costs and increase the possibility of providing financial services to everyone (Yawe & Prabhu, 2015). A situation where all societies can access cost-effective financial services or products online is known as "digital financial inclusion". The country's financial system can now serve a community from all walks of life, especially the impoverished and those who were previously financially excluded, thanks to digital financial inclusion (Tay et al., 2022). Digital banking solutions have given rural women entrepreneurs more financial management autonomy despite their lack of formal education. With the help of digital banking, women have broken down barriers and taken advantage of chances to improve their business endeavors and stabilize their incomes (Aryal, 2024). In these cases, accounting tools embedded in digital platforms enable better tracking of income, spending, and growth, empowering users to manage and report on their own micro-entrepreneurial activity. Expanding on accounting's contribution to financial inclusion, recent technological advances, such as artificial intelligence (AI) and blockchain, have altered accounting's contribution to this process in a substantial way. This means that accounting systems, when integrated with digital technologies, can help track how financial resources are used in underserved communities, ensuring that inclusion is not only about access but also about fair and transparent distribution. With finance and accounting at the forefront of its revolutionary capabilities, blockchain technology has rapidly evolved and been widely adopted across a variety of industries. Blockchain's transparency and immutability offer new possibilities for financial accountability, particularly in tracking aid flows, ESG metrics, and social impact investments. Blockchain's decentralized and impenetrable features can improve climate-related financial disclosures, investment strategies, and green financial products (Almadadha, 2024). Advanced cryptographic techniques are used by blockchain technology to protect data and transactions. To guarantee that only legitimate transactions are added to the blockchain, this technology relies on so-called consensus mechanisms, such as Proof of Work and Proof of Stake, which are used to validate and confirm the accuracy of each transaction (Rathore, 2019). These methods act as verification tools that help prevent fraud and ensure that only accurate and authorized transactions are recorded in the system. Still, the broader impact of these technologies on social equality remains a pressing concern. *"Inclusive development is a key policy priority since growth processes have not always helped lower-income groups"* (Paunov, 2013, p. 3). This claim emphasizes how important it is to use technological advancements to close the gap in wealth. However, these tools alone are not enough, without proper regulation, accessible infrastructure, and financial education, technology could deepen existing inequalities. Since innovation propels growth, its effects on income equality must be considered. Blockchain is one of the main technologies promoting financial transparency. It may lessen fraud, enhance auditing procedures, and build a more just financial system. Though blockchain and other financial technologies present encouraging prospects, their advantages ae not always shared equally. The OECD therefore asks a key question: "Do innovation and the resulting technological change necessarily lead to increased inequalities?" (Paunov, 2013, p. 3). This highlights the importance of using technological progress carefully. While digital tools can support financial inclusion, they cannot substitute for effective regulation, education, and infrastructure. Without these foundations, such tools risk exacerbating inequality rather than alleviating it. This is why the design of financial technologies must be responsive to the real needs of marginalized communities. When properly designed, they can help bridge the digital divide. For example, mobile banking and other fintech services like apps for saving, borrowing small amounts, or sending money, have made it easier for people without access to traditional banks to manage their finances. In addition to that, many ICT-based solutions, from health and education apps to tools supporting agriculture and small businesses—have made a real difference in the lives of low-income populations. However, regulatory frameworks that guarantee equitable and inclusive financial participation are just as important as technology access. Additionally, the OECD notes that ICTs did not widen the gap between leading and lagging firms, i.e. the evidence suggests no "digital divide" in terms of impacts. This realization emphasizes how important it is for financial institutions and policymakers to make sure that technology development advance financial inclusion rather than exacerbates inequality (Paunov, 2013). Traditional obstacles that frequently impede access to financial services, such as geographic distance and administrative expenses, have been lessened by digital banking services, e-payments, and alternative funding models. The financial sector has seen innovation as a result of this digital transformation, making services more accessible, inclusive, and suited to the unique requirements of disadvantaged groups in society (Wanof, 2023).

10.3 Conclusion

Significant progress has been made in how accounting can help advance economic inclusion, particularly through more equitable resource distribution, technological innovation, and transparent financial reporting. Case studies such as digital banking platforms, blockchain applications, and microfinance initiatives illustrate how these tools can improve access to financial services for underserved communities.

However, the continued existence of financial exclusion, due to limited digital access, complex financial systems, and a lack of targeted education, highlights that technology alone is not enough. Technology companies, financial institutions, and governments must work together to address these issues. Practical financial education, inclusive policy design, and internet infrastructure must all work together to guarantee that digital tools actually reach the people who need them the most.

Creating meaningful opportunities for participation in the economy is the core goal of financial inclusion, which goes beyond simply providing access to digital goods. A focus on underserved populations, accountability, and transparency must direct financial reform initiatives. A more inclusive financial system is not only desirable, it is achievable if inclusion remains a central priority in financial planning and development.

References

Acumen. (n.d.) About us. Retrieved February 10, 2025, from https://acumen.org/about-us/

Almadadha, R. (2024). Blockchain technology in financial accounting: Enhancing transparency, security, and ESG reporting. *Blockchain, 2*(3), 312–333. https://doi.org/10.3390/blockchains2030015

Aryal, A. (2024). From digital divide to digital empowerment: Transforming marginalized communities. *Social Innovations Journal, 25*. Retrieved February 09, 2025, from https://socialinnovationsjournal.com/index.php/sij/article/view/8242

Bokan, N., Bašić, E., & Tonković Bušljeta, A. (2024). Inequality on the rural-urban axis: women in rural areas: a European Perspective. *Hrvatski Geografski Glasnik, 86*(1), 23–45. https://doi.org/10.21861/HGG.2024.86.01.04

Burgess, R., & Pande, R. (2005). Do rural banks matter? Evidence from the Indian social banking experiment. *American Economic Review, 95*(3), 780–795. Retrieved January 19, 2025, from https://www.jstor.org/stable/4132740

Burns, J., & Jollands, S. (2020). Acting in the public interest: Accounting for the vulnerable. *Accounting and Business Research, 50*(5), 507–534. https://doi.org/10.1080/00014788.2020.1770940

Callies, L., Giorgis-Audrain, A., & Krizan, L. (2021). The importance of transparency, accountability and intersectionality in the implementation of international assistance. In A. Fitz-Gerald (Ed.), *Pandemic: 2021 global trends report* (pp. 53–57). Balsillie School of International Affairs. Retrieved February 07, 2025, from https://balsillieschool.ca/wp-content/uploads/2023/04/Graduate-Fellows-Anthology-2021-revised-A.pdf#page=59

Carnegie, G. D., & Napier, C. J. (2012). Accounting's past, present and future: The unifying power of history. *Accounting, Auditing & Accountability Journal, 25*(2), 328–369. https://doi.org/10.1108/09513571211198782

Cnaan, R. A., Scott, M. L., Heist, H. D., & Moodithaya, M. S. (2023). Financial inclusion in the digital age: Lessons from rural India. *Journal of Social Policy, 52*(3), 520–541. https://doi.org/10.1017/S0047279421000738

Copa-Cogeca. (2020). Reflection on the European Commission Communication on gender equality strategy. *Copa-Cogeca*. Retrieved February 07, 2025, from https://www.womenentrepreneurshipplatform.org/uploads/1/0/9/4/109400817/copa-cogeca_reflection_on_the_european_commission_communication_on_gender_equality_strategy.pdf

Dumay, J., Guthrie, J., & Farneti, F. (2010). Gri sustainability reporting guidelines for public and third sector organizations. *Public Management Review, 12*(4), 531–548. https://doi.org/10.1080/14719037.2010.496266

European Commission. (2023). *Corporate Sustainability Reporting Directive (CSRD)*. European Commission. Retrieved Februrary 07, 2025, from https://finance.ec.europa.eu/capital-markets-union-and-financial-markets/company-reporting-and-auditing/company-reporting/corporate-sustainability-reporting_en 07 February 2025.

European Parliament. (2022). Long-term vision for the EU's rural areas—Towards stronger, connected, resilient, and prosperous rural areas by 2040. *European Parliament*. Retrieved February 07, 2025, from https://www.europarl.europa.eu/doceo/document/A-9-2022-0269_HR.html Retrieved January 19, 2025.

Friede, G., Busch, T., & Bassen, A. (2015). ESG and financial performance: Aggregated evidence from more than 200 empirical studies. *Journal of Sustainable Finance & Investment, 5*(4), 210–233. https://doi.org/10.1080/20430795.2015.1118917

Galović, T. (2016). *Uvod u inovativnost poduzeća* (1st ed.). Ekonomski fakultet Sveučilišta u Rijeci. Retrieved February 09, 2025, from https://www.efri.uniri.hr/upload/tg.el._izd-uvod_u_inovativnost.pdf

Gunasilan, U. (n.d.). Digital transformation technologies reshaping financial reporting, transparency, and accountability in public sector organizations. *Accountancy Business and the Public Interest, 40*(7). ISSN: 1745-7718.

Gyu, D., Choi, K., Kim, S.-R., & Soo, R. H. (2017). Accounting transparency, business strategy, and accounting conservatism. *Korean Accounting Review, 42*(6), 31–79. https://doi.org/10.24056/KAR.2017.10.001

Idowu, A. (2014). Corporate social responsibility in Nigerian banking industry: When will the lip-service games end? *Journal of Economics and Sustainable Development, 5*(22), 21. https://doi.org/10.7176/JESD

Inoue, T., & Hamori, S. (2011). How has financial deepening affected poverty reduction in India? Empirical analysis using state-level panel data. *Applied Financial Economics, 22*(5), 395–408. https://doi.org/10.1080/09603107.2011.613764

Klapper, L., El-Zoghbi, M., & Hess J. (2016). *Achieving the sustainable development goals: The role of financial inclusion. CGAP*. Retrieved January 19, 2025, from https://www.cgap.org/sites/default/files/Working-Paper-Achieving-Sustainable-Development-Goals-Apr-2016_0.pdf

Lionzo, A. (2012). *Gli studi di Financial Accounting di matrice nordamericana.* FrancoAngeli. Retrieved April 09, 2025. https://francoangeli.it/Libro/Gli-studi-di-financial-accounting-di-matrice-nordamericana.-Fondamenti-epistemologici-e-percorsi-scientifici?Id=20951

Manetti, G., Belluci, M., Como, E., & Bagnoli, L. (2015). Investing in volunteering: Measuring social return of volunteer recruitment, training and management. *Voluntas: International Journal of Voluntary and Nonprofit Organizations, 26*, 2104–2129. https://doi.org/10.1007/s11266-014-9497-3

Mazumder, M. S. U., & Lu, W. (2015). What impact does microfinance have on rural livelihood? A comparison of governmental and non-governmental microfinance programs in Bangladesh. *World Development, 68*, 336–354. https://doi.org/10.1016/j.worlddev.2014.12.002

Niaz, M. U. (2022). Socio-economic development and sustainable development goals: A roadmap from vulnerability to sustainability through financial inclusion. *Economic Research—Ekonomska Istraživanja, 35*(1), 3243–3275. https://doi.org/10.1080/1331677X.2021.1989319

Nicholls, J., Lawlor, E., Neitzert, E., & Goodspeed, T. (2012). A guide to social return on investment. *The SROI Network*. Retrieved February 07, 2025, from https://socialvalueuk.org/resources/a-guide-to-social-return-on-investment-2012/

Nnaomah, U. I., Aderemi, S., Olutimehin, D. O., Orieno, O. H., & Ogundipe, D. O. (2024). Digital banking and financial inclusion: A review of practices in the USA and Nigeria. *Finance & Accounting Research Journal, 6*(3), 463–490. https://doi.org/10.51594/farj.v6i3.971

Ozili, P. K. (2022). Financial inclusion and sustainable development: An empirical association. *International Journal of Sustainable Development, 45*(3), 123–138. https://doi.org/10.1108/JMB-03-2022-0019

Paunov, C. (2013). *Innovation and inclusive development: A discussion of the main policy issue* (OECD Science, Technology and Industry Working Papers, 2013/01). https://doi.org/10.1787/5k4dd1rvsnjj-en

Rathore, B. (2019). Blockchain revolutionizing marketing: Harnessing the power of distributed ledgers for transparent, secure, and efficient marketing practies. *Internation Journal of New Media Studies, 6*(2), 34–42. Retrieved February 10, 2025 from https://www.ijnms.com/index.php/ijnms/article/view/123

Rodriguez Lopez, A., Rodriguez Gutierrez, G., & Rubio Martin, G.-M. (2023). Anti-corruption barriers financial transparency and accounting quality in political parties: Evidence from Spain. *Revista De Contabilidad-Spanish Accounting Review, 26*(1), 164–178. https://doi.org/10.6018/rcsar.464091

Rubino, F., & Veltri, S. (2017), La Critical Accounting a l'attenzione nei confronti delle tematiche sociali: il contributo agli studi di migrazione. *IPEJM*, 3, 1–16. https://www.impresaprogetto.it/sites/impresaprogetto.it/files/articles/ipejm-articolo_n_3_3-2017-rubino_veltri.pdf Retrieved 07, April 2025,

Tay, L. Y., Tai, H. T., & Tan, G.- S. (2022). Digital financial inclusion: A getaway to sustainable development. *Heliyon, 8*(6), e09766. https://doi.org/10.1016/j.heliyon.2022.e09766

Taylor, D., Osei-Tutu, F., & Awuye, I. S. (2024). The role of accounting standards in financial inclusion. *International Review of Financial Analysis, 96*(Part A), Article 103594. https://doi.org/10.1016/j.irfa.2024.103594

Šikić Mićanović, L. (2012). Skriveni Životi. Prilog antropologiji ruralnih žena. Institut društvenih znanosti Ivo Pilar, Zagreb. *Društvena istraživanja, 21*(4), 1041–1044. https://doi.org/10.5559/di.21.4.14

Van, D. T. T., & Nguyen, H. L. (2019). The impacts of financial inclusion on economic development: Cases in Asian-Pacific countries. *Comparative Economic Research, 22*(1), 1–16. https://doi.org/10.2478/cer-2019-0001

Wanner, J., & Janiesch, C. (2019). Big data analytics in sustainability reports: An analysis based on the perceived credibility of corporate published information. *Business Research, 12*(1), 143–173. https://doi.org/10.1007/s40685-019-0088-4

Wanof, M. I. (2023). Digital technology innovation in improving financial access for low-income communities. *Technology and Society Perspectives, 1*(1), 26–34. https://doi.org/10.61100/tacit.v1i1.35

Wong, M. C. S., & Yap, R. C. Y. (2019). Social impact investing for marginalized communities in Hong Kong: Cases and issues. *Sustainability, 11*(10), 2831. https://doi.org/10.3390/su11102831

World Bank. (2007). *India's Self-Employed Women's Association (SEWA): Empowerment through mobilization of poor women on a large scale. World Bank.* Retrieved February 10, 2025, from https://documents.worldbank.org/pt/publication/documents-reports/documentdetail/692491468771277275

World Bank. (2017). *The global Findex Database 2017: Measuring financial inclusion and the Fintech revolution. World Bank.* Retrieved January 19, 2025, from https://documents1.worldbank.org/curated/en/099650005162214653/pdf/P16477001277440f10b8080dc6f51daf2dc.pdf

Yao, M., He, D., Xianrong, Z., & Xiaobo, X. (2018). Impact of payment technology innovations on the traditional financial industry: A focus on China. *Technological Forecasting and Social Change, 135*, 199–207. https://doi.org/10.1016/j.techfore.2017.12.023

Yap, S., Lee, H. S., & Liew, P. X. (2023). The role of financial inclusion in achieving finance-related sustainable development goals (SDGs): A cross-country analysis. *Economic Researh-Ekonomska Istraživnja, 36*(3), 2212028. https://doi.org/10.1080/1331677X.2023.2212028

Yawe, B. L., & Prabhu, J. (2015). Innovation and financial inclusion: A review of the literature. *Journal of Payments Strategy & System, Henry Stewart Publications, 9*(3), 215–228. School of Economics, Makerere University & Judge Business School, University of Cambridge. https://doi.org/10.69554/SXTJ4645

Yunus, M. (1999). *Banker to the poor: Micro-Lendind and the battle against world poverty.* PublicAffairs. Retrieved February 10, 2025, from https://journals.sagepub.com/doi/abs/10.1177/0486613405285433?journalCode=rrpa

Vedrana Stermasi is PhD candidate at the University of Dubrovnik, Croatia. Holds a Master's degree in Tourism Economics and Management from the University of Bologna. Currently serves as a guest lecturer at Libertas University in Dubrovnik. Research interests include tourism management, sustainable development, and the reconciliation of professional and personal life in the tourism industry. Living in a rural island setting, she draws inspiration from the unique dynamics of small communities, where tourism is both an opportunity and a challenge. This environment fuels her passion for exploring responsible tourism models that balance economic growth with local identity and sustainability. She has actively participated in academic and industry discussions, including the 6th International Congress on Rural Tourism 2024, and Women in Tourism Split 2023. Her Latest publication is; Is the Reconciliation of Career and Personal/Family life Possible? Example of DMO Managers in Croatia.

Chapter 11
Developing Sustainability Reporting in the Pioneer Case Study of Beach Establishments in Italy: First Results

Maria-Gabriella Baldarelli and Macarena Paz Velasco Rosales

Abstract The chapter has the objective to describe the process of implementation of the first sustainable report for beach establishments in Italy, using GRI standards especially focusing on human resources indicators. The interdisciplinary literature perspective is using Neo-Institutional theory framework about sustainability reporting process implementation in territories. The empirical research considers one of most important hospitality territories in Italy: Rimini. The results of the research cases are used to focus on the main topics, that are necessary to combine the GRI model with the measurement and disclosure of inclusion practices.

11.1 Introduction

In the present state of art, the process of "standardization" of Social, Environmental and Sustainability Reporting is considered the main solution to the level of credibility of it. Some examples are the different processes and results of "Standardization" that are facing the problem.

The first is about the CSRD (Corporate Sustainability Reporting Directive, Directive (EU) 2022/2464) that is introducing mandatory sustainability reporting for a wide range of Firms in the EU and It is demanding the publication of information in the annual financial report and not in a distinct document.

The second is about the ESRS (European Sustainability Reporting Standards), that consist of standards by which the CSRD is applied and They are settled by EFRAG (European Financial Reporting Advisory Group), they provide the specific framework for what and how to report. European Sustainability Reporting Standards (ESRS) (Moscariello & Pizzo, 2024).

M.-G. Baldarelli (✉) · M. P. V. Rosales
University of Bologna, Bologna, Italy
e-mail: maria.baldarelli@unibo.it

M. P. V. Rosales
e-mail: macarenapaz.velasco@unibo.it

M. Baldarelli et al. (eds.), *Accounting and Accountability for Social Inclusion*, CSR, Sustainability, Ethics & Governance, https://doi.org/10.1007/978-3-032-09271-7_11

The focus on GRI (De Villiers et al., 2022) is very important to implement one model, that was applied by the end of nineties and so has several years of experience.

The research design, in order to read the process of implementation of GRI model, is based on neo-institutional theory (Di Maggio & Powell, 1991) and especially the use of this framework for Sustainability Reporting (Bebbington et al., 2009; Larrinaga-Gonzàlez, 2007).

Additionally, In previous works (Baldarelli, 2017) some drivers about the implementation of neo-institutional theory in territories have been analyzed and especially in respect of the territory of Rimini. This chapter is a good occasion to continue to answer to the research question(s) that emerged at the end of the previous research. Among them: "One doubt is that only by people is it possible to change and so why Rimini? Because there are special people? And which characteristic must these people have to be "special" or is it so simple; that the open mind and attention to the world is able to create a "virtuous- circle "? The reply is in following research steps" (Baldarelli, 2017, pp. XII–151). The chapter has the objective to continue the analysis to give some answers to the reach questions underlined above.

The research cases are focusing on beach establishments (also named: *bagni*), that are intrinsically linked to beach tourism in the Italian Riviera (Pommier & Engel, 2021). Traditionally family-owned, most of these organizations take pride in their long heritage linked to tourism development in the cities or towns where they belong. In an attempt to protect and promote micro and small business investments in coastal regions, Italian legislation allowed for the automatic renewal of beach establishment concessions, enabling family-owned businesses to operate through generations.

Several issues have arisen regarding this concessions model: on the one hand, it has been argued that it discourages competition, and on the other, established concessional payments have been considered low in relation to the business's profitability (Di Lascio, 2022).

In 2006, the Bolkstein Directive was introduced in the European Union. This set of guidelines aims to promote service competition across the EU states by reducing trade barriers and regulating the country's discretion in granting business operation authorizations, directly affecting beach establishment concessions. Several attempts have been made by the Italian Government to comply, repeatedly failing and extending concession renewals; the latest one is set to last until 2027.

Public opinion also shapes the circumstances, fueling negative perceptions of the *bagni* through mainstream and social media; confrontations on-site between clients and establishment owners are reported every summer.

Under this scenario, beach establishments face extreme uncertainty; not only have they invested in infrastructure, furniture, and tools, but they have also allocated resources to equipment, employee training, and facility improvements. They have also built upon differentiating services to appeal to diverse clients and develop their brand identities. Additionally, beach establishments face increasingly strict European regulations regarding environmental sustainability and social responsibility, further complicating the scenario.

Previous research has demonstrated that sustainability reporting and stakeholder engagement can have positive modulating outcomes on clients (Berezan et al.,

2013; Solis-Radilla et al., 2019) and enhance organizational reputation (Crossley et al., 2021). Strengthening social and environmental accountability and improving stakeholder relationships can also drive political support (Botero & Zielinski, 2020), underlining the benefits of proactively implementing voluntary Sustainable Reporting practices and supporting the progress of this innovative project that offers practical guidance for Rimini's, and Italian, beach establishments as they aim to improve their operations, preparing for upcoming regulatory changes.

11.2 Theoretical Framework: Neo-Institutional Theory and Sustainability Reporting

Literature is investigating the reasons why some firms assume Social, Environmental and Sustainability Reporting (SR), and what drivers occur in the external (societal) and inside firm) environment for reporting (Adams, 2002; Solomon & Lewis, 2002). Numerous scholars underline that the reasons for social/environmental/sustainability exposures are primarily due to external "shocks" (Laughlin, 1991; Larrinaga-Gonzalez & Bebbington, 2001). Other hypotheses underlines that there are several factors that drive firms to make and issue sustainability reporting (Campbell, 2000; Gray & Bebbington, 2000, 2001). Among Other contributions Larrinaga-Gonzàlez (2007) and Bebbington et al. (2009) have implemented the neo-institutionalist theories (Di Maggio & Powell, 1991) as a theoretical framework to explain the standardisation of Sustainability Reporting and to recognise the drivers of institutional transformation.

Institutional literature underline the institutional stability and inertia (DiMaggio & Powell, 1983) and that institutionalization pushes to homogenization of organizations. This process is named "isomorphism"and derives from the necessity for organizations to meet the environmental, social and sustainable expectations that increase reputation and legitimacy and that increase their business success Isomorphism emerges by way of three mechanisms: coercive, normative and mimetic (DiMaggio & Powell, 1983) and Scott (1995) sustained that legitimacy is supported by three pillars: regulative, normative and cognitive (Table 11.1).

Sustainability Reporting is the result of a mixture of these three mechanisms, taking different weights in different contexts. Larrinaga-Gonzàlez (2007) hinted that sustainability disclosure is becoming more and more institutionalized and may be the outcome of more general sustainability awareness being institutionalized in some settings, rather than a such institutionalised practice in its own right.

Furthermore, in recent decades, the accounting discipline has increasingly evolved in response to global shifts towards sustainability and corporate transparency, emphasizing a broader scope of organizational accountability beyond financial performance alone (Carnegie, 2022; Cooper et al., 2005; Gray, 2002; Gray et al., 2014), becoming a fundamental instrument for Corporate Social Responsibility (CSR) and stakeholder communication.

Table 11.1 Mechanisms/Structures of institutionalization

Di Maggio and Powell (1983)	Scott (1995)	Examples
Coercive mechanisms: the law or the market lead organizations to comply and to align with the norms in order to gain legitimacy and survive. Consequently behavior becomes very similar in all of them	***Regulative structures:*** the law or the market involve the capacity to establish rules, inspect conformity and manage sanctions in order to influence future behavior	Consumer boycotts lead companies to change structures and practices Environmental regulation makes companies to adopt new technologies **In the context of SR**, regulative structures and activities would include reporting regulations and their enforcement, as well as the threat of regulation of reporting: CSRD (Corporate Sustainability Reporting Directive, Directive (EU) 2022/2464; ESG; ESRS
Normative mechanisms: diffused through professionalization, formal education and professional networks, lead individuals to act according to shared social values and norms	***Normative structures*** based on social values and norms, leading individuals to act according to societal expectations organizations: -Legitimate authority of norms and values; -Organizations genuinely think that given their role in society have to acquire some structure or engage in some practices:	Deontological codes shape practice in many professions, such as doctors or accountants **In the context of SR**, normative structures refer to rules that are followed on moral/ethical grounds or in order to conform to norms established by referential bodies (i.e. EMAS; GRI; awards for best environmental, social or sustainability reports, such us ESRA, EERA, ACCA Awards)
Mimetic mechanisms: Organizations imitate (mimetic process) those peer organizations that seem to be more successful and legitimate	***Cognitive structures:*** There are taken for granted symbols, meanings and roles in social action that support the legitimacy of organizations The social construction of roles and organizations varies over time and space and contribute to stability Cognitive structures form a culturally supported and conceptually support of legitimacy. Their existence is very difficult to prove empirically	The waves in the use of some concepts and techniques by organization are associated with vogues (imitation) rather than with rationality **In the context of SR,** convergence is taking place in some organizational fields where reports are evolving rapidly (from environmental to CSR(Corporate social responsibility)

Source Authors' elaboration of Larrinaga-Gonzalez (2007, p. 156)

Corporate reporting has adapted to meet these challenges as one of the primary means of internal and external communication. The inclusion of non-financial issues into reporting has allowed the expansion of instruments like integrated reporting, which has evolved from a complement to financial reporting for capital allocation and value creation (de Villiers et al., 2017), to become an integrated thinking tool that provides organizations with a broader understanding of their impacts, facilitating strategic planning and improving decision-making processes (Guthrie et al., 2017). As (Del Baldo, 2018) posits, sustainable reporting is the catalyst, while IR has become a tool to drive change.

Adopting integrated reporting practices early may provide SMEs a competitive edge by helping them comply proactively with evolving regulatory demands (De Villiers et al., 2014).

Sustainable reporting on its own has also proved in the mid-term to improve social and environmental value creation for SME companies implementing it (Massa et al., 2015), and self-disclosure of sustainable practices has shown to provide better alignment with clients' expectations (Solís-Radilla et al., 2019), ultimately increasing their satisfaction (Berezan et al., 2013).

Communication and reporting of sustainable practices are used by organizations for enhanced reputation and legitimacy (Crossley et al., 2021), although (Hummel & Schlick, 2016) state that high sustainability performers prefer higher quality disclosures to communicate superiority. In contrast, poor performers prefer lower quality disclosures to help them maintain their legitimacy by hiding their insufficient sustainable practices. Often, organizations may use these tools to shape and control environmental narratives, gaining higher influence in policies, while engaging in practices of pinkwashing (Baldarelli et al., 2016) or greenwashing.

This highlights the importance of using standardized and quality-assured methods for sustainable reporting, to avoid distorted practices and stakeholder suspicion (Gianfelici, 2024).

GRI has been the most popular standard for non-mandatory non-financial disclosures (Carungu et al., 2022; de Villiers et al., 2022) Besides its comprehensive and well-known model, the availability of documents and training material for self-assessment free of charge makes it a highly accessible and practical tool for organizations starting the journey of sustainable reporting.

Although some authors like (Del Baldo, 2017) highlight the importance of a fitted solution for SMEs capable of adapting to the organizational context, reducing implementation barriers, and enhancing stakeholder engagement.

After selected literature review, in the next section the process implementation of GRI is described.

11.3 The GRI Implementation in Beach Establishments: Methodology and Stages of the Project

Research design is involving methodology to try to respond to the changing of regulations and to prepare the *bagni* for change and guided by the principle of improving their services and inclusion.

This case study assesses the development and implementation of a sustainable report for four beach establishments in the city of Rimini in the Emilia-Romagna Region in Italy. Together, these *bagni* account for more than 20,000 visitors per year. Three are family-owned, while one is a slightly broader organization representing a partnership of multiple beach establishments and their owners.

All of the owners are actively involved and regularly present at the beach establishments. In total, beach establishments account for 38 employees.

The motivations of beach establishment owners to develop a sustainable report varied, although most focused on the need to mitigate risks associated with the new regulations affecting beach establishment concessions. Owners also emphasized their drive to improve their services by sharing best practices, building sustainable businesses and increasing their industry standards. They also reported *bagni* operators' negative reputation and stressed the sense of unfairness this perception created in them. They view sustainability reporting as an opportunity to demonstrate their positive contributions and counteract public skepticism, highlighting the lasting value they provide to the community.

Furthrmore, the project let them to be aligned to the new regulations in the UE regulation concerning green and social standards for business management. For that reason, four beach establishments in Italy (Emilia Romagna Region) promoted the development of the research project to implement sustainable reporting system with a learning agreement wih the Center of Avdvanced Studies in Tourism of University of Bologna (named also: CAST).

The research working group was composed firstly by the scientific coordinator delegated by the CAST to the supervision of the project and the PHD student. Furthermore, Two independent consultants has been involved in. The project was one of the responses to the growing uncertainty regarding the forthcoming changes in Italian public concession law. The project also aimed to improve client services by adopting best practices in beach establishment management aligned with green and social standards.

A series of on-site interviews were conducted with *bagni* owners to understand their motivations and expectations of the project, identify their primary stakeholders, understand their operations, and assess their economic, social, and environmental impacts. This analysis reviewed waste management practices, cleaning and maintenance products, work and inclusive practices, and resource consumption, focusing on water and energy.

Beach establishment owners were also supported in compiling the UNI/PdR 92:2020, a guide for environmental sustainability, service quality, safety, and accessibility practices. *Bagni* owners were also asked to compile a Social and Environmental questionnaire by Banca Etica to assess their advancement in sustainable practices compared to other businesses.

Employee and customer satisfaction surveys were also done to collect information regarding stakeholder satisfaction and their alignment with sustainable business practices.

GRI topics were chosen following the materiality principle Table 11.2 shows the general GRI index depicting the main topics considered in the report.

All the data and activities considered in the report refer to the summer of 2024, except for information related to materials, water, and electricity consumption, which reflects the previous season, along with the financial information corresponding to the most recent fiscal year.

The kick-off started with an initial meeting to provide beach establishment owners with an overview of the project's objectives, timeline, and expected results. This was followed by individual interviews with family groups or partners to collect insights related to their motivations, challenges, expectations, organizational and sustainable practices, and particularities of their businesses.

Several communications between the consultants and the business owners followed these interviews to gather specific data regarding their utility consumption and compliance with sustainable and social practices. Owners were very open

Table 11.2 GRI index of the sustainable report

GRI index
GRI 2: General Information
GRI 3: Material Topics
GRI 201: Economic Performance
GRI 204: Procurement Practices
GRI 207: Taxes
GRI 301: Materials
GRI 302: Energy
GRI 303: Water and Effluent
GRI 304: Biodiversity
GRI 305: Emissions
GRI 306: Waste
GRI 401: Employment
GRI 403: Occupational health and safety
GRI 404: Training and education
GRI 405: Diversity and equal opportunity
GRI 406: Non-discrimination
GRI 413: Local Communities
GRI 416: Customer Health and Safety
GRI 418: Customer privacy

Source https://www.globalreporting.org

to sharing the information with the consultants, though one of the *bagni* faced more significant challenges delivering the necessary data.

Beach establishment owners were also asked to help identify stakeholders and assess their impact. They also completed a survey on sustainable practices by Banca Etica to assess their progress in sustainability compared to other businesses.

With the help of the external consultants, an assessment of their compliance with the UNI/PdR 92:2020 was also done. The UNI/PdR 92:2020, is a voluntary Italian reference standard published by UNI (the Italian National Standardization Body) for best practices in environmental sustainability, accessibility, quality, and safety for beach establishments.

An on-site online client survey was designed and implemented to understand clients' perspectives on sustainable business practices and collect feedback on the beach establishment services. A total of 307 replies were collected during the summer of 2024.

The questionnaire contained six demographic questions, one satisfaction question, one net promoter score question (NPS), ten questions assessing the importance of different sustainable practices, nine questions evaluating sustainable performance at beach facilities, and one open-ended space for comments.

An employee survey was also designed and conducted online. This questionnaire included three demographic questions, six questions to assess the importance given to sustainable practices, six questions for evaluating the performance of the *bagni* on them, and seven organizational climate questions. The participation rate was low since 10 out of 38 employees answered the questionnaire. A possible explanation for this limited engagement is that most employees hold temporary contracts for the summer season, as they are usually high school graduates. While some will return next summer, most employees are unlikely to do so, reducing the incentive to participate.

GRI guidelines and standards were used as the primary framework for the project. Items of the GRI were reviewed and assessed to determine their suitability and relevance to the industry and beach establishment operations.

All the data collected was analyzed, calculated, and presented as suggested in the GRI Guidelines; the report was written following these guidelines. A final chapter with recommendations for improvement for the beach establishment was added. Beach establishment owners and a representative of the CAST reviewed the final draft.

The report's launch was held at an open social presentation.

11.4 The GRI Implementation in Beach Establishments: Some Results About Stakeholders

For the implementation of Sustainability Reporting the stakeholder map was developed to better understand the stakeholders involved in the beach establishment operations and support the project's decision-making process. Potential stakeholders were presented to beach establishment owners using data collected from previous interviews. They were asked to add any other stakeholders, finalizing a list of 11 stakeholders. *Bagni*'s owners also assessed stakeholders' impact on power, legitimacy, urgency, influence, interest, and involvement.

A salience map was developed by evaluating their impact on Urgency, Power, and Legitimacy, and definite stakeholders (Mitchell et al., 1997) were identified for each *bagni*. Table 11.1 shows these results.

Beach establishment owners appear to be definite stakeholders for all the beach establishments; meanwhile, authority, state, regional, or local, appears important to most of them. Clients appear to be definite stakeholders for two of them.

The results, that are shown below (Table 11.3), reflect the differences between each beach establishment's history, context, and operations. Figure 11.1 shows a stakeholder map and a salience map for one of the beach establishments.

These results help *bagni* owners identify the stakeholders they should give more attention to and, therefore, the topics they should prioritize in their improvement plans and communication strategy, allowing a more efficient allocation of their resources, with a focus on relationships.

About Client Survey Results, the survey was done for several reasons: first, clients were primary stakeholders for two of the beach establishments, so it is essential to understand what matters to them and how much it matters; second, best practices of the UNI PdR 92:2020 suggest the implementation of client survey is to understand

Table 11.3 Definite stakeholders for each beach establishment

Beach Establishment	A	B	C	D
Owners	x	x	x	x
Employees				
Clients	x		x	
Suppliers				
Citizens				
Community	x			
Locale/Regional Authority	x		x	
State Authority	x	x	x	
Employee Family				x
Lifeguard	X			
Bagnini Cooperative	X			

Source Authors' elaboration

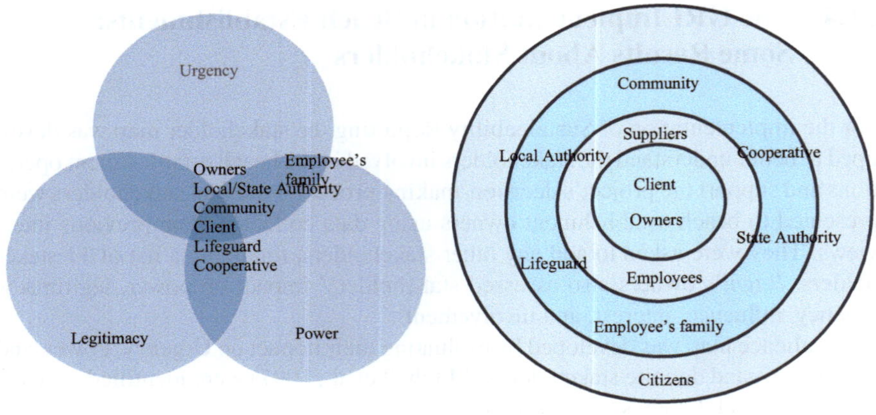

Fig. 11.1 Example of stakeholder map for one of the bagni. *Source* Authors' elaboration

how services could be improved; third, one of the primary objectives of the bagni owners with the implementation of the sustainable report is to find ways to improve their operations and services, which can be done through the analysis of the perception and opinions of clients. Finally, final-user perceptions and satisfaction levels can play a crucial role in sustainable tourism, driving operational improvements through environmental initiatives (Merli et al., 2019) or framing authority policies that encourage responsible tourism (Marin et al., 2009).

The survey was designed to understand clients' perception of importance and evaluation of several sustainable and service issues. Surveys were administered online; a QR code was available at the establishments, inviting clients to participate; *bagnis*' owners also sent their regular clients a direct link to the survey so they could participate. A total of 307 replies were collected.

Most of the clients belong to the age range of 36 to 55 years. More men responded to the survey, which does not necessarily mean fewer female clients, since most clients came to the beach, mainly with family, friends, and partners. Regarding the frequency of visits, most visits are made annually or more than once a year. Table 11.4 shows the demographic composition of the respondents of the survey.

As stated before, satisfaction levels can be used in sustainable tourism to shape strategy and initiatives; satisfaction was measured directly with a question related to their overall satisfaction and a net promoter score question (willingness to recommend). With an average satisfaction of the visits of 4.48 out of 5, most respondents are satisfied with the bagni services. The average net promoter score is 4.6, implying a high willingness to recommend the visit (Table 11.5).

Ten factors were evaluated in importance from 1 to 5; on average, all were important for the clients. The factors with the highest evaluation were health and safety at work, followed by compliance with environmental and social laws, showing the interest of clients regarding responsible business through compliance with regulations and standard workforce procedures (Table 11.6).

Table 11.4 Survey respondents' demographics

Demographics	Number of respondents
Age Group	
Less than 18	8
18–24	29
25–35	81
36–55	141
56 +	48
Gender	
Female	127
Male	175
Nonbinary	2
Prefer not to say	3
Companions	**Who came with you?**
Other	9
With friends	79
With Friends, partner	13
With Friends, a partner, and others	1
With Family	98
With Family, friends	10
With family, friends, and a partner	4
With family and partner	1
Alone	29
Alone, with friends	1
Alone, with friends, or with a partner	1
Alone, with family	2
Alone, with family, friends, and other	1
alone, family, friends, partner	2
Alone, partner	1
Partner	55
Frequency of visit	
Annual	97
More than once a month	55
More than once a year	79
First time	76

Source Authors' elaboration

Table 11.5 Satisfaction levels of client survey respondents

	Satisfaction	NPS
1—Not Satisfied	10	3
2	4	5
3	23	21
4	61	53
5—Very Satisfied	209	225
Total	307	307

Source Authors' elaboration

Table 11.6 Importance of attributes for client's survey respondents

Attribute	Very important	Important	Neutral	Minor importance	Not important	Average
Impact on the environment of activities	190	92	19	2	0	4.55
Social impact of our initiatives	194	85	18	3	0	4.57
Transparency in sustainability practices	175	103	21	3	0	4.49
Social responsibility	179	108	14	2	0	4.53
Engagement with the local community	171	104	23	2	0	4.48
Health and safety at work	222	70	12	0	0	4.69
Relationships with involved stakeholders	205	78	19	2	0	4.60
Compliance with environmental and social laws	218	75	10	1	0	4.68
Implementation of inclusive practices	203	81	12	3	0	4.62
Implementation of sustainability practices	193	89	15	1	0	4.59

Source Authors' elaboration

Table 11.7 Evaluation of organizational practices by client survey respondents

	Excellent (5)	Very good (4)	Good (3)	Barely sufficient (2)	Insufficient (1)	Average
Cleanliness of the beach and the structure	160	52	62	12	11	4.14
Courtesy and Professionalism of the staff	161	57	66	8	10	4.16
Quality of activities	104	65	77	36	11	3.73
Quality/Price relation	117	55	84	25	18	3.76
Inclusive Practices	137	46	76	18	9	3.99
Sustainable Practices	132	44	78	22	11	3.92
Compatibility of the structure with the environment	132	58	73	24	11	3.93
Access and assistance for reduced mobility	151	64	58	15	9	4.12
Commitment to Diversity	156	44	51	10	12	4.18

Source Authors' elaboration

Table 11.7 shows the results of the client's evaluation on several business practices. On average, most organizational practices and services were evaluated as very good; the highest evaluation was received by the commitment to diversity, followed by courtesy and professionalism. The quality of activities received the lowest evaluation, followed by the quality/price relation.

Despite the high satisfaction levels and NPS, some clients perceived attributes as insufficient. Quality/price is the attribute that accounts for a higher number of insufficient responses, where 18 respondents have a negative perception.

11.5 The GRI Implementation in Beach Establishments: Employee Survey's Results

UNI PdR 92:2020 also suggests putting in place a system to collect employees' feedback for improvements and preventive actions. Even though Employees were not assessed as primary stakeholders, an employee survey can help beach establishment operators to improve internal management practices, enhance workplace satisfaction, and align new initiatives more closely with staff needs and expectations. It is also seen as a best practice in people management resources.

The survey was conducted after the season ended, and it was not mandatory, so few replies were received. One of the beach establishments had an ongoing employee survey conducted as in previous years, resulting in mostly positive outcomes.

11.5.1 *Materiality Assessment*

Considering the interviews, the surveys, and the data collected, a double materiality assessment determined the inclusion of the different topics in the report. Each topic chosen was also associated with a sustainable development goal (SDG) to better understand its general impact. Table 11.8 shows the list of topics selected and their alignment to SDGs. More than one-third of the topics relate to SDG 8, decent work and economic growth.

A materiality map was also developed (Fig. 11.2).This chart features the most important topics for the organization and its stakeholders. This results in important matters for both, for one of them, and none. Primary issues from the assessment are law and regulation compliance, economic value for the community, health and safety at work, local sourcing, and employment.

Each of the sections portrayed in the chart will require a different approach from the organizations. On the one hand, the organization should actively work to raise awareness among stakeholders about issues they consider important but have not yet been fully recognized. On the other hand, the organization should seek feedback regarding stakeholders' concerns on topics it does not perceive as significant, ensuring it integrates these needs and aligns its business model with shared priorities.

After the presentation of main results of GRI implementation in Beach Establishments, in the next section discussion and conclusion are presented.

11.6 Discussion and Conclusion

Following neo-institutional theory, the isomorphism is guided by mechanisms and especially in the cases analyzed the coercive mechanisms (Di Maggio & Powell, 1983) are prevalent. But the previous voluntary process, that involved the Rimini territory cultural change was very important to contribute to GRI implementation (Baldarelli, 2017). In the past years, normative and mimetic mecanisms prevailed underlining the urgency of cultural changing and increasing the greater sensitivity to the application of sustainability reporting tools. So, the other mechanisms, such as normative and mimetic are important in the present state of art, because the owners of the fourth Bagni decided to start the implementation process and perhaps the other two mechanisms are the result of the cultural emancipation that is underline above (Table 11.9).

Table 11.8 Materiality topics linked to SDGs. The table was developed by consultants and is included in the reports

Topic	Impact	Description	SDGs
Economic value for the community	positive	Value creation, improvement of the city's reputation	8, 11
Locally sourced	positive	Locally distributed economic value	8, 11
Employment	positive	Social value	8, 11
Health and work safety	positive	Social Value	8
Social corporate responsibility	positive	Shared objectives, social value	8
Energy	negative	Resource consumption	[illegible]
Diversity and Equal Opportunity	positive	Social value	5, 10
Inclusion and non-discrimination	positive	Social Value	5, 10
Taxes	positive negative	Local economic impacts Competitivity loss	9
Water	negative	Natural resource consumption	9
Waste	negative	Resource consumption and the potential increase in contamination	6
Biodiversity	negative	Biodiversity loss	14, 15
CO_2 emissions	negative	Increase in greenhouse gases in the atmosphere	13

Source Authors' elaboration

In fact, Beach establishments trace their heritage across multiple generations, thanks to the automatic renewal of the beach concessions that were allowed to protect the local economy and small business investments. Family-owned beach establishments have significantly contributed to developing tourism and coastal economies.

In 2006, the EU adopted the Bolkestein Directive (Directive 2006/123/CE) and a series of guidelines that aim to liberalize the European service market by lowering

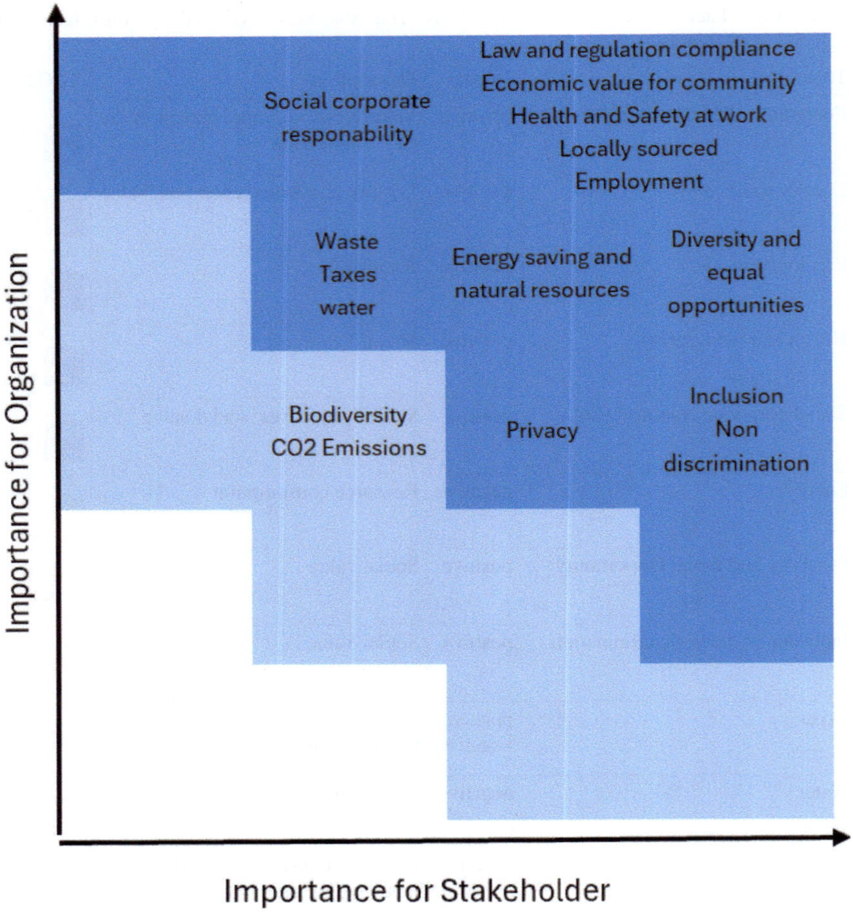

Fig. 11.2 Materiality map. *Source* Authors' elaboration along with research group collaboration

entry barriers and promoting competitiveness through the EU states, thus requiring, among other things, for public concessions to be awarded through transparent and competitive procedures.

However, Italy has not been able to implement these measures. Consecutive governments between 2006 and 2020 have applied multiple extensions of the concessions, avoiding the competitive bidding processes and maintaining the status quo of family-operated businesses. Surprisingly, under Giuseppe Conte's administration in 2018, concessions were extended through 2034,[1] further postponing compliance with European regulations.

[1] Crisi di governo, cosa cambia per i balneari. Accessed 12/03/2025.

Table 11.9 Institutional theory implementation in Rimini territory

Mechanism Di Maggio and Powell (1983, p. 164)
Coercive: (1) From 2003 the government pushed Italian chamber of commerce to implement CSR and on 2006 Low- compulsory SER for Social enterprises (2) Coercive market pressures: the development of other tourist destinations pushed Rimini to think of a Social responsible Territory (3) Some coercive sectors pressures: rules related to work safety, climate, environmental emissions, etc..(such as: gas and waste industries)
Normative: The SER is the answer to a background of social responsibility culture and "possible" intrinsic motivation Training course for enterprises Accounting professions involvement and the association of Rimini enterprises with strategic plan activities
Mimetic: (1) Others Italian territories were involved in this process (Italian chamber of commerce) (2) It is imitation, but not "pure" (vogues imitation) and implies a rational choice of: the Chamber of Commerce, public administration to create network about responsible and sustainable territory

Source Baldarelli (2017, pp. XII–148)

An infringement procedure against Italy was initiated in 2020 by the European Commission to push the Italian government towards compliance with the Bolkstein Directive. The commission has also openly criticized the Italian government's technical round table results regarding land availability for concessions, further complicating Italy's compliance with the directive.

Italy's Council of State intervened in 2021, declaring automatic renewals incompatible with EU law and urging governmental action to align with European standards. In September 2024, the Italian government declared that beach concessions would open to public offer starting from June 2027, eventually ending decades of automatic renewals.

In synthesis about the Institutional theory mechanisms (Di Maggio & Powell, 1983): coercive, normative and mimetic, the coercive mechanism is especially evidenced in 2006, by the EU adopted the Bolkestein Directive (Directive 2006/123/CE) and a series of guidelines that aim to liberalize the European service market. Furtermore, between 2006 and 2020 have applied multiple extensions of the concessions, avoiding the competitive bidding processes and maintaining the status quo of family-operated businesses. Finally on September 2024 the Italian government declared that beach concessions would open to public offer starting from June 2027, eventually ending decades of automatic renewals (Bolkestein Directive -Directive 2006/123/CE).

Normative mechanism (Di Maggio & Powell, 1983) is reading the Sustainability Reporting implementation, that is also the answer to a background of social responsibility culture, because Bagnis' Owners decided to collaborate both to the project, and among each other. Especially, the last process is relatively new and very difficult to start in firms that are market competitors like the promoters.

Mimetic mechanism (Di Maggio & Powell, 1983) is considering the Sustainability Reporting implementation as the process that is very important for the consolidation of the collaboration network. That process can be seen similar to other italian territories, because the objective of the Bagni that had been involved in, to Institutionalize the initial collaboration with a more formal contract, that is named Network Contract and that is considered by Italian Low (Table 11.10).

Some main results can be considered relative to mimetic and regulative mechanisms (Di Maggio & Powell, 1983). For example, in the social sphere, beach establishments reported a high desire to involve the community; two recalled a long family tradition related to Rimini's tourism development through beach activities and beach establishments. They all regularly organize sportive, religious, or cultural events open to the community. Three out of four have hired young people from a social project or with some disability. One of them had hired retired employees.

Furthermore, some elements of novelties are emerging. In fact, Beach establishments also showed high commitment to inclusiveness. They all display easy access features, including ramps and specialized chairs for clients with reduced mobility. Also, some beach establishment owners and their families have participated in autism training to enhance their service and support for their diverse clients. In the summer of 2024, they received more than 170 visitors with disabilities. One of the beach establishments has obtained the certificate for the inclusive tourism protocol for the LGBTQ + community.

Table 11.10 Institutional theory—Bagni of rimini territory

Mechanism Di Maggio and Powell (1983, p. 164)
Coercive: (1) In 2006, the EU adopted the Bolkestein Directive (Directive 2006/123/CE) and a series of guidelines that aim to liberalize the European service market (2) between 2006 and 2020 have applied multiple extensions of the concessions, avoiding the competitive bidding processes and maintaining the status quo of family-operated businesses (3) September 2024, the Italian government declared that beach concessions would open to public offer starting from June 2027, eventually ending decades of automatic renewals. Bolkestein Directive (Directive 2006/123/CE)
Normative: The Sustainability Reporting implementation is also the answer to a background of social responsibility culture because Bagnis' Owners decided to collaborate both to the project and among them
Mimetic: The Sustainability Reporting implementatio is consolidating the collaboration creatin a network, that imitate other italian territories with the objective to Institutionalise that collaboration with a more formal contract, that is named Network Contract that is considered by Italian Low

Source Author's elaboration

Regarding sustainable practices, all the establishments presented sustainable-oriented practices; they all sourced from local suppliers, reducing CO_2 emissions and supporting local businesses; they have implemented water and energy-saving systems, such as solar panels, solar showers, LED lights, and aerators for water dispensers; use of water-based paint and differentiated garbage disposals as commitment to environmental care.

One of the beach establishments also stated that they had chosen a particular type of beach umbrella to reduce visual contamination and ensure the use of recycled materials.

All establishments have assessed their work risks and maintained an updated Risk Assessment Document (DVR) to ensure compliance with health, safety, and workforce laws. Every facility employee has a contract and follows shift schedules that adhere to labor regulations.

Two beach establishments are mainly owned by women, and three have hired female employees.

Furthermore, in conclusion this case study presents the development of a sustainability report for beach establishments, based on GRI standards. It represents a key milestone for the future advancement of sustainable practices in the Rimini area and for beach tourism as a whole.

It highlights that, despite the absence of previous measurements or formal public communication, many beach establishments had already adopted social and environmental practices, driven by a genuine commitment to responsible business. This existing groundwork makes the path toward formal sustainability standards more accessible and meaningful.

The report also opens a new channel for dialogue between beach establishments and their stakeholders, aiming to raise industry standards and promote ongoing improvement in environmental and social performance.

Moreover, the experience illustrates how collaboration between different actors, such as the university, independent consultants, the cooperative, and the beach establishments themselves, can generate shared value for society. By combining technical knowledge, territorial presence, and long-standing local engagement, these partnerships can lead to more effective and inclusive pathways for sustainable transformation.

Finally, it shows that international reference frameworks such as the GRI can be effectively adapted to the beach tourism sector, and in particular to small or family-owned businesses, supporting the creation of relevant indicators and the implementation of improvement plans—both essential for addressing future challenges and fostering truly sustainable tourism.

Reading the process using Institutional Theory, the analysis is underlining the presence of all three mechanisms (Di Maggio & Powell, 1983) even if at the beginning seemed prevalent coercive one. But after more attentive analisys regulative and mimetic mechanisms emerge. Moreover, some new elements are emerging, that can be added to Isomorphism process. These elements are originated by some features, that are cacterizing only Rimini Territory (Baldarelli, 2017).

References

Adams, C. A. (2002). Internal organisational factors influencing corporate social and reporting beyond current theorising. *Accounting Auditing & Accountability Journal, 15*(2), 223–250.

Baldarelli, M. G. (2017). Territory entities process to implement social and environmental accounting and reporting: some drivers and actions in theory and praxis, Atti del Convegno Sidrea 2016- IL GOVERNO AZIENDALE TRA TRADIZIONE E INNOVAZIONE, XII Sezione – Aziende Non-Profit Etica e Responsabilità Sociale, Volume Elettronico – ISBN 978-88-917-3660-4, 131–154.

Baldarelli, M. G., Del Baldo, M., & Vignini, S. (2016). Pink accounting in Italy: Cultural perspectives on discrimination and/or lack of interest. *Meditari Accountancy Research, 24*(2), 269–292. https://doi.org/10.1108/MEDAR-10-2015-0065

Bebbington, J., Higgins, C., & Frame, B. (2009). Initiating sustainable development reporting: Evidence from New Zealand. *Accounting, Auditing & Accountability Journal, 22*(4), 588–625. https://doi.org/10.1108/09513570910955452

Berezan, O., Raab, C., Yoo, M., & Love, C. (2013). Sustainable hotel practices and nationality: The impact on guest satisfaction and guest intention to return. *International Journal of Hospitality Management, 34*(1), 227–233. https://doi.org/10.1016/j.ijhm.2013.03.010

Botero, C. M., & Zielinski, S. (2020). The implementation of a world-famous tourism ecolabel triggers political support for beach management. *Tourism Management Perspectives, 35*, 1–13. https://doi.org/10.1016/j.tmp.2020.100691

Campbell, D. J. (2000). Legitimacy theory or managerial reality construction? Corporate social disclosure in marks and spencer plc corporate reports, 1969–1997. *Accounting Forum, 24*(1), 80–100. https://doi.org/10.1111/1467-6303.00030

Carnegie, G. D. (2022). Accounting 101: Redefining accounting for tomorrow. *Accounting Education, 31*(6), 615–628. https://doi.org/10.1080/09639284.2021.2014915

Carungu, J., Molinari, M., Nicolò, G., Pigatto, G., & Sottoriva, C. (2022). Implementing SDGs and mandatory non-financial reporting in corporate practices: Insight from an Italian global player. In *SIDREA series in accounting and business administration: Part F28* (pp. 61–84). Springer. https://doi.org/10.1007/978-3-030-90355-8_3

Cooper, C. (2005). Accounting for the public interest: Public ineffectual or public intellectuals? *Accounting Auditing & accountability Journal, 18*(5), 592–607.

Cooper, D. F., Grey, S., Raymond, G. & Walker, P. (2005). *Project risk management guidelines: Managing risk in large projects and complex procurements*. John Wiley & Sons.

Crossley, R. M., Elmagrhi, M. H., & Ntim, C. G. (2021). Sustainability and legitimacy theory: The case of sustainable social and environmental practices of small and medium-sized enterprises. *Business Strategy and the Environment, 30*(8), 3740–3762. https://doi.org/10.1002/bse.2837

De Villiers, C., La Torre, M., & Molinari, M. (2022). The Global Reporting Initiative's (GRI) past, present and future: Critical reflections and a research agenda on sustainability reporting (standard-setting). *Pacific Accounting Review, 34*(5), 728–747. https://doi.org/10.1108/PAR-02-2022-0034

De Villiers, C., Rinaldi, L., & Unerman, J. (2014). Integrated reporting: Insights, gaps and an agenda for future research. *Accounting, Auditing & Accountability Journal, 27*(7), 1042–1067. https://doi.org/10.1108/AAAJ-06-2014-1736

De Villiers, C., Venter, E. R., & Hsiao, P. C. K. (2017). Integrated reporting: Background, measurement issues, approaches and an agenda for future research. *Accounting and Finance, 57*(4), 937–959. https://doi.org/10.1111/acfi.12246

Del Baldo, M. (2017). The implementation of integrating reporting IR in SMEs. *Meditari Accountancy Research, 25*(4), 505–532. https://doi.org/10.1108/MEDAR-11-2016-0094

Del Baldo, M. (2018). Integrated reporting in small and medium enterprises: Issues and perspectives from Italy. *Current Issues in Corporate Social Responsability*, 195–215. https://doi.org/10.1007/978-3-319-70449-4_13

Di Lascio, F. (2022). La Regulacion de las concesiones de playa en Italia: un objetivo inalcanzable? Revista Aragonesa de Administración Pública. http://documenti.camera.it/leg18/pdl/pdf/leg.18.pdl.came

Di Maggio, P. J., & Powell, W. W. (1991). *New institutionalism in organizational analysis*. University of Chicago Press.

Di Maggio, P. J., & Powell, W. W. (1983). The iron cage revisited: Institutional isomorphism and collective rationality in organizational fields. *American Sociological Review, 48*, 147–160. https://doi.org/10.2307/2095101

Gianfelici, C. (2024). *Rendicontazione di Sostenibilità e washing. Fondamenti teorici ed evidenze empiriche*. Aracne.

Gray, R. H. (2002). The social accounting project and Accounting Organizations and Society Privileging engagement, imaginings, new accountings and pragmatism over critique? *Accounting, Organizations and Society, 27*, 687–708.

Gray, R., Adams, C. A., & Owen, D. (2014). *Accountability, social responsibility and sustainability*. Accounting for society and environment, Pearson.

Gray, R. H., & Bebbington, K. J. (2000). Environmental accounting, managerialism, and sustainability: Is the planet safe in the hands of business and accounting? *Advances in Environmental Accounting and Management, 1*, 1–44.

Gray, R. H., & Bebbington, J. (2001). *Accounting for the environment* (2nd ed.). Sage publications.

Guthrie, J., Manes-Rossi, F., & Orelli, R. L. (2017). Integrated reporting and integrated thinking in Italian public sector organizations. *Meditari Accountancy Research, 25*(4), 553–573. https://doi.org/10.1108/MEDAR-06-2017-0155

Hummel, K., & Schlick, C. (2016). The relationship between sustainability performance and sustainability disclosure—Reconciling voluntary disclosure theory and legitimacy theory. *Journal of Accounting and Public Policy, 35*(5), 455–476. https://doi.org/10.1016/j.jaccpubpol.2016.06.001

Larrinaga Gonzàlez, C. (2007). Sustainability reporting. Insight from neoinstitutional theory. In J. Unerman, J. Bebbington & B. O' Dwyear (Eds.), *Sustainability accounting and accountability* (pp. 150–167) Routledge.

Larrinaga, G. C., & Bebbington, J. (2001). Accounting change or institutional appropriation?—A case study of the implementation of environmental accounting. *Critical Perspectives on Accounting, 12*(3), 269–292. https://doi.org/10.1006/cpac.2000.0433

Laughlin, R. C. (1991). Environmental disturbances and organizational transitions and transformations: Some alternative models. *Organization Studies, 12*(2), 209–232. https://doi.org/10.1177/017084069101200203

Marin, V., Palmisani, F., Ivaldi, R., Dursi, R., & Fabiano, M. (2009). Users' perception analysis for sustainable beach management in Italy. *Ocean and Coastal Management, 52*(5), 268–277. https://doi.org/10.1016/j.ocecoaman.2009.02.001

Massa, L., Farneti, F., & Scappini, B. (2015). Developing a sustainability report in a small to medium enterprise: Process and consequences. *Meditari Accountancy Research, 23*(1), 62–91. https://doi.org/10.1108/MEDAR-02-2014-0030

Merli, R., Preziosi, M., Acampora, A., & Ali, F. (2019). Why should hotels go green? Insights from guests experience in green hotels. *International Journal of Hospitality Management, 81*, 169–179. https://doi.org/10.1016/j.ijhm.2019.04.022

Mitchell, R. K., Agle, B. R., & Wood, D. J. (1997). Toward a theory of stakeholder. *Academy of Management Review, 22*, 853–886.

Moscariello, N., & Pizzo, M. (2024). *Climate Change and Corporate Reporting in Europe. Standard Setting and Disclosure Practices*. Cambridge Scholars Publishing.

Pommier, B., & Engel, A. M. (2021). Sustainability reporting in the hospitality industry. *Research in Hospitality Management, 11*(3), 173–175. https://doi.org/10.1080/22243534.2021.2006937

Scott, W. R. (1995). *Institutions and organizations*. SAGE Publications.

Solís-Radilla, M. M., Hernández-Lobato, L., Callarisa-Fiol, L.J., & Pastor-Durán, H. T. (2019). The Importance of Sustainability in the Loyalty to a Tourist Destination through the Management of Expectations and Experiences. *Sustainability, 11*(15), 4132. https://doi.org/10.3390/su11154132

Solomon, A., & Lewis, L. (2002). Incentives and disincentives for corporate environmental disclosure. *Business Strategy and Environment, 11*(3), 154–169. https://doi.org/10.1002/bse.328

Maria-Gabriella Baldarelli , PhD, CPA, is Associate Professor of Accounting, at University of Bologna, Department of Management- Rimini Campus. Full professor availability. Envited professor at Sophia University Institute. SIDREA board member until 2018. She is a member of international scientific networks: the Centre for Social and Environmental Accounting Research (CSEAR) and the European Business Ethics Network (EBEN). Key-note Speaker 2nd International Conference on Economics, Business, Finance and Governance (ICEBFG) by Economics and Business Faculty of University of Bandar Lampung- Bali- Indonesia- Dic. 4-5, 2019. Research interests includes: accountability and gambling enterprises; corporate social responsibility; ethical, social and environmental accounting and accountability, sustainability in tourist enterprises; responsible and accessible tourism for blind people, economy of communion; gender accounting; accounting history, accounting education and Feminist Economics.

Macarena Paz Velasco Rosales is PhD student at University of Bologna, Alma Mater Studiorum in Future of the Earth, Climate Change and Social Challenge, associated with the Department of Management. She attended and concluded (from—to) September 2020—July 2021 Bologna Business School, the Global Master in Business Administration, Green Energy and Sustainable Businesses. Doctoral Cooloquium 34th Anual conference EBEN-European Business Ethics Network and presented some paper at some conferences and published some chapters in edited books.

Chapter 12
Social Inclusion in Higher Education: Accountability Practices and Challenges in Ex Transition Country

Lorena Mošnja-Škare and Ksenija Černe

Abstract Social inclusion should be considered as the society's mission, goal and challenge. Transition countries moved slower towards catching up accountability practices in developed countries, accompanied by modest advancements in corporate responsibility or sustainability reporting. Transition processes left many people in worsened socioeconomic position, with twofold consequences. The problems arose regarding getting them back on the scene, i.e. developing models of involving in normal life, educational, cultural and working community and on the other hand, unemployment and low life standard pushed the problems of different vulnerable groups as inferior topics. Decades after the beginnings of transition, the raising awareness of social inclusion is noticed, with current detailed regulatory requirements in line with EU legislation. Here we analyse the experiences in Croatia, focusing on the public higher education sector inclusion activities under strict funds limitations, and related accounting practices by presenting the case study of public university and its contributions to the goal of making higher education accessible and supportive to vulnerable groups. It offers examples of inclusion activities embedded in academic life and captured by accounting solutions as well as suggested fields for improvements to reduce the gap between declarative and real inclusive practices.

12.1 Introduction

The debate upon social inclusion as the society's mission towards the more sustainable world has been spread in this chapter to the ex-transition environments with lower development level of accountability practices in comparison with more developed countries, accompanied by modest advancements in corporate responsibility reporting, non-financial or sustainability reporting. Moreover, transition processes

L. Mošnja-Škare (✉) · K. Černe
Juraj Dobrila University of Pula, Pula, Croatia
e-mail: lmosnja@unipu.hr

K. Černe
e-mail: ksenija.cerne@unipu.hr

M. Baldarelli et al. (eds.), *Accounting and Accountability for Social Inclusion*, CSR, Sustainability, Ethics & Governance, https://doi.org/10.1007/978-3-032-09271-7_12

have swept through those countries, leaving many people in their worsened socioeconomic position, with twofold consequences. On one hand the problems arose regarding getting them back on the scene, i.e. developing models of their involving in normal life, educational, cultural and working community and on the other hand, unemployment and low life standard pushed the problems of different vulnerable groups into the background as inferior topics. Decades after the beginnings of transition processes, the raising awareness of social inclusion necessity could be noticed. It grew across corporate responsibility principles acceptance towards accountability practices followed by nonfinancial reports disclosure in addition to traditional financial reports, with current more detailed regulatory requirements in line with EU legislation. Except few CSR business leaders, public sector has offered more initiative for social inclusion enhancement in post-transition environments. Here we analyse the experiences encountered in Croatia, after the transition processes, focusing on the public higher education sector social inclusion activities and related accounting practices. The empirical study—the case-study method is employed, based on selected Croatian public university and its contributions to the goal of making higher education accessible and sustainable to many vulnerable groups of people. After selected research findings synthesis, recent frameworks and inclusion policy guidance as well as academic debate developed in the following section, it is considered how does the social inclusion really works in everyday students' life, how it is embedded in academic community and captured by accounting solutions, testing for the gaps between declarative and real-life inclusive practices, opening as well the fields for further improvements. To enable tracking the progress of social inclusion activities and outcomes achieved, a set of indicators is listed from double perspective—students' benefits and institution's benefits. Thus, universities' commitment and accountability in the field of social inclusion activities create positive reflections to both sides, contributing in same time also to all other stakeholders' and the whole society's prosperity and sustainability.

12.2 Social Inclusion in Academic Environments

12.2.1 Academic Debate: Social Inclusion in Higher Education—Declarative or Real Commitment

Inclusive education is recognized as an extremely important process that contributes to overall social inclusion achievements. "A move to an inclusive system requires the identification and removal of barriers that prevent all learners being present in mainstream settings and participating fully in learning opportunities that allow them to achieve (not only in academic subjects, but also in wider terms that impact on social inclusion)" (European Agency for Special Needs and Inclusive Education, 2018, p. 28). The goal to provide equal learning opportunities and achievement potentials for all the learners is valuable, and in same time challenging due to many implementation obstacles.

As debated in Haug (2017, pp. 210–211) "In all countries, there is a gap between formulations and realizations of inclusive education (Göransson & Nilholm, 2014; Graham & Jahnukainen, 2011; Nes, 2010; Smyth et al., 2014). Changes are slow, few and there are many setbacks."… "Research literature presents several obvious explanations about implementation difficulties, and about the differences between countries regarding how to understand and practise inclusive education. Competing initiatives (Florian, 2014; Hardy & Woodcock, 2015; Kreitz-Sandberg, 2015), national traditions (Graham & Jahnukainen, 2011; Miles & Singal, 2010; Mitchell, 2005) and lack of far-reaching changes explain weak implementation".

However, besides the common implementation difficulties, here we analyze another aspect that could significantly influence the progress of inclusive achievements.

The academic debate on social inclusion in higher education has been evolving multidimensionally. Among many contributions to the current debate, here we focus on institutional practices with dual approach to social inclusion and its endorsement—publicly and formally, while sticking to exclusive activities in the real everyday academic life ("institutional decoupling", Mampaey, 2017). The debate relates also to measurement of inclusion where easier access to higher education presented by enrollment metrics is not enough, it should be followed by structural changes in providing institutional support, academic and mental advising, inclusive pedagogy training and institutional culture reform. Moreover, according to the results of the case study at an elite UK university with widening participation schemes for students from underrepresented groups, those students must invest effort in identity work to fit in. (Fernando & Kenny, 2021, p. 1).

So, both debates bring to the conclusion that neoliberal governance with performance-based fundings, leaves scarce resources and time for supportive politics for those in need, that are more dependent on charitable initiatives than systematic approaches, disabling in such a way the equity agenda. In this way, instead of inclusive schemes implementation, social stratification schemes remain or even get deeper.

Such gap between rhetorical commitments to inclusion as the reputational raising instrument and the actual implementation of practices that foster inclusivity, destroys the mission of universities expected to be leaders in inclusive, socially responsible practices.

So, considering policy vs. practice, an image vs. substance, inclusion processes that really bring benefits to disadvantaged students, should go above just diversity metrics under the comprehensive framework that includes whole educational practices transformation, revising curricula, training faculty in inclusive pedagogy, facing with barriers and providing resources to meet specific needs of disadvantaged students, and finally, universities' organizational culture evolving. The current debate within the Academy of Management Learning & Education, as stated above and broader (Kottmann et al., 2019), deserves attention, we can consider it as the warning of transforming the imperative of social responsibility practised by inclusive universities to just another marketing instrument in competitive universities' environment characterised by continuous decrease of state budget funding. Considering the gap between declarative inclusion policy and real practice found at elite universities, what to expect in other, less prestigious universities or the ones functioning in developing economies or ex-transition countries, with particularly scarce resources at disposal for higher education development? That rises another research question upon the real inclusive practices in higher education of ex-transition countries. Motivated by current academic debate on formal versus real inclusion in higher education, as well as case studies led by this idea explored at elite universities, this chapter provides a case study of social inclusion in higher education of Croatia, as an ex-transition country, based on public, legally and functionally integrated University of Pula. The goal is to discover the real inclusive university practices existing in ex-transition economy under scarce resources and strong state budget funding limits, that particularly affect smaller universities. It was challenging to make an insight on the topic, not at large or elite universities, but on smaller ones to check if there are any inclusive practices going on, either on formal or material basis.

12.2.2 Social Inclusion Within Higher Education in Ex-Transition Countries

While the goals, policies and strategies of social inclusion are established both in ex-transition and non-transition countries, and they are all facing with the challenges of accessibility and support to disadvantaged students, there are still some differences that influence and shape the current inclusive practices in ex-transition countries.

Many ex-transition countries are still coping with challenges arosen during the transition process from centrally planned to market economies like structural unemployment, wealth concentration, informal economy. Moreover, transition processes have swept through those countries, leaving many people in their worsened socioeconomic position.

"In the beginning of the new era, the real income of the majority of citizens living in the Central Eastern European region was significantly below the average for member-countries of the European Union, and a considerable proportion were at the poverty level. Since that time—regardless of how much the world changed around us—the real income of a significant proportion of the population has remained unchanged, and many among the impoverished have become mired at the low level of their earlier living standard. And there are a non-negligible number of people whose standard of living has discernibly deteriorated" (Kornai, 2006, p. 228).

There were twofold consequences. On one hand the problems arose regarding getting them back on the scene, i.e. developing models of their involving in normal life, educational, cultural and working community and on the other hand, unemployment and low life standard pushed the problems of different vulnerable groups into the background as inferior topics. Particularly in Southeastern European transition countries like Croatia, there were very limited fiscal resources available for social inclusion programs and integration of marginalized groups like people with disabilities, elderly people, rural population, minorities like Roma population, and in Croatian post-war period—also veterans and their families, single parents and other groups. Educational system reform was expected to deliver experts with market-relevant skills and as well as market policies, to target vulnerable groups who had limited access to quality education.

"The translation of the value of social inclusion into practice is highly problematic due to the lack of financial resources" (Mampaey, 2017), "higher education institutions are increasingly confronted with resource stringencies due to the neo-liberalisation of higher education" (Slaughter & Rhoades, 2004).

While resources stringencies are met even in stable, stronger non-transition economies with well-established frameworks and social institutions, ex-transition countries had particularly scarce, more limited and hardly obtainable resources to implement effective inclusive policies in comparison with non-transition economies. Moreover, "educational systems that use early selection to place students in different educational tracks are less socially inclusive with regard to higher education than education systems that use later selection", i.e. systems with a high degree of selectivity or where selection takes place early are less likely to integrate students from these backgrounds in higher education (Orr et al., 2017a, 2017b in Kottmann et al., 2019, p. 10). The former are related to ex-transition and the latter to non-transition countries.

So, ex-transition educational systems with early selection processes are considered to be less socially inclusive, while struggling more severely with the lack of resources to cope with the inclusivity challenges in comparison with non-transition educational systems. That leads to lower expectations regarding higher education access and support to disadvantaged and vulnerable groups in academic environments of this group of countries. In same time, it motivated this empirical research performed in ex-transiton country to get the real insights into the inclusive policy and practice based on the case-study related to one Croatian public university, similar to the qualitative case-study research on this topic as performed for the selected Flemish university belonging to the group of non-transition countries (Mampaey, 2017).

12.2.3 Inclusive Policy in Higher Education, Its Framework and Indicators in the Literature

Social inclusion is expected to be the mission involved in any segment of life of the twenty-first century society, it particularly stands for academic society and its accountability to foster social inclusion in higher education environments.

In the European Higher Education Area, the Bologna Follow-Up Group (BFUG) on Social Dimension, its Widening Participation for Equity and Growth strategy (2015) and its Principles and Guidelines to Strengthen the Social Dimension of

Higher Education (2020) present the major framework for social inclusion policies at national as well as at institutional level.

Universities are expected to provide access to higher education and to ensure equitable outcomes for all students, as well as vulnerable, marginalized groups. Actually, as noticed by O'Shea et al. (2016, p. 5) "Providing access is only one part of the social inclusion equation." The International Association of Universities acknowledges: "access without a reasonable chance of success is an empty phrase" (Devlin, 2013, p. 939 in O'Shea et al., 2016, p. 5). So, in an equitable and diverse learning environments, all the students should have equal opportunities not only to participate, but to succeed in educational processes.

Macheridis and Paulsson (2021) discussed the processes of accountabilization that have been transforming the higher education institutions to become accountable for their performance. Accountability contributes to professors' assessments of student performance, focusing on student's individual features, not just on the student as a member of some different or vulnerable group. Moreover, students belonging to such groups usually don't require special practices, but prefer inclusion pedagogy benefitial for all students, since sometimes too obvious accommodation could have opposite effect by stressing the differences, instead overcoming them in a way that all students feel supported and valued. There was research about students' experiences of their perception of being included (Tobbell, 2020, pp. 11–12): "… inclusive relationships were enabled by the experience of positive emotion which underpins the formation of effective learning relationships which is part of feeling included. Further, feeling included demands that students can exercise their own identities, where the practices of the institution do not allow for this, inclusion is not fostered. Feeling included is also supported by continuous communication between learners and teachers, learners and the institution and learners and fellow learners."

Comprehensive accountability frameworks should be developed to promote ethical practices, sustainability, and inclusivity to serve diverse student populations with equitable starting positions towards successful acquisition of learning outcomes. The implementation of accountability measures can enhance also the higher education institution performance in successful social inclusion. There is a strong need to establish the framework of indicators that could enable tracking the social inclusion outcome and to adopt the internationally agreed set of indicators to enable comparisons among institution in this field of their performance.

Here we highlight the valuable potential indicators overview as proposed by Veidemane, Kaiser and Craciun (2021, pp. 51–52) derived from a broad list of indicators from different studies and academic literature, policy documents and large-scale projects:

- "The number of new entrants with a low social economic background as a percentage of the total number of new entrants, normalised by the regional percentage of population with low socio-economic background.
- The number of new entrants who are the first student in his/her immediate family, as a percentage of the total number of new entrants, normalised by the regional level of higher education attainment.

- The number of new entrants with disabilities as a percentage of total number of new entrants. Disabilities refer to health, sight, hearing, speech impairments, and learning disabilities.
- The number of new entrants with migrant background as a percentage of total number of students, normalised by the regional percentage of population with migrant background.
- The number of new entrants with ethnic minority background as a percentage of total number of students, normalised by the regional percentage of population with ethnic minority background.
- The number of new entrants older than 29 years as a percentage of total number of new entrants.
- The number of (fe)male new entrants as a percentage of the total number of new entrants."

According to Fuller et al. (2004, pp. 315–316). there are "four key issues for supporting disabled students' learning, based on disabled students' own experiences and reflections. First, their accounts highlight the need for both variety and flexibility in all aspects of teaching and learning—what works for one student may not be a good option for another. Second, there is a need to ensure quality as well as parity of provision in comparison with non-disabled peers. Third, access to information for both the disabled students themselves and for lecturers is evidently an important basis for ensuring the key principles of variety, flexibility, quality and parity can be achieved…Finally, the actions and attitudes of staff are manifestly important in themselves and in relation to the other issues highlighted in this study. It is a common experience that creating an inclusive learning environment is likely to have benefits for all students, not least those disabled students who, for whatever reason, do not make their needs known."

Hand in hand with the learning process, the same supporting issues should be applied to the assessment process. "Assessment in higher education should not disadvantage diverse students because of characteristics or abilities extraneous to the outcomes being judged. All students should be supported to achieve and demonstrate capability in an equitable manner"… what leads us to the concept of assessment for inclusion: "assessment that recognises diversity in student learning, and endeavours to ensure that no student is discriminated against by virtue of features other than their ability to meet appropriate standards" (Tai et al., 2023, pp. 483–484).

While in theory, it is clear that it is necessary to stick to academic standards in making assessments with necessary adjustments of the examination process, recent researches raise the questions (Ashworth et al., 2010, p. 221) such as: "Are tools designed specifically to create consistency in standards giving staff permission to create new frameworks to make judgements in a more inclusive way? Or could it be that ambiguities in criteria disguise a lowering of standards for students with complex disabilities? From this standpoint, the concept of 'reasonable adjustments' does not take into account the complexities of academic judgement, and, therefore, the legal requirement, while sound in intention, is considerably more contentious in application. "

That brought the literature on inclusive assessment to move, according to Nieminen (2022, p. 72): "from technical (the accommodation model) to social (accessible assessment design) conceptualisation of the inclusivity in assessment", i.e. "the one that locates the inaccessible and exclusionary elements of assessment design before assessment is conducted."

Hockings (2010, pp. 46–47) has provided the valuable synthesis of publicly funded UK studies research results with implications for policy and practice of inclusive learning and teaching:

1. "The need to see students as individuals, to learn about and value their differences and to maintain high expectations of all students.
2. The need for teachers to create safe learning environments in which students can express their ideas, beliefs, requirements and identities freely in an atmosphere of mutual trust and respect, empathy and open mindedness.
3. The need to establish at the outset clear rules of what is expected from students with tight control and close monitoring to develop confident learner identities and behaviours.
4. The need for teachers to create student-focused 'universal' programmes, modules and lessons that engage all students meaningfully by encouraging them to draw on and apply their own and others' knowledge.
5. The need for teachers to anticipate, recognise and provide for individuals' specific physical, cultural, academic and pastoral needs, particularly at critical periods (e.g. transitions, examinations).
6. The need for shifts in negative beliefs about, and attitudes towards, student diversity that currently inhibit the development of inclusive learning and teaching.
7. The need to challenge and change policies, practices, systems and standards that inhibit the participation of students in any subject or constrain teachers' capacity to engage all their students.
8. The need for greater involvement of students in the negotiation of the curriculum, assessment and in the development of teachers.
9. The need for adequate time, resources and a safe environment in which staff at all levels can develop a shared understanding and commitment to student diversity and inclusive practice. Such understanding and commitment should be a key component of staff recruitment, training, development and reward.
10. The need for adequate and relevant central services to support students and staff; integrating strategies for teaching and learning, widening participation and disability; and co-ordinating the efforts of academics and specialist support staff in central service centres.
11. The need for collection and analysis of institutional, quantitative and qualitative data for the evaluation and improvement of inclusive learning and teaching strategies, policies and practices."

Although the majority of research on inclusive pedagogy focuses at providing the same opportunities for all the students independently of their belonging to any vulnerable group, actually it is necessary to understand also the vice-versa mutual reflections: the vulnerable groups of students actually contribute to teachers' professional development enriching their experiences and building added value for the whole university. According to Moriña (2020, p. 1213) "Universities should not only work on the access, permanence and success of students with disabilities; they should also make use of the great resource that these students pose as an example to others: they have a strong will and are eager to learn and excel, and they show great motivation and interest, despite the adversities they have to overcome … The data provided by this study suggest that inclusion is possible and that disability, far from being interpreted as a difficulty, is an additional value in a university that moves forward and away from the deficit lens, acknowledging that every student is important and has something to contribute, both to the university itself and to society."

12.3 Social Inclusion in Croatian Higher Education

There are many documents developed in the context of social dimension of higher education in Europe such as Widening Participation for Equity and Growth strategy (2015), Principles and guidelines for strengthening the social dimension of higher education in the European area of higher education (2020), Implementation guidelines—Erasmus + and European Solidarity Corps Inclusion and Diversity Strategy (European Commission, 2021), Policy Recommendations (Bologna with Stakeholders Eyes for an Innovative, Inclusive and Interconnected EHEA by 2030, 2024) and others.

In accordance with this framework, the Croatian National Group for Improving the Social Dimension of Higher Education has developed the Plan of Measures for Enhancing the Social Dimension of Higher Education for the period 2023–2025 and revised the definitions of vulnerable and underrepresented groups:

- students whose parents have a lower education level—higher education, particularly at higher level is still less accessible to students from families with lower parental education;
- students with lower socio-economic status—lower economic status reduces the probability of enrolment in higher education as well as participation in mobilities, summer schools and raises the rate of giving up of studying, particularly for employed students;
- students with additional family obligations, that could present financial, time psychological load, particularly students-parents (usually older students), students taking care for family member with disabilities, students with brothers/sisters under the age of 26 in the regular education system;
- students from single-parent families or without parents;

- students, children of Croatian veterans—children of dead, imprisoned or missing Croatian veterans and children of the Croatian war veterans with most severe disabilities;
- students coming from alternative care systems that need financial and psychological support, since after the age of 18, they no longer consume alternative systems protection;
- Roma students according to Support program for the education of members of the Roma national minority for the period 2021 to 2023;
- students with disabilities in accordance with Guidelines for improving the support system for students with disabilities in higher education in the Republic of Croatia;
- older students who can now, under new regulation, study as full-time students even if they are employed;
- employed students, challenged to combine working and studying obligations, which can also use the benefits of working across the student's service under new regulation;
- students with three-year high school—that should firstly attend the fourth year to enable the enrolment to study, or otherwise to enrol in the short professional study before their enrolment in undergraduate study program;
- homeless students;
- students traveling to study—which is time consuming;
- students from rural, transport-isolated and/or deprived areas—with lower access to studying, with strong need for dormitory accommodation;
- students refugees and asylum seekers—facing with obstacles like language knowledge, fees, health insurance;
- LGBT students;
- female students in technical fields, male students in humanities—the need for alleviating gender stereotypes.

12.3.1 Building Capacity to Strengthen Accountability for Equality, Diversity and Inclusion Practices—The Case-Study of Juraj Dobrila University of Pula, Croatia

Juraj Dobrila University of Pula has been developing as an inclusive academic community that values diversity and promotes equality. According to the University document Recommendations for inclusive communication with people with disabilities: "Understanding the specific needs of people with disabilities is the key to creating an environment where everyone can participate equally and realize their full potential. Effective and decent communication, apart from facilitating daily interaction, contributes to breaking down prejudices and stigmatization related to disabilities." These Recommendations include the guidelines for effective communication with people with physical disabilities, impairments of vision, hearing, speech problems. The University nourishes the approach for any academic community member to actively meet and include people with disabilities in their academic environment, to give them the opportunity to contribute and realize their full potential.

Methodology—A Case Study

This empirical study is performed under the framework of Croatian higher education system. It is aligned with the Bologna process and is structured as a binary system offering two types of studies: university undergraduate, graduate, postgraduate studies and professional studies as short-cycle professional undergraduate studies, undergraduate and graduate specialist professional studies. There are nine public and four private universities in Croatia. According to State Bureau of Statistics there were 148.383 students enrolled in higher education institutions in Croatia in academic year 2023/24, out of which 58,4% were female students. Faculties enrolled 83,6% of students, polytechnics 14,5%, art academies 1,8%, and colleges 0,1%.

Here we present qualitative single case study research of real inclusive practices implementation based on selected public university, located in Pula, at the south of Istrian county, considered as most developed Croatian county after the Town of Zagreb and Zagreb county, out of 21 Croatian counties. This university was selected as an average university, since it is neither the largest or the oldest one, neither belongs to the group of newly established ones. It was founded in 2006 (although its constituents have longer history dating from 1960s), and belongs to the group of smaller universities like the ones located in Zadar, Dubrovnik, Varaždin, Slavonski Brod, while larger, traditional universities are situated in Zagreb, Split, Rijeka and Osijek.

There are no entry examinations for all the students who passed the state graduate exam after high scool, except for art studies.

Under this case study, the data were collected from national documents and guidelines, as well as research papers, university strategic plans, rules, documents and brochures, university bodies' decisions, students' questionnaires (internal survey) as provided by the University DEI office, financial model and reports as provided by accounting and reporting office, workshops held by internal and external experts, interview with the head of the DEI office, discussions held during faculty council sessions, as well as own authors' archives and experiences acquaired during current mandate of vice rector for academic topics, enrollment process and student support, and ex mandate of vice rector for resources management, but also as teachers facing with DEI topics in everyday practice. We also combined the methods of induction and deduction searching for the answers to the research questions upon the differences between formal and real inclusive policy and practices implementation, considering the current contribution from the literature that has identified decoupling processes. The research combined the study of the institutional framework and relevant university documents that declared its commitment to inclusivity goals, the detailed investigation of socially inclusive real practices in everyday life and the overview of inclusive practices outcomes as considered from the students' own attitudes and experiences.

Considering that Mampaey (2017) has discussed possible decoupling reasons—the neo-liberalisation of higher education, uncertainty about effective inclusive practices, resistance of key constituencies and resource stringency, the latter was particulary interesting to explore in an ex-transition country that is seriously struggling with the lack of resources. Such environment is expected to particularly contribute to the gap between declarative and real inclusive activities, so it was interesting to test the existance of such a gap based on this case study with the results presented as follows. Moreover, in order to narrow any potential gap, the model of indicators classified in three groups was developed to enable tracking the progress of social inclusion activities and outcomes achieved that should provide significant feedback to guide further inclusive governance.

Current Inclusion Practices

University of Pula has developed many activities to improve equality, diversity and inclusion across the whole academic society of Pula. To coordinate those activities performed by university's faculties and departments, Office for Equality, Diversity and Inclusion (EDI) was established with the scope of work:

- to provide gender/sexual equality, ensure visibility and inclusiveness of LGBTIQ + persons, encourage a culture of non-violence, the values of tolerance and justice, and to increase the inclusiveness awareness of students and employees,
- to ensure inclusion and support for students with disabilities and students belonging to other vulnerable and underrepresented groups.
- The activities are focused on equalizing the study opportunities of all students who, due to illness, impairment or disorder, have permanent, temporary or occasional difficulties in fulfilling their daily academic obligations.

(https://www.unipu.hr/rektorat/ured_za_ravnopravnost_raznolikost_i_inkluzivnost, accessed January 10, 2025)

Students are informed about the Office for Equality, Diversity and Inclusion activities and its contacts at the beginning of each academic year, during the Orientation Day. News and notices are regularly announced on the University's website.

Students with disabilities

There were 1,32% students with disabilities studying at University of Pula in academic year 2024/25, according to the Office for EDI Report to Ombudsperson for persons with disabilities, 2024.

The support is provided for students with any type of disabilities like motoric problems, sensory impairments, physical or mental illnesses or disorders, specific learning difficulties (such as dyslexia, dysgraphia, dyscalculia), ADHD, autism or other health conditions. Learning difficulties and motoric problems were the most frequent type of disabilities at Pula University according to the Report as cited above.

The Office for EDI collects the data about the students with disabilities to improve the services offered and for statistical reasons, by questionnaires and interviews with students, in accordance with GDPR rules. The data set, as suggested by Coordination of the ombudsman for persons with disabilities consists of:

1. personal data (including type of the disability or difficulty),
2. information about the study (department, field of study, study program level, academic year—of enrolment and current study year, full time or part time status, changes of study program, ECTS earned, possible temporary breaks of study, study progress, the use of direct enrolment rights, accommodation in the students dormitory and the necessary adjustments, received financial support or scholarship from University funds),
3. data on previous adjustments (during previous education),
4. necessary support and adjustments during studying (like adjustment of tests, adaptation of the literature, individual study plan development, space adjustment, peer (fellow) support, educational assistance, personal assistance, specialized transport, student accommodation benefits, specialized equipment, psychological counselling, career counselling, support group, education in the field of academic and life skills, support during international mobility programs, etc.),
5. additional data (gathered in collaboration with alumni—about the post-studying period activities like graduation, employment, break of study).

The University ensures the accessibility to study programs for students with disabilities even from the first moment they start to think about their enrolment in studies.

Enrolment process priority

Candidates with physical disability of 60%, with certain types and severity of disability or impairments, are entitled to priority for enrolment in undergraduate studies as full-time or part-time students, over the approved enrolment quota, but the candidates still must exceed the required points threshold and pass special knowledge or skills tests for particular study programs.

Teaching and examinationprocess adjustments

Status, conditions and methods of studying are regulated by the Rulebook on studying for students with disabilities at Juraj Dobrila University in Pula.

According to this Rulebook, students with disabilities are those students with long-term impairments, disabilities or illnesses who in the interaction encounter obstacles in the environment that prevent them from fully and effectively fulfilling their students' obligations in accordance with the study program and syllabuses. These are students with: motor disorders, visual impairments, hearing impairments, chronic diseases, with mental illnesses and disorders, with learning difficulties (dyslexia, dysgraphia, dyscalculia, ADHD), with other health conditions or difficulties that may affect the course of studies.

Recommendation for adjustments of teaching or/and examination process are prepared based on the student's request, appropriate documentation, and an individual interview to eliminate or reduce possible obstacles during the study (according to the Rulebook on recommendations for adjustments of the teaching and exam process).

There are many teaching adjustments offered, such as digital form of teaching materials, lectures audio recordings, extended deadlines to fulfil students' obligations or alternative methods applied, while keeping the same learnings outcomes acquainted by all students. Also, examination process adjustments are often performed such as extended exam time, adequate exam form (oral or written), graphical adjustments of exam materials, individually performed exams, etc.

The application for teaching and/or examination adjustments can be submitted by students with:

- impairment of neuromuscular-skeletal and movement-related functions,
- impairment of sensory functions (vision, hearing),
- specific learning difficulties, impairment of language, voice and speech functions,
- impairment of organs and organ systems (includes all organ systems),
- chronic diseases,
- behavioural disorders and mental health impairments,
- multiple impairments.

A student with a disability may miss 15% of classes more than the total number of absences allowed for each individual course. More than 15% of classes missing were allowed only in case of providing the medical or other documentation indicating the student was prevented from attending classes.

In cases where absences are not allowed, the teacher in charge of the course, with the opinion of the Office for Equality, Diversity and Inclusion, will consider justified absences, considering all the circumstances of each individual case.

It is necessary to emphasize that adjustments in the category of students with behavioral disorders and mental health impairments are particularly challenging, not only from the perspective of teachers but also from the perspective of professionals, given that there is a whole range of different cases, and thus situations that require adjustments. Given that this type of disability is very often not manifested physically, or at first glance to a professor, it is difficult to assess what can be expected and what will be needed. For this reason, we believe that this segment should be given special attention, not only in the context of psychological counseling, but with the involvement of experts exclusively for this field who will be able to react ad hoc, advise and instruct professors about adjustments, and even organize training specifically for this type of adjustments. After all, studying is very often occupational therapy for such students, so this is another reason to pay additional attention to this.

Peer support

Continuous support is organized as peer support, i.e. fellow student assistant' support, organized upon the invitation to students wishing to help to their fellows with disabilities that attend the same study program. Student assistant is hired to provide assistance in various aspects of student life, not only the physical or learning assistance but also in solving administrative procedures, obtaining the literature and performing many academic tasks. There is also the course "Peer Support for Students with Disabilities" that provides the undergraduate, graduate or postgraduate students with the competences and academic, practical, socio-emotional and communication skills necessary to provide the help as needed.

Although commendable as an initiative and support, peer support is only part of the support that students with disabilities need. Currently, there is no possibility for students with disabilities to obtain a teaching assistant set by the state or paid by ministry, as is the case for primary and secondary school pupils, nor a personal assistant who would be available continuously throughout the day. This shortage is mainly addressed by teaching assistants paid for by students and their families, through associations for people with disabilities, sometimes by the presence of parents throughout the day at faculty, and various other individual initiatives and solutions.

Financial benefits

Free tuition relates to full-time students with determined percentage of physical disability of 60% and above

- who enrolled in the first year of studies for the first time,
- who achieved at least 30 ECTS points in previous academic year by the time of enrolment in the next academic year.

Partial subsidy of participation in the costs of studies is provided for the students with physical disability of 60% and above:

- who achieved from 23 to 29 ECTS points in one academic year. The number of missing ECTS credits is multiplied by the cost of one ECTS point minus 50%.
- who achieved less than 23 ECTS points in previous academic year. They pay half of the amount of tuition fee.
- who re-enrolled for the prolongation of their studies (the so-called senior year). They pay half of the full amount of tuition, except for students who have only a final/diploma thesis left to complete their studies, who pay a minimum participation of 6 ECTS points minus 50%. This stands for full-time as well as part-time students.

Part-time students with physical disability of 60% and above pay half of the full amount of tuition during their regular study period and for the prolongation as it is stated above.

Those rights are related to the number of years corresponding to twice the regular duration of study program, and to the enrolment in new study program of the same level after previous uncompleted study program.

In addition, all life-long education programs performed at the university are free of charge for students with disabilities.

Accommodation subsidies

Students with residence outside Pula and with disabilities have the right to subsidized accommodation in a student dormitory with following conditions:

Students with disabilities—60% or more confirmed organ damage or more serious impairment of functional abilities (according to regulated types and levels), including students with disabilities in doctoral studies, acquire the direct right to subsidized accommodation throughout the entire calendar year if they have achieved at least 1 ECTS credit in the current academic year, and at least 15 ECTS credits on average in the previous years of study.

Students with disabilities—50% confirmed organ damage or less serious impairment of functional abilities (according to regulated types and levels), acquire additional 400 points in the scoring process upon their application at the public tender for accommodation in Student dormitory, as announced by the University of Pula Student Centre.

Transportation costs financial support

The Ministry of Science, Education and Youth of Croatia provides partial financial support for transportation costs for full-time students with disabilities with at least 60% physical impairment or more serious impairments of functional abilities.

The University also provides them with the organized transport services.

Scholarships

The Ministry of Science, Education and Youth provides the additional points in the ranking process for the students with disabilities when they apply for state scholarships for full-time students studying in STEM field or for students with poor socio-economic status. In addition to state scholarships, Juraj Dobrila University of Pula announces a public call for students with disabilities scholarships every academic year.

Students with disabilities have right to additional financial support during their stay abroad under the international student exchange programs (more about Erasmus program inclusion topics—in Härtel & Marterer, 2023).

Adaptation of buildings to the needs of students with disabilities

The students' dormitory facilities are built following Croatian Rulebook on ensuring the accessibility of buildings for people with disabilities and reduced mobility. They have flat floors for free movement without obstacles. There are rooms with their own bathrooms, fully adapted for people with disabilities and reduced mobility, located on the ground floor. It is possible to evacuate from the ground floor level, directly to the field, in case of emergency. All public spaces on the ground floor and basement are fully accessible to people with reduced mobility. The entrance to the ground floor is enabled by a sloping lifting platform located in the windshield. The entrance to the basement is also enabled by a slight ramp. In the basement, there are parking spaces for students with disabilities/reduced mobility. A tactile line of guidance is provided from the porch, through the entrance area to the notice board and the elevator. Tactile line guidance is also provided in the restaurant, from the front door to the toilet. The elevator buttons are marked with Braille. By choosing the finishing coverings and dimensioning the space, all the necessary preconditions for a safe and undisturbed use of the building by students with disabilities are ensured.

Ramps and elevators are also provided in other university buildings to enable easy approach to classrooms and other spaces, particularly in new buildings that are more convenient for adjustments than the older ones.

The Accessibility plan of premises, procedures and policies of the Juraj Dobrila University of Pula in relation to people with disabilities comprises assessments of the organizational (soft) accessibility aspects and architectural accessibility of the space, as well as the plan for improving the elements of accessibility. This plan suggests complementing the definitions of the social model of disability, reasonable adjustments and universal design, also to describe with further details the dimensions of accessibility in the university acts.

Regarding the architectural accessibility, under this plan for each building, current situation is described in detail with specific proposal for improvements where still needed to fit to persons with disabilities—regarding the entrance area, communications/corridors, toilets, free spaces around the furniture in rooms, classrooms, workspaces, position of advertising board, ramps and elevators as well as the parking lots.

Accessibility of Website

Also, in addition to buildings adjustments, according to the Accessibility statement, Juraj Dobrila University in Pula strives to make its websites accessible in accordance with the Law on Accessibility of Websites and Software Solutions for Mobile Devices of Public Sector Bodies of the Republic of Croatia (Narodne novine 17/19) transposing Directive (EU) 2016/2102 of the European Parliament and of the Council of October 26, 2016 on the accessibility of websites and mobile applications of public sector bodies (SL L 327, 2 December 2016). The University's web pages are adapted to students and any person from vulnerable and underrepresented groups by using accessibility settings that include the following options: changing the font size, changing the page layout, and changing the page contrast. Further improvements of web content accessibility through more than one sense are expected in accordance with the Web Accessibility Initiative Guidelines for ensuring the accessibility of online content.

Psychological Counselling

To provide psychological support and help to students, Juraj Dobrila University in Pula has established a Psychological Counselling Centre which organizes individual or group sessions to educate students in various areas necessary for successful study, such as communication and social skills, learning strategies, organizational skills, overcoming test anxiety, and the like. The main purpose of counselling is to increase personal satisfaction, personal competence and academic success of students. Around half of the users are students with different disabilities and disorders.

Students' feedback

According to the internal survey Experiences of students with disabilities at Juraj Dobrila University of Pula (Rotta, 2024), 75% of students with disabilities have easily or very easily adapted to the University environment (physical obstacles, social life, support by peers, professors, staff), while 12,5% reported hard adaptation (none has reported very hard adaptation), the rest couldn't estimate. Moreover, 62,5% of students made close friendships with other students at the University and 75% stated they didn't miss the family support during their student life. The percentage of 12,5% were not independent in performing the students' obligations while 25% were partially independent and 62,5% were completely independent. The adaptation of teaching or examining process was necessary for 62,5% students. According to the students' assessment, in 60% of cases, the adaptation was helpful, while for 40% of students it was partially helpful, and no one reported that they were useless. Although the professors were officially informed about the need for modifications, in only 20% of cases the students didn't have to explain the necessary adaptations directly to professors, while further explanations were required rarely (20%), often (20%) or always (20%). Regarding successfulness in students' tasks performance, 37,5% of them manage to fulfil them very easily or easily (25%), while also 25% of students hardly manage to fulfil the tasks (very hard—0%). Many students (62,5%) are acquainted with the services offered by Office for EDI, but the rest of them still is not aware of activities provided by the Office. The satisfaction by the Office services was also explored to assess if the students' requests and inquiries were adequately addressed by the Office—such as finding students' assistants, adjusting classes and exams, timely information, scholarship information, etc. The requests were fully solved by Office for 50% students, partially solved for 25% of students, not solved for 12,5% while the others didn't contact the Office. Considering the access to all the necessary information and resources, such as literature, assistive technology, staff support needed to successfully perform the student duties, half of the students have all information and resources as needed, 25% of them reported the partial access, while others couldn't estimate. Noone has expressed the need for another special equipment or additional services to be provided by the University.

Students from the alternative care system

University of Pula facilitates access to its study programs to future full-time and part-time students coming from the alternative care system where they lived until the age of 18 years old instead in a parental home, applying the following measures:

- enrolment in the first year of undergraduate professional studies, undergraduate university studies, integrated undergraduate and graduate university studies outside the approved quota, and according to the enrolment criteria with the consent of the Ministry of Education, Science and Youth;
- enrolment in the first year of studies without paying participation in the costs of studies and tuition fees;
- enrolment in the next academic year without paying participation in study costs or tuition fees, provided that at least 30 ECTS credits have been earned in the previous academic year.
- This also stands for single parents.

A student can consume the rights for as many years as corresponds to the regulated duration of study, at most one year longer, or two years longer for integrated undergraduate and graduate university studies.

Students with lower socioeconomic status

The criteria for determining the lower socio-economic status of students studying at the Juraj Dobrila University in Pula and the incentives that facilitate access to studies for students of lower socio-economic status are determined by university's internal acts.

The University announces an annual call for applications for support and facilitated access to studies for students with lower socio-economic status that includes:

- awarding scholarships,
- one-off financial support,
- procurement of computers, literature or other adequate equipment and
- exemption of students from paying tuition fees in whole or in part.

The rights above are granted to students who meet the following general criteria:

- they are Croatian citizens or European Union citizens with registered residence in the Republic of Croatia who have approved the status of a foreigner with permanent residence in the Republic of Croatia,
- they are full-time students at the University of Pula.

The support is approved for students based on a ranking list determined according to the following special conditions:

- The average monthly income per member of the joint household[1] does not exceed 65% of the budget amount determined each year by the relevant regulation;
- Statement on the members of the joint household has been submitted as part of the application form.

Scoring for the ranking list is based not only on monthly income per student's household member, but also other criteria such as parent-student status, student without one or both parents, student with a physical disability of at least 60%, student with brother or sister with developmental disabilities who are not included in the regular education system, student who studies outside the place of residence, student whose family is a beneficiary of permanent financial assistance, student with one or both parents with a 100% physical disability, student whose sibling is of preschool age or involved in the regular primary, secondary and higher education system.

In 2024/25 academic year, there were 1,43% of total students who applied for financial support.

The support cannot be granted to students:

(1) who did not meet the requirements for enrolment in a higher year of study,

[1] According to Croatian legislation, a joint household is a community consisting of spouses or partners, children and other relatives who live together in the same residence, work, earn income in another way and spend it together. A child who does not live in the same residence with the family and is in school is also considered a family member, until the completion of regular schooling, and at the latest until the age of 29.

(2) who have acquired a total number of less than 42 ECTS points in the study programme divided by the number of enrolments in the previous academic years, not including the current academic year;
(3) who changed their study programme in the academic year of application on call;
(4) who enrolled in a study programme at the same level of study as a full-time student three times.

In addition, instalment payment (four instalments during first/winter semester of academic year) of tuition fees may be granted to full-time and part-time students of the Juraj Dobrila University in Pula, enrolled in undergraduate university studies, graduate university studies, integrated undergraduate and graduate university studies and undergraduate professional studies, provided that their average monthly income per member of a joint household does not exceed 65% of the statutory budget amount as determined at the national level every year.

Also, students of lower socio-economic status, as well as students from alternative care, students without parents, students with disabilities and students who are parents of small children, are provided with more favourable accommodation conditions in the Student Dormitory.

The Student Union provides one-time assistance in the form of vouchers for shopping in stores to student parents of small children, which aims to alleviate the socio-economic difficulties of these students.

In addition to the mentioned forms of financial support for vulnerable and under-represented groups of students, directly by awarding grants, scholarships or indirectly by financing the work of a separate office to support these students, aids, equipment, accessibility of websites, peer support, student assistants, platforms, adaptation of facilities to student standards, work of counselling centres, etc., the University regularly reported to the Ministry of Science, Education and Youth about the allocation of a minimum of 1% of state budget program funding total amount as provided for University, to support students with disabilities and 1% to support students with lower socio-economic status. This was continuous process during the previous cycle of program funding, and the practice of financial support continued.

It is also worth to mention that two university departments offer online study programs, which makes it especially convenient for students with disabilities as well as part-time students or students from distant rural areas, to access higher education because of online studying flexibility enabling the balance of education with other commitments.

The University has recently adopted the Rulebook on recognition and evaluation of prior learning, i.e. of competencies acquired through formal, non-formal and informal education, based on learning outcomes as required by the certain program. This also contributes to educational inequalities reduction. The students can be exempted from parts of the study program with aligning outcomes, making it easier for students coming from less favourable educational and socioeconomic environments, for part-time and older students.

Plans and Improvements

Despite of many inclusion programs that have been evolving, there are still areas for further improvements. Institutional and management commitment to inclusive learning should be clearly recognizable in institution's mission, strategic documents, policies, procedures, plans of inclusive activities by university and its departments, in accordance with the University of Pula vision as stated in its Development Strategy 2021–2026:

> The vision of our university is to become a prestigious inclusive centre of scientific and teaching excellence and a modern entrepreneurial university founded as a platform for the creation of human capital and an engine for the development of the social community of Istria County and beyond.

Therefore, to follow its vision, the University should be—in one word—sensible, in any aspect of inclusive organizational culture, supported by developed collaboration with non-profit organizations, ministry and local governments to foster inclusive activities.

All the stakeholders like students, faculty, administration, community should understand the institution's commitment to social inclusion and should get involved in decision-making regarding social inclusion to identify the opportunities for improvements.

The stakeholders are in the first place, the students who are expected to value diversity not only in their academic society but also once they become academic citizens to acknowledge it in their working environments and whole society. The academic management should coordinate the inclusive activities at departments and university level, matching the equality goals with funds allocated for their accomplishment. The professors (teachers) should be aware of individual differences and invest the efforts in inclusive teaching, curriculum development and assessments to ensure equal opportunities but also equal learning outcomes acquired by all students. Their contribution to inclusivity could be recognized by promotion criteria. Also, administration staff and student services should be adequately educated and deeply committed to handling diversity.

As part of University's commitment to providing support to all the students in need, there are many activities planned period:

- individualization program: continuous preparation of individual adaptation proposals for students with disabilities;
- in addition to peer support, introduction of professor—mentorship to monitor the course of studies and provide support to students with disabilities;
- providing transportation for students to the dislocated campus part;
- organization of an annual event with lectures and workshops and the awarding of prizes for the most successful students with disabilities, on the International Day of Persons with Disabilities (December 3rd);
- cooperation with the student union in party organizations;
- organization of the workshop "Put yourself in their shoes" (walking with obstacles blindfolded or in a wheelchair, etc.);

- continuity of sensitization educations, workshops for teaching and non-teaching staff on the topic of raising awareness and accessibility for people with disabilities, which are currently regularly organized within the framework of individual projects from EU funds (or independently, outside the projects), where not only the elements of physical accessibility but also the ways of communication, treatment, and support for this vulnerable group of students are elaborated on case examples;
- regular updates of brochure about all the rights and opportunities that students with disabilities can exercise at the University;
- recommendations to employees on how to communicate with people with disabilities;
- procurement of equipment (computers and scanners) for University Library so that library materials can be transferred into audio formats for visually impaired students and students with learning difficulties (dyslexia, dysgraphia), and those who, due to physical impairment or motor impairments, are unable to hold a book, handle it, focus or move their eyes. This initiative is based on the provisions of the Law on Copyright and Related Rights and the Marrakesh Treaty, ratified by Croatia, which obliges member states to ensure the availability of library materials and other content in accessible formats for people with disabilities, thereby contributing to their education, employment and social integration by equal access to knowledge and information;
- organization of "living" libraries;
- application of EU projects to improve the architectural accessibility for the rest of the buildings that still need adjustments, to purchase equipment for students with disabilities;
- strengthening the cooperation with associations of persons with disabilities;
- development of measures for other underrepresented groups of students;
- promotion of gender equality;
- creation of a gender equality action plan;
- development of guidelines for gender inclusive language;
- preparation of the Rulebook on protection against sexual harassment and other forms of gender discrimination;
- surveys related to motherhood and discrimination

(Interview with Head of Office for equality, diversity and inclusion Sara Rotta).

As further improvement of existing materials and acts, the detailed document should be prepared in line with Guidelines for improving the support system for students with disabilities in higher education in the Republic of Croatia (Kiš-Glavaš, 2016), that would comprise at one place the information upon:

- availability of teaching materials to students before the start of the semester,
- audio recordings of lectures,
- availability of e-learning forms and digital repositories of teaching materials,

- providing the personal assistant for some teaching forms (laboratory exercises, with chemicals or electronic devices, etc.) and peer support,
- alternative contents for field teaching or similar forms,
- availability of computers, typists, sign language translators, communication mediators, when necessary,
- provided digitalized teaching literature accessible to students with visual impairments and reading difficulties (audio books, easy-to-read books, audio periodicals, video/DVD books with subtitles and/or sign language, Braille books, large print books),
- systematic implementation of an individually adjusted knowledge, competences and skills testing process (by extended time for solving written exams, oral instead of written test and vice versa, etc.)
- monitoring the share of students with disabilities in the student population, continuous analysis and evaluation, identifying specific needs, problems and limitations, searching for the needs for changes in education process, student life, etc.

In the near future, besides the ordinary surveys upon the satisfaction of users by social inclusion activities performed, it is also necessary to establish and to track key performance indicators related to social inclusion to monitor the progress towards broader participation of target groups and disparities reduction or elimination. Some examples are provided in the next section.

Accounting and Accountability for Social Inclusion

Accounting is usually considered as the information support for making business decisions, meeting the financial objectives in the first line. This approach has been complemented by additional requirements set by corporate social responsibility trends that contributed to the development of sustainability accounting. Under the sustainability accounting, besides the environmental issues, social equity topics are expected to be embraced proactively to attain the sustainability goals. Global Reporting Initiative, as considered to be the golden standard for sustainability reporting, provides the guidelines for environmental, social and governance performance disclosure. According to Jeyaretnam (2023) "As accountants, we can play a pivotal role in aligning corporate strategies and financial reporting with the SDGs (sustainable development goals). Integrating these goals into our practices can facilitate positive social and environmental impacts, fostering a more inclusive and equitable society." Sustainability accounting disclosures not only contribute to companies' and institutions' transparency, enhancing their responsibility for equality and inclusivity achievements, but also enables the marginalized groups to actively address their needs based on the reported data—"But accounting also allows marginalized social groups to raise awareness of problems like economic inequality and exclusion. For example: applying administrative and accounting criteria to social welfare programmes can bring to light how a programme might privilege some groups and exclude others. This exclusion, made visible by accounting categorizations, can lead such groups to take initiative in developing alternative solutions and innovative policies to help address these issues… Reflecting on this social and behavioral role of accounting gives us better tools to navigate the multifaceted challenges of our time, fostering greater accountability and transparency in the pursuit of a more equitable and sustainable society" (Duenas, 2024).

The facts as stated above also stand for accounting and accountability practices in higher education institutions. The accounting role is to provide the relevant information for accountable actions to reach inclusive higher education goals. The information system should enable collecting, monitoring, planning, analyzing and reporting the data upon the disadvantaged groups access, enrolment and participation statistics, measuring their performance including the retention and study completion rates. Those information enable the evaluation of outcomes and inclusive policies effectiveness, enabling tracking the progress and strategies or action plans adjustments as needed. Accountability practices in higher education are expected to provide equitable access, develop an inclusive institutional culture, remove the barriers, ensure transparent reporting and involve all the stakeholders towards inclusivity goals achievement.

University of Pula as one of nine public universities in Croatia is mostly financed by state budget. As the budget user, it applies the budget accounting and all related institutional framework requirements with detailed regulation of financial planning process, financial reporting, business books and documents, accounting principles, policies and methods, bookkeeping rules and defined chart of accounts in use. The budget accounting framework is used to allocate the resources intended for social inclusion purposes, to transparently present the financing of the needs of marginalized groups by specific funds targeted to reduce disparities, and finally to assess the social impact of policies, programs, and projects performed for vulnerable groups of students.

Budget classifications are employed such as economic classification, location and organizational classification, functional classification, classification by programs and activities, and classification by financial sources. Those classifications are also applied to accounting for social inclusion at University of Pula.

Economic classification is based on chart of accounts and here they reflect the nature of the expenses related to a particular social inclusion activity. So, there are different type of expenses like: scholarships for students with disability and lower socio-economic status, fees for peer supports, transport costs, salaries and work contracts fees for experts in psychological counselling centre, salaries in the Office for EDI, etc. Under functional classification, all the expenses are classified as higher education expenses. Regarding organizational classification, the expenses are classified under Rectorate as the administration unit offering services for all the departments at the university. According to program classification, there is a separate activity recognized under financial plan that relates to social inclusion expenses which comprises the work of Office for EDI, psychological counselling centre, scholarships awarded, peer support expenses, equipment purchasing, and all related expenses invested to reach the social inclusion goals. The expenses are also classified by the source of their financing, e.g. the scholarships are financed by state budget or University's own resources; peer support by own resources; counselling costs from University Student centre donations, etc. The building adjustments to enable appropriate accessibility are usually financed under EU infrastructural projects funds.

In such a way, the accounting information presented by different criteria is always available for university management or other stakeholders, for ministry reporting or statistical reporting, for analysis of trends across the years and relation with achieved outcomes of social inclusion activities. In 2024 the funds for supports to students with lower socio-economic status rose 65% in comparison with 2023 expenses, psychological counselling expenses increased for 4%, peer support for 21%, etc.

Under annual or periodical financial reporting, expenses and revenues are reported for each program or activity (so the same stands for social inclusion activities), using separate set of accounts and financial sources codes. In such a way clear accountability mechanisms are established.

Since the university has its own internal audit department, the internal and independent audits would further contribute to the University accountability and commitment to social inclusion.

Moreover, it would be advisable to involve the marginalized groups in the budgeting process, so they can feel their power to participate in selection of priorities and resources allocation. The Office for EDI communicates the possibilities to take a part of resources allocation process to students, such as participating as a member of e.g. scholarships award committee, or as a student representative in different university's bodies.

Besides the financial information as provided by the university's accounting information system that enable tracking the funds allocation and financial support of diversity groups over time, additional non-financial information could be useful to present the outputs of inclusion activities such as peer assistance provided, inclusive education workshops organized, accommodation benefits, etc. In addition to the output as measured by financial metrics, it is necessary to establish the goals and related outcomes metrics for measuring social inclusion accomplishments and development. Although some indicators are already collected, this process of data upon real outcomes tracking should be organized systematically on continuous basis.

The data should be organized in three groups:

1. Access to higher education—enrolment
2. Teaching and learning performance, study experience
3. Graduation.

1. Enrolment metrics—access outcomes:
- Percentage of students enrolled from underrepresented/diverse groups in total and by the group type, for each level of the study,
- Demographic data upon students from underrepresented/diverse groups,
2. Teaching and learning performance, study experiences and participation outcomes:
- Retention/withdrawal rates for underrepresented/diverse groups in total and by the group type, for each level of the study,

- Students' feedback—indicators of satisfaction with inclusion environments and programs, sense of participation, inclusion,
- The use of digital infrastructure and technology like online learning platforms, assistive technologies (type and frequency),
- The use of support services, counsellors' and mentors' help (type and frequency),
- Campus physical obstacles removed, accessibility improvements by type and building,
- Intervention needs identified and resolved (type and frequency),
- Participation in management and budgetary process (number of diverse groups' students in university's bodies, actions suggested and realized).

3. Graduation

- Completion rates for underrepresented groups in total and by the group type, for each level of the study,
- Completion data in relation to support programs used by graduates over studying.

For each indicator the measure should be stated, its starting value, planned annual value, realized indicator value and outcome explained. The benchmarking process is necessary to monitor the progress, and outcomes should be transparently publicly reported.

Since the indicators are groups based, it is necessary to provide clear definition of underrepresented, marginalized, vulnerable, diverse groups to be included in the analysis, since too many groups could make the process more expensive without related results achieved. But the main groups should be traced since "by focusing solely on underrepresented student groups, it did not consider other classifications such as vulnerable and disadvantaged groups as proposed by the latest Principles and Guidelines of the BFUG on Social Dimension" (2020).

On the other hand, there are also beneficial outcomes, not only for the students in focus, but also for university resulting from its accountability, commitment and efforts invested in social inclusion progress.

- Contribution to teaching excellence—relates to innovation of the creative teaching process, employing critical thinking upon diverse perspectives, development of methods and learning environment where every student can participate, to reach the successful results for all students (measurable by the number of new teaching methods applied, inclusive academic projects developed…),
- Contribution to research excellence—relates to development of new research perspectives, innovative approaches to complex social problems, and enhancing interdisciplinarity (measurable by the number of related research projects, publications, conferences participation or organization…),
- University contribution to inclusive society—University as a promotor of social equality, raising awareness upon social inclusion as inevitable transformation in the local, regional and wider community (measurable by the number of workshops, seminars, lifelong education programs upon social inclusion offered to community),
- University contribution to employment—relates to contribution to the labour market by delivering the graduates with market-relevant competences and skills

among the people with previously poor access to higher education system (measurable by employed graduates from vulnerable groups in six months/a year after graduation),
- Funds raising—enhancing the social dimension of higher education raises the university's attractiveness to donors, industry partners, funds providers (measurable by the amounts of funds increased based on social inclusion incentives),
- University visibility and reputation—the university becomes widely recognizable for its commitment to social inclusion and more competitive in global education market (measurable by progress at relevant university rankings lists, the number of new international partners and students attracted…).

Accounting system enhanced by broader diversity-focused information system should provide financial and non-financial information upon the measurable outcomes as previously stated to track progress in social inclusion developments from students' as well as from institution's perspective, and to derive in such a way integral conclusions upon its evolution process milestones.

This case study analysis points out the role of accounting and accountability in addressing social inclusion in higher education:

- accounting information system organization for processing of financial incentives and transactions to enable adequate resource allocation for inclusive purposes, in such a way social accountability reduces misallocation of resources in higher education, what is particularly important in an ex-transition country with scarce resources,
- transparent reporting system provides relevant information to internal and external stakeholders participating in social inclusive processes developments, particularly enabling the disadvantaged students' representatives to take a part of governance actions,
- in addition to financial metrics, non-financial information set on real outcomes are included in the model to better and in more comprehensive way enable the evaluation of inclusion policies implemented by responsive governance,
- accounting and accountability developments contribute to the general capacity building for the real progress of inclusive processes, not only declarative ones,
- finally, accountability, commitment and efforts invested in social inclusion progress are highlighted as contributors to university's teaching and research benefits, to its reputation and visibility.

12.4 Conclusion

This chapter deals with the case study of social inclusion activities in public university from an ex-transition country, by providing an overview of the current accountability and accounting practices in this field, and by presenting its further improvements as planned. The fact is that the University of Pula operates in Croatia, an ex-transition country burdened with complex consequences of transition, with very limited resources for social protection financing, just like in many other South-Eastern European ex transition countries, much lower than e.g. in Central European countries that have achieved better transition process outcomes. In such circumstances, it is inevitable to develop targeted support for lower social status and other vulnerable groups and to make the developed models sustainable. The universities are expected to become the leaders in the community, committed to handling diversity and receptive for best good practices that could be followed by other institutions, companies, authorities on local, regional or national level. The practices presented are probably not ideal, and find themselves with plenty of room for improvements, but could serve as one step closer to social inclusion mission worldwide or as the basis for comparisons with similar models in ex-transition countries or other ones. Despite of the scarce resources for operating in an ex-transition country, the university practices as described confirmed that inclusive processes presented far more than just a formal commitment, but the real dedication to mission accomplishment under available limited funds. So, this empirical study has contributed to the current literature and the debate upon declarative vs. real inclusive practices implementation in higher education by the evidence provided that the gap between declarative commitment and real inclusive activities implementation can be overcome, even under the circumstances of very scarce resources and limited budget funds that are main feature of ex-transition countries struggling with numerous obstacles and consequences of the processes that marked their economic history after 1990s. The accounting practices described, suggested data-basis of financial and non-financial indicators for tracking progress in social inclusion developments could be further analysed in depth, compared to different indicators models as suggested by previous research or improved in accordance with new requirements by users, as they appear. The set of standardized indicators could be introduced to enable high quality comparisons of social inclusion in higher education of a given country, region or broader. To attract the incentives and strengthen the efforts in inclusion activities development, the universities should become aware that they not only contribute to the success of their students, but also to its own benefits. The long-term benefits contribute to university's' sustainability by its recognition and better visibility, enhanced competitiveness, creative teaching methods and innovation capacities, stronger national and international partnerships and community relationships, as well as better allocation and use of resources. The path to achieve the benefits both for students and for institution begins with leadership commitment and stakeholder engagement in clear inclusion strategies, policies, measurable goals set, followed by efficient resources allocation tracked by accounting system and monitored by evaluation systems of inclusion outcomes achieved. In such a way the gap between formal declaration and real inclusive practices should get substantially reduced in many cases. Higher education institutions must become a leader and driver of inclusion in the entire society, regardless of whether it is a small university operating in ex-transition country like the one in case, or large university centre in the most developed countries worldwide. The models are specific, but the mission is common.

Research Funding This chapter has been partially supported by Juraj Dobrila University of Pula, under the project "Accounting as the support to sustainable business" and by the European Union-NextGenerationEU, IIP_010140, "Development of the AI-Supported Model upon Financial and Non-financial Sustainability Information", UI-INFINE.

References

Ashworth, M., Bloxham, S., & Pearce, L. (2010). Examining the tension between academic standards and inclusion for disabled students: The impact on marking of individual academics' frameworks for assessment. *Studies in Higher Education, 35*(2), 209–223. https://doi.org/10.1080/03075070903062864

Bologna Follow-up Group (BFUG) Advisory Group 1 for Social Dimension (2020, March). Principles and guidelines to strengthen the social dimension of higher education in the EHEA. BFUG_HR_UA_69_5_2_AG1 PAGs.

Bologna with Stakeholders Eyes for an Innovative, Inclusive and Interconnected EHEA by 2030. (2024, February). Policy recommendations.

Claeys-Kulik, A. L., Jorgensen, T. E., & Stöber, H. (2019). *Diversity, equity and inclusion in European higher education institutions*. European University Association.

Croatian National Group for Improving the Social Dimension of Higher Education (2023, September). Plan of measures for enhancing the social dimension of higher education for the period 2023–2025.

Devlin, M. (2013). Bridging socio-cultural incongruity: Conceptualising the success of students from low socio-economic status backgrounds in Australian higher education. *Studies in Higher Education, 38*(6), 939–949.

Državni zavod za statistiku (State Bureau of Statistics), Priopćenje (Announcement) OBR-2024-4-5. https://podaci.dzs.hr/2024/hr/76955. Accessed 21 April 2025.

Duenas, N. (2024, May). The role of accounting in solving great challenges. https://telfer.uottawa.ca/telfer-knowledge-hub/better-canada/the-role-of-accounting-in-solving-grand-challenges. Accessed 15 March 2025.

European Agency for Special Needs and Inclusive Education. (2018). In S. Symeonidou (Ed.), *Evidence of the link between inclusive education and social inclusion: A review of the literature*. Odense

European Commission. (2021). Implementation guidelines—Erasmus+ and European solidarity corps inclusion and diversity strategy.

Fernando, D., & Kenny, E. J. (2021). Negotiating a sense of fit in elite higher education: Exploring the identity work of "Widening Participation" students. *Academy of Management Learning & Education, 20*(2), 2025. https://doi.org/10.5465/amle.2019.0358.Accessed14April

Florian, L. (2014). What counts as evidence of inclusive education? *European Journal of Special Needs Education, 29*(3), 286–294. https://doi.org/10.1080/08856257.2014.933551

Fuller, M., Healey, M., Bradley, A., & Hall, T. (2004). Barriers to learning: A systematic study of the experience of disabled students in one university. *Studies in Higher Education, 29*(3), 303–318. https://doi.org/10.1080/03075070410001682592

Göransson, K., & Nilholm, C. (2014). Conceptual diversities and empirical shortcomings-a critical analysis of research on inclusive education. *European Journal of Special Needs Education, 29*(3), 265–280. https://doi.org/10.1080/08856257.2014.933545

Graham, L., & Jahnukainen, M. (2011). Wherefore are thou, inclusion? Analysing the development of inclusive education in New South Wales, Alberta and Finland. *Journal of Education Policy, 26*(2), 263–288. https://doi.org/10.1080/02680939.2010.493230

Hardy, I., & Woodcock, S. (2015). Inclusive education policies: Discourses of difference, diversity and deficit. *International Journal of Inclusive Education, 19*(2), 141–164. https://doi.org/10.1080/13603116.2014.908965
Härtel, P., & Marterer, M. (2023). *Guidelines on development and implementation of inclusion and diversity strategies within the framework of the erasmus+ and European solidarity corps programmes (2021–2027). Styrian Association for Education and Economics & SALTO inclusion and diversity (Education and Training).* Agency for Mobility and EU Programmes.
Haug, P. (2017). Understanding inclusive education: Ideals and reality. *Scandinavian Journal of Disability Research, 19*(3), 206–217. https://doi.org/10.1080/15017419.2016.1224778
Hockings, C. (2010). Inclusive learning and teaching in higher education: a synthesis of research. EvidenceNet. www.heacademy.ac.uk/evidencenet. https://www.advance-he.ac.uk/knowledge-hub/inclusive-learning-and-teaching-higher-education-synthesis-research. Accessed 15 January 2025.
János, K. (2006, April). The great transformation of Central Eastern Europe: Success and disappointment. *The Economics of Transition, 14*(2), 207–244. The European Bank for Reconstruction and Development. Accessed 3 February 2025.
Jeyaretnam, T. (2023). Accounting inequality: Tackling moral progress through Jeyaretnam. https://www.linkedin.com/pulse/accounting-inequality-tackling-moral-progress-through-jeyaretnam. Accessed 13 April 2025.
Kiš-Glavaš, L. (2016). Smjernice za unapređenje sustava potpore studentima s invaliditetom u visokom obrazovanju u Republici Hrvatskoj/Guidelines for improving the support system for students with disabilities in higher education in the Republic of Croatia. https://mzom.gov.hr/UserDocsImages/dokumenti/Obrazovanje/VisokoObrazovanje/RazvojVisokogObrazovanja/Smjernice%20za%20unapređenje%20sustava%20potpore%20studentima%20s%20invaliditetom%20u%20visokom%20obrazovanju%20u%20Republici%20Hrvatskoj.pdf. Accessed 18 December 2024.
Koluder, N. (2002). The accessibility plan of premises, procedures and policies of the Juraj Dobrila University of Pula in relation to people with disabilities. EduMotion, Juraj Dobrila University of Pula, under the project, financed by EFRR: Prenamjena zgrade bivšeg vojnog objekta - Mornaričke bolnice za potrebe istarskog sveučilišta. https://www.unipu.hr/_download/repository/A2.2.%20Plan%20pristupačnosti%20prostora%2C%20procedura%20i%20politika%20UniPu%20u%20odnosu%20na%20osobe%20s%20invaliditetom.pdf. Accessed 10 January 2025.
Kornai, J. (2006). The great transformation of central eastern Europe. *Economics of Transition, 14*(2), 207–244.
Kottmann, A., Vossensteyn, J. J., Kolster, R., Veidemane, A., Blasko, Zs., Biagi, F., & Sanchez-Marrioluengo, M. (2019). Social Inclusion Policies in Higher Education: Evidence from the EU. EUR 29801 EN.
Kreitz-Sandberg, S. (2015). As an Educator You Have to Fix Many Things on Your Own. Teachers Perspectives on Organizing Inclusions in Various Welfare Contexts. Rights of Children in the Nordic Welfare States, 145–167.
Law on Accessibility of Websites and Software Solutions for Mobile Devices of Public Sector Bodies of the Republic of Croatia (Narodne novine/Official Gazette 17/19).
Macheridis, N., & Paulsson, A. (2021). Tracing accountability in higher education. *Research in Education, 110*(1), 78–97. https://doi.org/10.1177/0034523721993143
Mampaey, Jelle. (2017). An organisational perspective on social exclusion in higher education: A case study. Education as Change, 21(3), 1–19. https://doi.org/10.17159/1947-9417/2017/1492
Miles, S., & Singal, N. (2010). The Education for All and Inclusive Education Debate: Conflict, Contradiction or Opportunity? *International Journal of Inclusive Education, 14*(1), 1–15. https://doi.org/10.1080/13603110802265125
Mitchell, D. (2005). Sixteen Propositions on the Contexts of Inclusive Education. Contextualizing Inclusive Education. Evaluating Old and New International Perspectives, 1–21.

Moriña, A., Sandoval, M., & Carnerero, F. (2020). Higher education inclusivity: When the disability enriches the university. *Higher Education Research & Development, 39*(6), 1202–1216. https://doi.org/10.1080/07294360.2020.1712676

Nes, K. (2010). The First Decade of the 21st Century: A Backlash for Inclusion in Norwegian Schools? Zeitschrift für Inklusion, 2(11). http://www.inklusion-online.net/index.php/inklusion-online/article/view/139/139

Nieminen, J. H. (2022). Inclusive Assessment, Exclusive Academy, in Assessment for Inclusion in Higher Education, 63–73. *Routledge*. https://doi.org/10.4324/9781003293101-8

Orr, D., Usher, A., Haj, C., Atherton, G., & Geanta, I. (2017a). Study on the impact of admission systems on higher education outcomes: Volume I: Comparative report. Publications Office of the European Union.

Orr, D., Usher, A., Haj, C., Atherton, G., & Geanta, I. (2017b). Study on the impact of admission systems on higher education outcomes: Volume II: National cases study. Publications Office of the European Union.

O'Shea S.E., Lysaght, P., Roberts, J., & Harwood, V. (2016). Shifting the blame in higher education - social inclusion and deficit discourses. Research Online. University of Wollongong. https://ro.uow.edu.au/. Accessed 7 February 2025.

Rotta, S. (2024). *Experiences of students with disabilities at Juraj Dobrila University of Pula.* Internal Survey. https://www.unipu.hr/rektorat/ured_za_ravnopravnost_raznolikost_i_inkluzivnost

Slaughter, S., & Rhoades, G. (2004). *Academic Capitalism and the New Economy: Markets, State, and Higher Education.* Johns Hopkins University Press.

Smyth, F., Shevlin, M., Buchner, T., Biewer, G., Flynn, P., Latimier, C., et al. (2014). Inclusive Education in Progress: Policy Evolution in Four European Countries. *European Journal of Special Needs Education, 29*(4), 433–445. https://doi.org/10.1080/08856257.2014.922797

Tai, J., Ajjawi, R., Bearman, M., Boud, D., Dawson, P., de St, J., & Jorre, T. (2023). Assessment for inclusion: Rethinking contemporary strategies in assessment design. *Higher Education Research & Development, 42*(2), 483–497. https://doi.org/10.1080/07294360.2022.2057451

Tobbell, J., Burton, R., Gaynor, A., Golding, B., Greenhough, K., Rhodes, C., & White, S. (2020). Inclusion in higher education: An exploration of the subjective experiences of students. *Journal of Further and Higher Education, 45*, 284–295. https://doi.org/10.1080/0309877x.2020.1753180

University of Pula documents: Brochure for students with disabilities. (2024). Development strategy 2021–2026; Recommendations for inclusive communication with people with disabilities (2024); Rulebook on studying for students with disabilities at Juraj Dobrila University in Pula (2020); Rulebook on recognition and evaluation of prior learning (2024).

University of Pula - Office for Equality, Diversity and Inclusion. Various Documents, and instructions. https://www.unipu.hr/rektorat/ured_za_ravnopravnost_raznolikost_i_inkluzivnost. Accessed 10 January 2025.

Veidemane, A., Kaiser, F., & Craciun, D. (2021). Inclusive Higher Education Access for Underrepresented Groups: It Matters, But How Can Universities Measure It? Inclusive Universities in a Globalized World. Social Inclusion, 9(3), 44–57. https://doi.org/10.17645/si.v9i3.4163. Accessed 16 December 2024.

Working group on social dimension (2015). Widening Participation for Equity and Growth. A Strategy for the Development of the Social Dimension and Lifelong Learning in the European Higher Education Area to 2020. Ministerial Conference. chrome-extension://efaidnbmnnnibpcajpcglclefindmkaj/https://ehea.info/media.ehea.info/file/2015_Yerevan/71/5/Widening_Participation_for_Equity_and_Growth_A_Strategy_for_the_Development_of_the_SD_and_LLL_in_the_EHEA_to_2020_613715.pdf. Accessed 19 December 2024.

Lorena Mošnja-Škare PhD, is Professor of Accounting, at Juraj Dobrila University of Pula, Faculty of Economics and Tourism "Dr. Mijo Mirković", Croatia. Her research interests include: assets valuation topics, strategic and CSR accounting, SMEs accounting, internal auditing, European and international harmonisation of accounting, financial reporting, financial indicators in post-transition countries. She is a member of Editorial/Advisory Board of "Almatourism—Journal of Tourism, Culture and Territorial Development" (University of Bologna), "Economic Research" (Juraj Dobrila University of Pula), "UTMS Journal of Economics" (University of Skoplje), "Dubrovnik International Economic Meeting" (University of Dubrovnik), "Revija SIR*IUS" (Slovenski inštitut za revizijo, Ljubljana), "Journal of International Accounting, Auditing and Taxation" (Elsevier), a member of Scientific Committee of Corporate Governance Lab (Universita Roma Tre), Assembly member of CRIMPI—Research Center on Entrepreneurship and Small-medium Firms (Universita Carlo Bo, Urbino). Her collaboration with researchers from high education institutions includes: Facolta di Economia, Rimini, Universita di Bologna, Universita Carlo Bo, Urbino, Universita di Ferrara, Universita Roma Tre, University of Ljubljana, School of Economics and Business, Boston University, Charles Sturt University, Bathurst, University of Tartu, SouthEastern Oklahoma State University—John Massey School of Business, Rollins College - Crummer Graduate School of Business, Orlando, Charles W. Lamden School of Accountancy, San Diego State University.

Ksenija Černe PhD, is Associate professor of Accounting at Juraj Dobrila University of Pula, Faculty of Economics and Tourism "Dr. Mijo Mirković", Croatia. Her research interest areas are international accounting and harmonisation, intellectual capital accounting, SMEs accounting, and currently neuroaccounting and application of AI in accounting. She serves as vice-rector for academic affairs, enrollment and student support at Juraj Dobrila University of Pula.

Index

M. Baldarelli et al. (eds.), *Accounting and Accountability for Social Inclusion*, CSR, Sustainability, Ethics & Governance, https://doi.org/10.1007/978-3-032-09271-7

MIX
Papier aus verantwortungsvollen Quellen
Paper from responsible sources
FSC® C105338

If you have any concerns about our products,
you can contact us on
ProductSafety@springernature.com

In case Publisher is established outside the EU,
the EU authorized representative is:
Springer Nature Customer Service Center GmbH
Europaplatz 3, 69115 Heidelberg, Germany

Printed by Libri Plureos GmbH
in Hamburg, Germany